|H|A|C|K|E|R|S|

NEW
SAT
READING

10 PRACTICE TESTS

Author Sung-Hun Kim (Daniel Kim)

Graduated from Beuth University of Applied Sciences in Media Computer Science
SAT, TOEFL Instructor at Hackers Academia (2012-present)
OPIC Instructor at Samsung (Dogok) (2011)
TOEFL Instructor at Park Jung Language Academy (PJ English) (2008-2011)
English and TOEFL Instructor and Head Instructor at Chungdahm Institute (CDI) (2006-2008)

New **SAT Trends** Inside

Hackers New SAT Reading: 10 Practice Tests

First Published 2016

By ChampStudy
23, Gangnam-daero 61-gil, Seocho-gu, Seoul, Korea
(Tel: 02-566-0001 / Fax: 02-563-0622)

Online lectures	HackersIngang.com
Inquiries	publishing@hackers.com
ISBN	978-89-6965-001-6 (13740)

COPYRIGHT © 2016 by Daniel Kim
All rights reserved. No part of this publication may be reproduced, stored in a retrieval system, or transmitted, in any form or by any means, electronic, mechanical, photocopying, recording, or otherwise, without the prior written permission of the author and the publisher.

Printed in KOREA
Serial Number: 01-03-06

Additional attribution and copyright information on page 264

SAT is a registered trademark of the College Entrance Examination Board, which was not involved in the production of and does not endorse this book.

Complete SAT Preparation!

- New SAT Q&A
- SAT success stories
- Complimentary SAT material

Information Hub for Studying Abroad!

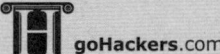

- University admissions qualifications
- Study abroad information Q&A
- Tips on part-time jobs & living abroad

PREFACE

How did this book come about? Given the availability of other books aimed at providing the same service (practice for the SAT Reading Test), one might demand justification for its existence. As any teacher who has just started teaching this subject can attest (I certainly felt this way), working through even a single SAT prep book initially appears daunting at best. Won't this behemoth provide enough content for a year's worth of lessons, if not two? So why another book? After some time, teaching becomes manageable and then, once you find your own pace and become comfortable with the style of the test, there just isn't enough material! Considering the—let's call it study span for lack of a better word—of a typical SAT student, the number of useful books that are freely available on the market has historically been lacking, and students asking "What should I do now? Should I just solve that same book again?" are a dime a dozen. Therefore, I believe that providing more material actually makes sense.

Different books represent the test in different ways. The experience of preparing students, the material used, the perceived difficulties regarding the test, the actual performance of students, and a slew of other factors all come together over time to shape a certain set of beliefs and certainties that I, as an instructor, do my best to channel into meaningful lectures. I can only hypothesize, but it is my guess that this acquired outlook lies at the heart of why some books turn out differently from others.

In this book, I have done my best to include the things I have learned while teaching, i.e., to build or utilize passages that are akin to what students will experience on the renewed version of the SAT, and to also include problems that are quite challenging that are of the kind that students usually have trouble with. And of course, there are lessons learned from existing material. Due to my job, I have spent years poring over it, and I often wished certain passages, questions, or answer choices had been written differently for a number of reasons. I have incorporated as many lessons and conclusions drawn from such instances as I could, and I hope that students will find in this book a substantial amount of meaningful practice.

As a student or test taker, you need to know the enemy. What kinds of passages can I expect? What do the questions look like? What does this particular question want from me? Where do I find the answer for a given question? How long does solving a test usually take me? What am I spending my precious minutes on? Where do I lose points? I would like for this book to answer these questions and, more importantly, to provide the practice needed to get better at beating the test. It is also my hope that teachers and instructors will recognize with a smirk the odd quirk inherent to SAT within these problem sets, and that they will use the material provided here to create challenging but helpful lessons around.

Daniel Kim

CONTENTS

HOW TO USE THIS BOOK	6
STUDY PLAN & GUIDELINES	10
ABOUT THE SAT	14
GUIDELINES FOR PREPARATION	18

TEST 1 — 24
Answer Keys & Performance Breakdown — 38
Answer Explanations — 39

TEST 2 — 48
Answer Keys & Performance Breakdown — 62
Answer Explanations — 63

TEST 3 — 72
Answer Keys & Performance Breakdown — 86
Answer Explanations — 87

TEST 4 — 96
Answer Keys & Performance Breakdown — 110
Answer Explanations — 111

TEST 5 — 120
Answer Keys & Performance Breakdown — 134
Answer Explanations — 135

TEST 6   144
Answer Keys & Performance Breakdown   158
Answer Explanations   159

TEST 7   168
Answer Keys & Performance Breakdown   182
Answer Explanations   183

TEST 8   192
Answer Keys & Performance Breakdown   206
Answer Explanations   207

TEST 9   216
Answer Keys & Performance Breakdown   230
Answer Explanations   231

TEST 10   240
Answer Keys & Performance Breakdown   254
Answer Explanations   255

How to Score Your Test   263
Answer Sheet   265

HOW TO USE THIS BOOK

01
Understand the New SAT and learn problem-solving strategies for the Reading Test.

About the SAT
Learn about the changes in the overall structure and content of the New SAT and its Reading Test by comparing them to current version of the actual exam.

Guidelines for Preparation
Familiarize yourself with the question types of the New SAT and acquire problem-solving strategies for the Reading Test.

02

Experience the feeling of taking the real test by working on questions that follow real-life exam trends.

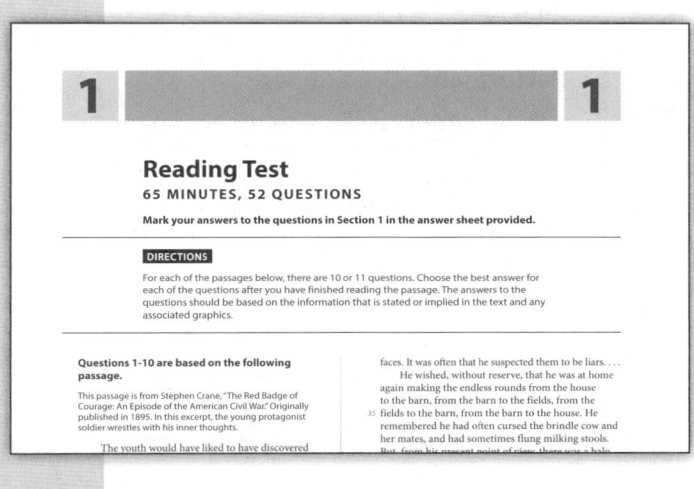

Practice Tests

10 practice tests modeled on the New SAT will help you get acquainted with the actual exam.

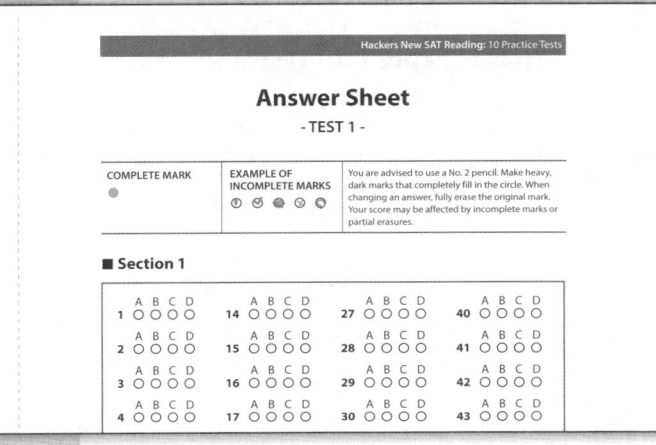

Answer Sheets

Mark your answers on answer sheets that are similar to those used for the actual exam. Answer sheets for each practice test are provided at the back of the book.

HOW TO USE THIS BOOK

Make progress toward your ideal score by checking your performance after every test.

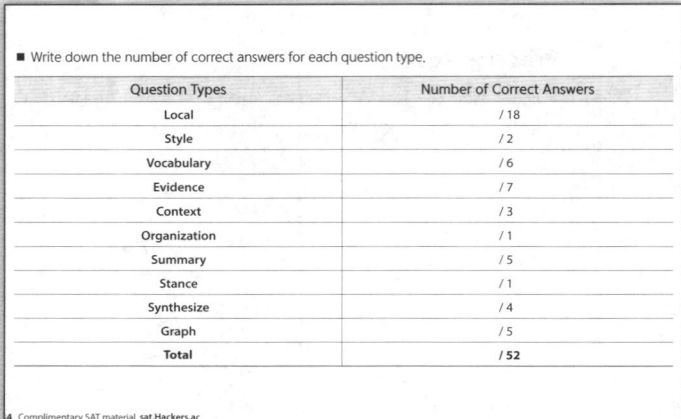

Performance Breakdown
The Performance Breakdown will give you a concise analysis of how you did on each test. You can use it to identify question types to work on, which will help you achieve maximum results.

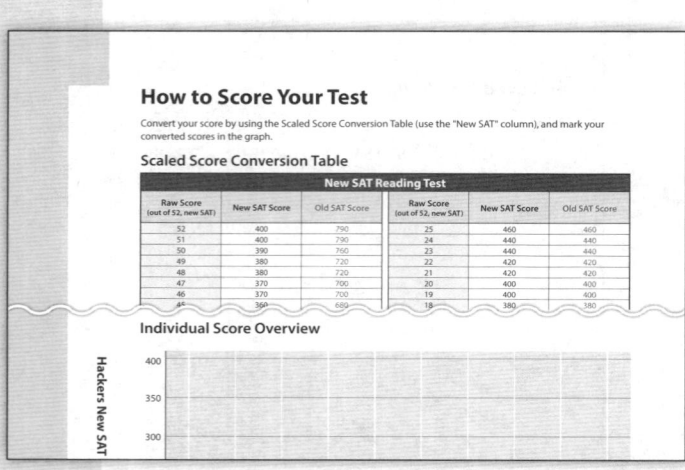

How to Score Your Test
Check how well you are doing by converting your raw score into an Actual Reading Test score. You can also keep track of your performance using the Individual Score Overview.

04

Improve your understanding of Reading Test questions by reviewing the comprehensive explanations provided.

Answer Explanations

Questions 1-10

1. (B) — Summary
B is the best choice because the youth (the protagonist) mainly wonders if his comrades are secretly afraid of battle, or if they really look forward to it as many of them claim. He wishes he could ask them directly. The long conversation in the latter part again shows the youth's fixation on bravery versus cowardice.

A is incorrect because the passage focuses on the feelings and doubts of one soldier. C is incorrect because a lack of courage is never admitted to in the passage, and no such communities have formed. D is incorrect because the passage does not describe "dire odds" that could be faced with bravado.

2. (A) — Local
A is the best choice because he fears he might be "derided" by the "unconfessed" (those who did not confess their fears).

A is incorrect because reliability in battle is not mentioned. C is incorrect because maturity and naivety are not compared. D is incorrect because it mixes up bravery and fear for the respective parties.

5. (D) — Local
D is the best choice because within these lines, he curses the cows and flings implements, which implies frustration or rage.

A, B, and C are incorrect because none of these are supported by the specified lines.

6. (C) — Local
The "present point of view" is in opposition to his former dislike of farm life. Now, he would give anything to return to that time. In other words, the time he used to hate looks much more appealing in retrospect.

C is the best choice.

A, B, and D are incorrect because none of them

Answer Explanations

Thorough explanations of the correct answers as well as the incorrect ones w ll help you gain a clear understanding of each and every question.

STUDY PLAN & GUIDELINES

2-Week Plan

Take the test. Grade and review the same day.

	Day 1	Day 2	Day 3	Day 4	Day 5
WEEK 1	Take TEST 1 / Grade and Review	Take TEST 2 / Grade and Review	Take TEST 3 / Grade and Review	Take TEST 4 / Grade and Review	Take TEST 5 / Grade and Review
	Day 6	**Day 7**	**Day 8**	**Day 9**	**Day 10**
WEEK 2	Take TEST 6 / Grade and Review	Take TEST 7 / Grade and Review	Take TEST 8 / Grade and Review	Take TEST 9 / Grade and Review	Take TEST 10 / Grade and Review

4-Week Plan

Take the test. Grade and review the following day.

	Day 1	Day 2	Day 3	Day 4	Day 5
WEEK 1	Take TEST 1	Grade and Review TEST 1	Take TEST 2	Grade and Review TEST 2	Take TEST 3
	Day 6	**Day 7**	**Day 8**	**Day 9**	**Day 10**
WEEK 2	Grade and Review TEST 3	Take TEST 4	Grade and Review TEST 4	Take TEST 5	Grade and Review TEST 5
	Day 11	**Day 12**	**Day 13**	**Day 14**	**Day 15**
WEEK 3	Take TEST 6	Grade and Review TEST 6	Take TEST 7	Grade and Review TEST 7	Take TEST 8
	Day 16	**Day 17**	**Day 18**	**Day 19**	**Day 20**
WEEK 4	Grade and Review TEST 8	Take TEST 9	Grade and Review TEST 9	Take TEST 10	Grade and Review TEST 10

Study Guidelines

Make a Plan
You might want to use one of the study plans outlined on the left. Being systematic often helps when you feel swamped (as you are likely to, preparing for SAT).

Take the Test
If you're just starting out, you don't need to time yourself as you solve the problems. Otherwise, try using a timer (65 minutes for the Reading Test) to get used to the time constraints of the test.

Grade and Review
Make sure you grade your efforts using the provided answer keys and keep track of your question type-specific performance by filling in the Performance Breakdown.

While the number of correct answers you get is an indicator of your skill (this is how good I am), it is your review of mistakes that will elevate you to the next level. *Take enough time to review your mistakes and understand what made your specific answer choice wrong.* If you are able to avoid making similar mistakes in the future, that means you have improved (obvious as it may seem). I like to think of it in terms of "I'm making fewer mistakes now." rather than "I'm getting more questions right." As you review, keep asking yourself: why did I get this question wrong?

Probable reasons:
1. I did not know the exact meaning of a keyword. (vocab problem)
2. I did not understand the meaning of the sentence/context.
3. I missed something in/misunderstood the question. (Happens more than you might think!)
4. I did not know where to look for the right answer. (This is where question types come in.)
5. I was running out of time and rushing.

After working through a few of these tests, it should become clear which of these reasons (though of course, there might be others as well) is holding you back.

SAT.Hackers.ac

Complete SAT Preparation!

SAT.Hackers.ac

Everything you need to know about the New SAT! `SAT Q&A`
Success stories from studying Hackers SAT! `SAT success stories`
Complimentary `SAT study material`

Information Hub for Studying Abroad!

goHackers.com

17,000 posts about `university admissions qualifications`
US/UK/Australia/Canada `study abroad information Q&A`
Tips on living abroad from overseas students! `Tips on part-time jobs & living abroad`

BEFORE YOU GET STARTED

- ABOUT THE SAT
- GUIDELINES FOR PREPARATION

ABOUT THE SAT

What is the SAT?

The SAT test is a standardized test used by many colleges in the United States to assess a student's eligibility in the admissions process. (As of 1997, "SAT" is not supposed to be an acronym anymore, so "SAT" simply means SAT.) Ideally, the results of the test show the test taker's readiness for university or college, so the majority of test takers will be high school students in their final three years. College Board, a private, nonprofit U.S. organization owns, creates, and releases SAT.

Even though high schools provide GPA as a measure of a student's academic performance, there is no guarantee that nationally, each school will adhere to the same grading standards and curricula (and, by implication, difficulties), which means that GPA in itself does not necessarily provide a reliable way to compare students' aptitude for college on a national level. What adds to this lack of score compatibility is the substantial number of foreign high school students (outside the U.S.) who apply for U.S. colleges.

As a result, many colleges use SAT and other such exams as a way to assess students' college readiness directly and regardless of background, based on the problems posed in these tests. (For instance, SAT tests critical reading, mathematics, and writing skills.)

2016 Redesign

A Host of Changes

College Board has started to administer the redesigned SAT in March 2016. The most conspicuous change is that the previous incarnation (henceforth referred to as the "old test") had a maximum score of 2400 while the 2016 redesign (called the "new test" from here on) has a maximum score of 1600 because the essay portion of the test is optional. The old test consisted of "Critical Reading" (200-800 points), "Writing" which means Grammar and the essay (200-800 points), and "Math" (200-800 points), whereas the new test consists of "Evidence-Based Reading and Writing" which in essence means Reading and Grammar (200-800 points), "Math" (200-800 points), and the optional essay.

Note the difference in weight. According to the information provided on the website of the College Board, Critical Reading—i.e., Reading—made up ⅓ of the score on the old test; it decides only ¼ on the new test. At the same time, Math goes from ⅓ on the old test to ½ on the new test.

Perhaps this is why the score report on the new test not only includes the total score (out of 1600), but also section scores. Reading, and Writing and Language are represented by individual section score (10-40) to show how well the test taker did on each.

The score reports also includes new cross-test scores and subscores. Cross-test scores are called "Analysis in History/Social Studies" and "Analysis in Science," and they are calculated using a number of questions taken from all of the mandatory sections (Reading, Writing and Language, and Math). The scores are meant to show performance for a certain subject area as opposed to test section. Subscores present certain performance statistics within each of the sections (Reading, Writing and Language, and Math). For Writing and Language, these are called "Expression of Ideas" and "Standard English Conventions." For Math, they are called "Heart of Algebra," "Problem Solving and Data Analysis," and "Passport to Advanced Math." For Reading, the new subscores are "Command of Evidence" and "Words in Context."

Another significant change affects multiple-choice questions that make up the bulk of the exam: the number of options for each question has decreased from five to four, and the penalty for choosing a wrong option has been dropped. On the old test, students guessing blindly had a 20% chance of picking the correct answer and scoring one point, and an 80% chance of picking the wrong answer and losing 0.25 points which means that on average, blind guessing would net students 0 points. The new test has only four answer choices and without a penalty involved, blind guessing will, on average, net students 0.25 points. Of course, this observation in itself does not mean the new test is easier because it does not take into account actual levels of difficulty or score conversion rules between the old and the new tests.

The new test's Reading section instantly feels different to test takers who have taken the old SAT because the sentence completion questions that only targeted knowledge of vocabulary has been eliminated. On the other hand, the new test features graphs, charts, and tables and ask questions based on their contents as well.

The Math section includes parts that do not permit the use of calculators. This was not the case on the old test. The new test also tests students' trigonometry skills and introduces "Grid-In Questions" which are basically a departure from standard multiple-choice options and more akin to a free response. Instead of choosing from a list of provided results, test takers have to use provided grids that allow them to freely enter numbers or fractions.

Finally, the number of sections has decreased for the test as a whole, but the time allotted to each section has increased on the new test which might or might not affect test takers' abilities to stay focused.

Overview of Structural Changes

	New test	Old test
Score Report	400-1600 Based on 2 section scores (200-800 each) Additional scores: 2 cross-test scores (10-40) 7 subscores (1-15) Optional essay score: (2-8)	600-2400 Based on 3 section scores (200-800 each)
Test Sections	1. Reading + Writing and Language 2. Math 3. Essay (optional)	1. Critical Reading 2. Writing 3. Math 4. Essay
Test Time	3 hrs (50 mins for optional essay)	3 hrs 45 mins (this includes 25 mins essay time)
Total Number of Questions	154 (155 with Essay)	170
Minutes per Question (excluding essay)	1.17	1.18
Answer Choices	4 options No penalty for incorrect answer choices	5 options ¼ point penalty for incorrect answer choices

Score Comparison Old vs. New

As of May 2016, the College Board has made Concordance Tables available on their website, which makes it possible to compare old and new SAT scores. Total-to-Total, Section-to-Section, and Section-to-Test conversions can thus be made between the two different score systems. As for Reading, we are comparing a top score of 400 (new test) against a top score of 800 (old test). Though one might assume that therefore, 200 on the new test might equal 400 on the old test, and that 350 on the new test might equal 700 on the old test, this is not the case. Test takers will have to achieve higher results on the new test to stay competitive. For instance, 370 on the new test equals 700 on the old. **The new test feels easier than the old, but this merely means that test takers are allowed fewer mistakes.**

To see the charts relevant for the Reading test (old SAT scores to new SAT scores, and raw points to scaled scores), please turn to page 263.

Changes to the Reading Test

Since this is a practice book for the Reading section of the redesigned SAT, changes specifically regarding this section will now be discussed in more depth.

From Afar

The Reading section on the new test differs in several significant ways from the old test. First of all, what used to be three Critical Reading sections will now be tested in a single, bigger Reading section: the old test had two reading sections each lasting 25 minutes with 24 questions each, and one reading section lasting 20 minutes with 19 questions. In other words, the old test gave test takers 70 minutes to deal with 67 questions. The new test has a single reading section lasting 65 minutes with 52 questions.

This means that test takers have more time per question on the new test (1.25 mins/Q in the new test as opposed to 1.04 mins/Q in the old test). Given that easier questions are usually answered quickly regardless of new or old test, this gain in time to chew on more difficult questions could be significant. However, sentence completion questions also need to be taken into account when considering this matter. (Read on.)

A Closer Look

A second decisive departure from the old test is the elimination of sentence completion questions that solely focused on the knowledge of vocabulary. This type of question heavily favored test takers versed in difficult, sometimes recondite vocabulary because all that was required to receive a point was a comparison of the words in the answer choices to the sentence supplied in the question. More than ¼ of the old test's questions were of this type. The new test does not enable test takers to quickly secure this many points based on pure vocabulary knowledge anymore.

Sentence completion questions, by nature, do not require as much time as passage-based questions (no larger context is provided or its comprehension required for solving a question), so the removal of these questions ought to partly negate the advantage that new test takers gain by having more time per question.

Worth mentioning in context of the elimination of sentence completion questions is the fact that one of the new subscores is called "Words in Context." This subscore's name implies that it will refer to passage-based vocabulary questions. Thus, it is reasonable to assume that one or two such vocabulary questions will appear per passage.

The new test introduces charts, graphs, or tables that complement the information provided in the passages. Two out of the five passages that make up the reading test have one or two charts or figures attached. Questions regarding this material can be very basic ("Tell me what is in the graph."), but they can also become more complex ("Synthesize information from both the graphic and a part of the passage.").

To take another look at structural changes, the old test featured two short (short means around 100 words) reading passages and a pair of short reading passages. In addition, there used to be a pair of medium-length passages, two single medium-length passages and a long passage. The new test features five medium-to-long passages with 10-11 questions each. Therefore, the new test might actually be less confusing in terms of time management. For instance, an old Critical Reading section might have had five sentence completion (vocab) questions, two short reading passages with two questions each, a medium passage with six questions, and another medium passage with nine questions. This made it difficult for many test takers to gauge how much time they should allot to each part of the section.

Close-Up

The redesigned Reading Test introduces question types that did not appear on the old test. A tenet prevalent in the design of the new test is that test takers have to provide evidence for their answers. This has been implemented in the form of evidence questions that ask test takers where they found the answer to the previous question. For example, question 17 asked "Why did Norman decide to return to his parents' house after ten years?" and the test taker chose option (B) "He had finally forgiven them." This is the correct answer. However, the next question now asks the test taker where they found this correct answer and presents them with four different line numbers to choose from. This favors test takers who have actually found the correct answer and evidence backing up this answer in the passage as opposed to other test takers who simply guessed the answer correctly or still others who "kind of felt" that it might be correct.

This question type informs the other subscores for the Reading section—"Command of Evidence" (the other one, "Words in Context," was mentioned above).

The old test and the new feature questions that ask test takers to synthesize information. This could happen in the form of information presented in two different lines from the same passage, or this could be information from two different passages in a pair of passages. This type of task has very much remained the same across revisions. However, graphs, tables, and charts (from now on simply called "charts") add a new dimension to this. The addition of charts means that text-chart relationships can now be asked for. For instance, such a question could ask whether an opinion presented in the passage agrees with the data presented by the chart. While not inherently more difficult than a text-text relationship, the difference in presentation and its novelty within the context of this test warrant a certain amount of practice.

Overview of Changes for the Reading Test

	New test	Old test
Structure	1 section containing **52 passage-based questions** Based on: 4 medium-to-long passages 1 medium-to-long pair	3 sections containing **19 sentence completion questions** **48 passage-based questions** Based on: 2 short passages 1 short pair 1 medium pair 2 medium passages 1 long passage
Time	65 minutes	70 minutes
Sentence Completion Questions	NO	YES
Charts, Graphs, and Tables	YES	NO
Evidence Questions	YES	NO

How to Approach the Reading Test

Time is the Enemy

The new test has around 3,200 words per test, several charts, and 52 questions. These questions have to be solved within 65 minutes. This means that time pressure (or lack of time) becomes a major factor in achieving a competitive score.

There will always be one paired passage on the test which will most likely feature eleven questions instead of ten. The increased difficulty of understanding two different points of view and the resulting presence of questions that ask test takers to synthesize information from both passages mean that a paired passage will probably require more time than a single passage.

Also, charts have to be considered. Some chart questions are actually quite simple while others have proven to be very tricky. More importantly, though, the simple fact that they represent *more* information to be considered could very well mean that an extra minute needs to be assigned to passages with charts when planning on how much time each passage should take. Failure to carefully read the sometimes extensive descriptions and legends that accompany such charts often results in misinterpretation of data.

Quick and Slow

A maxim that applies to both the old and the new test is to skim quickly, and to solve the questions slowly. A mistake a number of test takers make is to actually read the whole passage for comprehension before attacking the questions. This will invariably lead to a lack of time towards the end of the Reading section. Also, having read the whole passage usually means that by the time the questions are looked at, the relevant details have been forgotten (and have to be read again).

Instead, skimming quickly for main idea and major details only (checking each paragraph touching on first and last sentences and focusing on contrast words for important turning points) is all that time allows for. Skimming helps with summary and organization questions, and it also gives test takers an idea of where certain information is mentioned, which helps with evidence questions (questions that determine where the evidence backing up a certain fact can be found).

On the other hand, questions should be read slowly and carefully. Misinterpretation of questions (not understanding exactly what the question is asking for) is to blame for a tremendous number of mistakes. So is the misinterpretation of answer choices (not understanding precisely what the answer choice means). In addition, it takes time to carefully check what the passage states while solving questions.

In short: skim quickly and solve slowly.

Upgrade and Maintain your Vocabulary

Even though sentence completion questions have been eliminated from the Reading test, vocabulary still plays an essential role. Imprecise knowledge of what a word means, not knowing that a certain word's secondary or tertiary meanings exist, or confusing one word with another might have an even bigger impact on one's scores than the time factor. Answer choices for questions are almost always paraphrased or rephrased, and inference and circumlocution are used to such a degree that a weak command of vocabulary will inevitably drag down one's test score.

In short: studying vocabulary is still crucial for doing well on the redesigned Reading Test.

Refer to the Passage (not your opinion)

The correct answers to the questions refer to the passages on the test. Test takers are not asked for their opinions. This means that assumptions or conclusions that lack grounding in the passage are automatically wrong.

> Example Passage:
>
> *Practically everyone who can afford to uses shampoo to wash their hair. A number of researchers, however, assert that most of the shampoo products on the market could actually have detrimental effects on scalp and hair. A majority of the shampoos tested in a study contained a certain ingredient that might promote hair loss.*
>
> Question 1) The passage primarily serves to
>
> (A) advocate against the use of a product.
> (B) accuse researchers of making spurious claims.
> (C) present an opinion that could have broad implications.
> (D) …

In this tiny example passage, it is stated that most shampoo might actually be bad for one's hair. Therefore, a lot of test takers assume that the passage "advocates against the use of shampoo," which looks like it makes logical sense and choose (A). The problem is that the passage does not, in fact, recommend not using shampoo, so (A) is incorrect. (C) is correct because an *opinion is presented* (what the "number of researchers" asserts), and because *broad implications* is supported by the fact that "practically everyone who can afford to uses shampoo." (A significant number of people uses this hair product that could have detrimental effects.)

In short: if it is not supported by the passage, it is not correct.

Novels — Focus on the Characters

Each reading test contains an excerpt from a narrative (such as a novel). Such passages differ from the other passages in that the latter usually have a central idea that is presented with supporting details that back it up. Narrative pieces, on the other hand, usually revolve around one or more characters.

Thus, when dealing with novels, special attention ought to be paid to the main character(s): their central motivation, their feelings, and their relationships with other characters. These factors in essence are to a novel what a main idea is to another passage.

Question types

The revamped SAT Reading test features a new set of question types. Of course, there is significant overlap, but all things considered, thinking of this test as a new test rather than as a variation on an old theme is probably more helpful. Here are the types of questions that the redesigned SAT Reading test will ask.

- **Local**

    These questions, as their name suggests, are focused on a limited part of the passage. Line numbers or specific keywords often clearly pinpoint the area of the passage that is asked about. Close reading, exact comprehension of the question and the specified part of the passage are required.

- **Style**

    Style questions ask what effect a certain phrasing or the use of a rhetorical device has. This question type aims at a nuanced understanding of a certain part of the passage.

- **Vocabulary**

    Vocabulary means vocabulary in context of the passage. Many English words have several different meanings depending on context. Therefore, test takers have to understand the meaning of the word within the sentence or within the direct context of the sentence in which it is employed.

- **Evidence**

    These questions will ask the test takers to prove that they know where certain information can be found. Most commonly, they will ask where in the passage (each answer choice will have a range of line numbers) the best evidence supporting the correct answer for the previous question can be found.

- **Context**

    These are questions that ask why an author mentions a piece of information. Thus, the meaning of that piece of information is usually secondary to what it does in context. It could, for instance, support an assertion made previously or cast doubt on an argument.

- **Organization**

    These questions require test takers to identify the overall buildup of a passage. Rather than reading closely and looking at details (as in "local" questions), test takers have to skim and find the parts that make up the passage to be able to choose the correct answer.

▪ Summary

Summary questions ask the test takers to identify the best summary of the whole passage. Being able to skim is important for this question type as well.

▪ Stance

Stance questions are a variation of summary questions. They might appear when the passage is taken from a speech, and instead of finding the best summary of the whole passage, they ask for the attitude or stance of the speaker.

▪ Synthesize

These questions require test takers to put together information from two different sources. This question type will mostly appear with pair passages.

▪ Graph

Certain passages in the Reading section will be accompanied by charts, graphs, or tables. When this happens, questions will ask which statement about the data presented is true, which will require a close look at the data. Other questions will ask test takers to synthesize information from the graph and the passage to find the correct answer.

SAT.Hackers.ac

Hackers New SAT Reading: 10 Practice Tests

TEST 1

Answer Keys & Performance Breakdown
Answer Explanations

Reading Test

65 MINUTES, 52 QUESTIONS

Mark your answers to the questions in Section 1 in the answer sheet provided.

DIRECTIONS

For each of the passages below, there are 10 or 11 questions. Choose the best answer for each of the questions after you have finished reading the passage. The answers to the questions should be based on the information that is stated or implied in the text and any associated graphics.

Questions 1-10 are based on the following passage.

This passage is from Stephen Crane, "The Red Badge of Courage: An Episode of the American Civil War." Originally published in 1895. In this excerpt, the young protagonist soldier wrestles with his inner thoughts.

   The youth would have liked to have discovered another who suspected himself. A sympathetic comparison of mental notes would have been a joy to
Line him.
 5   He occasionally tried to fathom a comrade with seductive sentences. He looked about to find men in the proper mood. All attempts failed to bring forth any statement which looked in any way like a confession to those doubts which he privately
10 acknowledged in himself. He was afraid to make an open declaration of his concern, because he dreaded to place some unscrupulous confidant upon the high plane of the unconfessed from which elevation he could be derided.
15   In regard to his companions his mind wavered between two opinions, according to his mood. Sometimes he inclined to believing them all heroes. In fact, he usually admitted in secret the superior development of the higher qualities in others. He
20 could conceive of men going very insignificantly about the world bearing a load of courage unseen, and although he had known many of his comrades through boyhood, he began to fear that his judgment of them had been blind. Then, in other moments, he
25 flouted these theories, and assured himself that his fellows were all privately wondering and quaking.
   His emotions made him feel strange in the presence of men who talked excitedly of a prospective battle as of a drama they were about to witness, with
30 nothing but eagerness and curiosity apparent in their faces. It was often that he suspected them to be liars. . . .
   He wished, without reserve, that he was at home again making the endless rounds from the house to the barn, from the barn to the fields, from the
35 fields to the barn, from the barn to the house. He remembered he had often cursed the brindle cow and her mates, and had sometimes flung milking stools. But, from his present point of view, there was a halo of happiness about each of their heads, and he would
40 have sacrificed all the brass buttons on the continent to have been enabled to return to them. He told himself that he was not formed for a soldier. And he mused seriously upon the radical differences between himself and those men who were dodging imp-like
45 around the fires.
   As he mused thus he heard the rustle of grass, and, upon turning his head, discovered the loud soldier. He called out, "Oh, Wilson!"
   The latter approached and looked down. "Why,
50 hello, Henry; is it you? What you doing here?"
   "Oh, thinking," said the youth.
   The other sat down and carefully lighted his pipe. "You're getting blue, my boy. You're looking thundering peeked. What the dickens is wrong with you?"
55   "Oh, nothing," said the youth.
   The loud soldier launched then into the subject of the anticipated fight. "Oh, we've got 'em now!" As he spoke his boyish face was wreathed in a gleeful smile, and his voice had an exultant ring. "We've got 'em now.
60 At last, by the eternal thunders, we'll lick 'em good!"
   "If the truth was known," he added, more soberly, "*They've* licked *us* about every clip up to now; but this time—this time—we'll lick 'em good!"
   "I thought you was objecting to this march a little
65 while ago," said the youth coldly.
   "Oh, it wasn't that," explained the other. "I don't mind marching, if there's going to be fighting at the

end of it. What I hate is this getting moved here and moved there, with no good coming of it, as far as I can
70 see, excepting sore feet and damned short rations."

"Well, Jim Conklin says we'll get a plenty of fighting this time."

"He's right for once, I guess, though I can't see how it come. This time we're in for a big battle, and
75 we've got the best end of it, certain sure. Gee rod! how we will thump 'em!" . . .

The youth watched him for a moment in silence. When he finally spoke his voice was as bitter as dregs. "Oh, you're going to do great things, I s'pose!"

80 The loud soldier blew a thoughtful cloud of smoke from his pipe. "Oh, I don't know," he remarked with dignity; "I don't know. I s'pose I'll do as well as the rest. I'm going to try like thunder." He evidently complimented himself upon the modesty of this
85 statement.

"How do you know you won't run when the time comes?" asked the youth.

"Run?" said the loud one; "run?—of course not!" He laughed.

1

The passage is chiefly concerned with

A) the panic soldiers endure on the verge of battle.
B) a soldier trying to ascertain the emotions of others.
C) the camaraderie formed among those who lack courage.
D) a soldier's unjustified bravado in the face of dire odds.

2

Lines 10-14 indicate that the youth "was afraid to make an open declaration of his concern" because

A) he thinks whoever learns of it might mock him.
B) he does not want to implicate someone else.
C) he does not know how to put it in words.
D) he has never before confessed it to anyone.

3

The passage suggests that in judging his comrades, the youth might have been "blind" (lines 23-24) because

A) they might be just as afraid as he himself feels.
B) having known them for a long time has colored his perception.
C) they may have more courage than he ascribed them.
D) their excited talk of coming battles are obvious lies.

4

The youth's attitude towards the "men" in line 20 and the "men" in line 28 differs in that he believes

A) only the former can be relied on in battle since he has known them since childhood.
B) the former might be braver than he knows while the latter might not be as fearless as they claim.
C) the former display maturity while the latter are naïve in their excitement and keenness for battle.
D) the former might secretly be afraid of battle while the latter long to join the fighting.

5

The youth's attitude towards farm life as described in lines 35-37 can best be described as

A) longing.
B) tedious.
C) clumsy.
D) loath.

6

Which of the following is the most analogous to the youth's "present point of view" (line 38)?

A) A student finds that French is much easier thanks to having suffered through studying Latin.
B) A driver prefers driving at night because the same roads, congested during the day are free.
C) A runner realizes that the way behind him was not as arduous as he had thought at the time.
D) An engineer stops complaining and promptly finds the solution to the problem he is working on.

7

The author mentions the "brass buttons" in line 40 in order to emphasize the

A) impossibility of a wish.
B) magnitude of his excitement.
C) earnestness of a desire.
D) sagacity of his peers.

8

As used in line 59, "ring" most nearly means

A) circle.
B) clank.
C) quality.
D) reverberation.

9

The passage suggests that what the youth dislikes the most about Wilson is the latter's

A) bravado.
B) vociferation.
C) egoism.
D) sanctimony.

10

Which choice provides the best evidence for the answer to the previous question?

A) Lines 53-54 ("You're . . . you?")
B) Lines 64-65 ("I thought . . . coldly")
C) Lines 78-79 ("his voice . . . s'pose")
D) Lines 86-87 ("How . . . youth")

Questions 11-21 are based on the following passage and supplementary material.

In this passage, the author discusses an apparent difference between men and women.

A recent discussion I recently participated in centered on the preponderance of men among notably evil leaders in history. Indeed, rattling off the most malicious historical personae one remembers from school, there seems to be an undeniable lack of women. Why should this be the case? Do we seek the root causes in the absence of equal opportunities for women? Or is there some gender-based intrinsic difference that favors this outcome?

These questions piqued my interest, and I decided to look at more recent examples of such nefarious leadership since this might shed light on the question of equal opportunity. Since in our contemporary Western society, genocide and related activities would not serve as useful indicators, I decided on large-scale financial fraud as an adequate, modern-day substitute. Again, names of men such as Bernard Madoff, Walter Forbes, and Jeff Skilling headed the list of those who have ruthlessly and on a large scale swayed others to do their bidding not for the greater good, but for their personal enrichment alone.

Today's symptoms are reflective of what history books tell us even though today, we would like to think we live in an emancipated society. But how emancipated is it really? Is it emancipated enough to grant women equal opportunities to commit evil on a large scale? Or are men really, as certain people are fond of trotting out, from one planet and women from another?

Of course, the question of emancipation looms large. Without a sufficiently powerful title gracing your business card, you won't be able to run any grand schemes. Even today, stereotypes about women persist, and many experts hold that it will be a long struggle before women will hold even 20% of the top leadership positions within the nation's most successful companies. This means that while opportunities to be bad are by no means equal, neither are they nonexistent.

It turns out that studies have been conducted to answer the question of difference—not in perception, but in makeup. Many experts have devised tests and surveys that have been used to gather rather conclusive data from all over the nation. Men and women in different age groups and from different walks of life have undergone whole batteries of questions, and their answers are quite compelling: On average, men are 9% more prone to manipulating others for their own gain. They are also more likely (8%) to yearn for the admiration of others through attaining a higher social status or wealth.

Other psychologists have scrutinized the correlation between these tendencies and corporate promotions in many industries, and they have found a robust link between the two. In other words, the treacherous path leading to the upper echelons of power favors the ambitious and the cunning. While this finding in itself will not raise a lot of eyebrows, the existence of inherently gender-based differences in disposition came as a surprise. I suppose I ought to blame my personal environment for not yielding results quite as representative as those mentioned above.

It appears that the observation in the discussion I recently had was not a fluke after all. Though the environment we have created plays a part, part of the reason we have created the environment the way we have is that men are somewhat better at being bad. You cannot blame women for being devious sometimes just to deal with that fact.

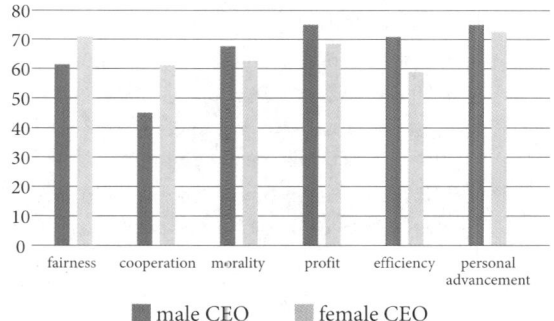

Poll About the Underlying Motivations of CEOs as Perceived by Their Employees (Independent Poll in Region D)

11

The primary purpose of the passage is to

A) call for support for female CEOs.
B) advocate equal opportunities for both sexes.
C) debunk the notion of gender-based differences.
D) investigate reasons for a puzzling peculiarity.

12

The passage suggests that the rationale behind looking "at more recent examples of such nefarious leadership" (lines 11-12) is that

A) men feature prominently among those who have committed large scale fraud.
B) the nature of the crimes that are committed centers more and more on money.
C) a certain factor governing society might have changed over time.
D) researching motives connected to gender is much easier in contemporary times.

13

The most likely purpose of the third paragraph (lines 22-29) is to

A) restate an inquiry in trying to ascertain which factor underlies a difference between genders.
B) assert that current times present changed circumstances thanks to social advances.
C) question those who would claim that we have achieved a certain level of emancipation.
D) shift the focus of the discussion from recent occurrences to those found in history.

14

The passage mostly suggests that opportunities for women to hold corporate leadership positions

A) are within 10% of those that men have.
B) will not be comparable to those of men soon.
C) are a reaction to the conduct of their male counterparts.
D) have changed at a drastic pace.

15

Which choice provides the best evidence for the answer to the previous question?

A) Lines 13-15 ("Since . . . indicators")
B) Lines 24-27 ("But how . . . scale")
C) Lines 34-36 ("many . . . positions")
D) Lines 48-51 ("men are . . . wealth")

16

As used in line 42, "makeup" most nearly means

A) contents.
B) personality.
C) configuration.
D) appearance.

17

Which choice best supports the author's claim that our society exists in its current form since men are better at being bad?

A) Lines 3-6 ("Indeed . . . women")
B) Lines 48-49 ("On average . . . gain")
C) Lines 52-55 ("Other . . . link")
D) Lines 57-60 ("While . . . surprise")

18

As used in line 9 and in line 57, "favors" most nearly means

A) facilitates.
B) honors.
C) sanctions.
D) supports.

19

The author indicates that his "personal environment" (line 61) is not representative because

A) his acquaintances that hold leadership positions are mostly men.
B) none of his acquaintances has ever committed contemptible acts.
C) the women he knows rival the men in shrewdness and ambition.
D) most of his acquaintances think that men should perform mission-critical jobs.

20

Which claim about female CEOs as compared to male CEOs is supported by the figure?

A) They believe they are better team players, but trail behind in terms of efficiency.
B) They are given more credit for ethical behavior, but less for wanting to advance the company.
C) They are seen as less able to optimize processes and more egoistical at the same time.
D) They are regarded as less egoistical, but also as being less conscientious.

21

The author of the passage would most likely consider the data in the figure to be

A) evidence for his belief that average women cannot become CEO.
B) representative of the perspective he thoroughly disagrees with.
C) not representative of the tendencies present on average.
D) an excellent illustration of the point he wants to convey.

Questions 22-31 are based on the following passage and supplementary material.

This passage is adapted from James Clerk Maxwell, "The Scientific Papers of James Clerk Maxwell," published in 1890. The passage describes an experiment.

When we mix together blue and yellow paint, we obtain green paint. This fact is well known to all who have handled colours; and it is universally
Line admitted that blue and yellow make green. Red,
5 yellow, and blue, being the primary colours among painters, green is regarded as a secondary colour, arising from the mixture of blue and yellow. Newton, however, found that the green of the spectrum was not the same thing as the mixture of two colours of
10 the spectrum, for such a mixture could be separated by the prism, while the green of the spectrum resisted further decomposition. But still it was believed that yellow and blue would make a green, though not that of the spectrum.
15 As far as I am aware, the first experiment on the subject is that of M. Plateau, who, before 1819, made a disc with alternate sectors of prussian blue and gamboge, and observed that, when spinning, the resultant tint was not green, but a neutral gray,
20 inclining sometimes to yellow or blue, but never to green. Prof. J. D. Forbes of Edinburgh made similar experiments in 1849, with the same result.

Prof. Helmholtz of Königsberg, to whom we owe the most complete investigation on visible colour, has
25 given the true explanation of this phenomenon. The result of mixing two coloured powders is not by any means the same as mixing the beams of light which flow from each separately. In the latter case we receive all the light which comes either from the one powder
30 or the other. In the former, much of the light coming from one powder falls on particles of the other, and we receive only that portion which has escaped absorption by one or other. Thus the light coming from a mixture of blue and yellow powder, consists
35 partly of light coming directly from blue particles or yellow particles, and partly of light acted on by both blue and yellow particles. This latter light is green, since the blue stops the red, yellow, and orange, and the yellow stops the blue and violet.

40 I have made experiments on the mixture of blue and yellow *light*—by rapid rotation, by combined reflexion and transmission, by viewing them out of focus, in stripes, at a great distance, by throwing the colours of the spectrum on a screen, and by receiving
45 them into the eye directly; and I have arranged a portable apparatus by which any one may see the result of this or any other mixture of the colours of the spectrum. In all these cases blue and yellow do *not* make green. I have also made experiments on the
50 mixture of coloured powders. Those which I used principally were "mineral blue" (from copper) and "chrome-yellow." Other blue and yellow pigments gave curious results, but it was more difficult to make the mixtures, and the greens were less uniform in
55 tint. The mixtures of these colours were made by weight, and were painted on discs of paper, which were afterwards treated in the manner described in my paper "On Colour as perceived by the Eye," in the *Transactions of the Royal Society of Edinburgh*,
60 Vol. XXI. Part 2. The visible effect of the colour is estimated in terms of the standard-coloured papers:—vermilion (V), ultramarine (U), and emerald-green (E). The accuracy of the results, and their significance, can be best understood by referring
65 to the paper before mentioned. I shall denote mineral blue by B, and chrome-yellow by Y; and $B_3 Y_5$ means a mixture of three parts blue and five parts yellow.

Test Results of Mixing "Mineral Blue" (B) and "Chrome-Yellow" (Y) Powders

Given Colour	Standard Colours*			Coefficient of brightness
	V	U	E	
B_8	2	36	7	45
$B_7 Y_1$	1	18	17	37
$B_6 Y_2$	4	11	34	49
$B_5 Y_3$	9	5	40	54
$B_4 Y_4$	15	1	40	56
$B_3 Y_5$	22	-2	44	64
$B_2 Y_6$	35	-10	51	76
$B_1 Y_7$	64	-19	64	109
Y_8	180	-27	124	277

*The standard colours are vermillion (V), ultramarine (U), and emerald-green (E).

22

Within paragraph 1, the phrases "well known" and "universally admitted" serve which of the following purposes?

A) They establish an assertive tone that underlines obvious facts to be built upon.
B) They establish a sarcastic tone that shows the author's stance towards a certain view.
C) They establish a confident tone about a fact that is subsequently qualified.
D) They establish a dubious tone that makes clear the author's uncertainty regarding colors.

23

The passage suggests that Newton would mainly characterize primary colors as those that are

A) visible.
B) a mixture of two colors.
C) indivisible.
D) part of the spectrum.

24

As used in line 20, the word "inclining" most nearly means

A) tending.
B) prompting.
C) tilting.
D) persuading.

25

The passage as a whole suggests that the results of Prof. J.D. Forbes' experiment could best be described as

A) inconclusive.
B) outdated.
C) legitimate.
D) mystifying.

26

Which choice provides the best evidence for the answer to the previous question?

A) Lines 7-11 ("Newton . . . prism")
B) Lines 45-49 ("and I . . . green")
C) Lines 49-52 ("I have . . . chrome-yellow")
D) Lines 65-67 ("I shall . . . yellow")

27

Which of the following best summarizes the findings of Prof. Helmholtz of Königsberg? Mixing blue and yellow powders is different from mixing blue and yellow beams of light because

A) the former will result in green due to absorption while the latter will result in green due to mixing.
B) the former only emits light that is not absorbed while the latter emits light from all its sources.
C) the former shows green thanks to absorption of light acting on blue and yellow particles.
D) the latter is a mix of all the light flowing from each color that includes green due to absorption.

28

The passage suggests that the author believes which of the following regarding experiments?

A) They must cover new, previously untested questions.
B) They should be conducted in a practical manner.
C) They have to be based on previous experiments.
D) They are not always conducted following the same motivations.

29

Which choice provides the best evidence for the answer to the previous question?

A) Lines 15-19 ("As far . . . gray")
B) Lines 21-22 ("Prof. J. D. Forbes . . . result")
C) Lines 40-45 ("I have . . . directly")
D) Lines 50-55 ("Those . . . tint")

CONTINUE ➡

30

Does the data in the table provide support for the author's claim that light coming off a mixture of blue and yellow powders will include green?

A) Yes, because the value of emerald-green increases each time that the value of yellow increases.

B) Yes, because the data shows that emerald-green often has the highest value among the three standard colors.

C) No, because the data does not provide any evidence that a mixture of yellow and blue light does not result in green.

D) No, because the data indicates that yellow powder alone also shows high amounts of emerald-green.

31

What statement is best supported by the data presented in the table?

A) The brightness of the mixture is directly dependent on the amount of yellow present in the mixture.

B) The vermillion value of 1 in $B_7 Y_1$ is due to yellow's quality of strongly suppressing vermillion.

C) The more yellow is present in the mixture of powders, the more it absorbs ultramarine.

D) Though both grow along with yellow, emerald-green is always greater or equal to vermillion.

Questions 32-41 are based on the following passage.

This passage is adapted from Charles Loring Brace, "The Dangerous Classes of New York and Twenty Years' Work Among Them." Originally published in 1872.

The source of juvenile crime and misery in New York, which is the most formidable, and, at the same time, one of the most difficult to remove, is the *overcrowding* of our population. The form of
5   the city-site is such—the majority of the dwellings being crowded into a narrow island between two water-fronts—that space near the business-portion of the city becomes of great value. These districts are necessarily sought for by the laboring and mechanic
10 classes, as they are near the places of employment. They are avoided by the wealthy on account of the population which has already occupied so much of them. The result is, that the poor must live in certain wards; and as space is costly, the landlords
15 supply them with (comparatively) cheap dwellings, by building very high and large houses, in which great numbers of people rent only rooms, instead of dwellings.
    Were New York a city radiating from a centre
20 over an almost unlimited space—as Philadelphia, for instance—the laborers or the mechanics might take up their abode anywhere, and land would be comparatively cheap, so that the highest blessing of the laboring class would be attainable—of separate
25 homes for each family. But, on this narrow island, business is so peculiarly concentrated, and population is so much forced to one exit—towards the north— and the poor have such a singular objection to living beyond a ferry, that space will inevitably continue
30 very dear in New York, and the laboring classes will be compelled to occupy it.
    To add to the unavoidable costliness of ground-room on this island, has come in the effect of bad government.
35   It is one of the most unpleasant experiences of the student of political economy, that the axioms of his science can so seldom be understood by the masses, though their interests be vitally affected by them. Thus, every thoughtful man knows that each new
40 "job" among city officials, each act of plunder of public property by members of the municipal government, every loss of income or mal-appropriation or extravagance in the city's funds, must be paid for by taxation, and that taxation always falls heaviest
45 on labor. The laboring classes of the city rule it, and through their especial leaders are the great public

losses and wastefulness occasioned.

Yet they never know that they themselves continually pay for these in increased rents. Every
50 landlord charges his advanced taxation in rent, and probably a profit on that. The tenant pays more for his room, the grocer more for his shop, the butcher and tailor and shoemaker, and every retailer have heavier expenses from the advance in rents, and each
55 and all charge it on their customers. The poor feel the final pressure. The painful effect has been, that the expense for rent has arisen enormously with the laboring classes of this city during the last five years, while many of the other living expenses have nearly
60 returned to the standard before the war.

The influence of high rents is to force more people into a given space, in order to economize and divide expense.

The latest trustworthy statistics on this important
65 subject are from the excellent Reports of the Metropolitan Board of Health for 1866. From these, it appears that the Eleventh Ward of this city, with a population of 58,953, has a rate of population of 196,510 to the square mile, or 16 1/10 square yards to
70 each person; the Tenth Ward, with 31,587 population, has a rate of 185,512 to the square mile, or 17 1/10 square yards to each; the Seventeenth Ward, with 79,563, has the rate of 153,006; the Fourteenth, with 23,382, has a rate of 155,880; the Thirteenth, with
75 26,388, has 155,224; and so on with others, though in less proportion.

32

The central problem described by Brace in the passage is that New York

A) has a higher rate of crime and poverty than other cities in America due to political corruption.

B) has attracted too many workers with its low rent prices and is running out of living space.

C) is crowded to the point where living costs rise which in turn causes other social problems.

D) is divided into sections that house different social classes which leads to friction among the latter.

33

The phrase in lines 5-7 ("the majority . . . water-fronts") primarily serves to

A) substantiate a statement about land prices.

B) describe the city as having an elongated shape.

C) explain the influx of inhabitants to New York.

D) suggest that water access drives up prices.

34

The "highest blessing of the laboring class" mentioned in lines 23-24 refers to

A) luxurious circumstances.

B) dwelling arrangements.

C) an impractical fantasy.

D) cities that cover a large area.

CONTINUE

35

The passage suggests which of the following statements about the high cost of living space?

A) It will go down once New York improves its transportation system.
B) Political corruption has recently begun to exacerbate the situation.
C) Workers cannot be considered free of blame regarding rent prices.
D) Sharing space has relieved most of the pressure on the lower classes.

36

Which choice provides the best evidence for the answer to the previous question?

A) Lines 14-18 ("landlords . . . dwellings")
B) Lines 28-31 ("and the . . . it")
C) Lines 32-34 ("To add . . . government")
D) Lines 61-63 ("The influence . . . expense")

37

As used in line 30, "dear" most nearly means

A) intimate.
B) beloved.
C) steep.
D) respected.

38

It can be inferred from the passage that the "thoughtful man" (line 39)

A) represents a minority due to his insight.
B) would readily work for the government.
C) is bent on righting the government's wrongs.
D) is the cause for the plight of the laboring classes.

39

The author indicates which of the following about members of the laboring class of New York?

A) They are unaware of their own plight.
B) They do not know they are shortchanged.
C) They should move to other cities like Philadelphia.
D) They can only enter certain wards of the city.

40

Which choice provides the best evidence for the answer to the previous question?

A) Lines 13-18 ("The result . . . dwellings")
B) Lines 19-23 ("Were . . . cheap")
C) Lines 35-38 ("It is . . . them")
D) Lines 45-49 ("The laboring . . . rents")

41

The most likely purpose of the final paragraph (lines 64-76) is to

A) illustrate an assertion.
B) show an improvement.
C) prove a theory.
D) clarify a boundary.

Questions 42-52 are based on the following passages.

These passages present different viewpoints on energy production. Passage 1 was written in 2014. Passage 2 was written in 2015.

Passage 1

Hardly anyone will dispute the fact that the United States, and everyone else for that matter, should move away from coal and gas, and invest in carbon-free energy instead. In addition to stemming
5 the greenhouse effect on a global scale, it is also in the interest of national security to work towards energy independence.

Another irrefutable fact is that nuclear power constitutes more than half of the pie that represents
10 the clean energy generated in our country. While about 67% of our electricity is derived from fossil fuels, 19% is produced in environmentally friendly nuclear power plants. Alternative sources such as wind and solar energy only contribute marginally.
15 Something that warrants immediate discussion, however, is the lack of support for our nuclear industry. Its potential is far from fully tapped. Its latent benefits are squandered each and every day that we fire fossil fuels instead of commissioning
20 new plants. All the while, we are falling miserably short of covering our energy requirements by relying on wind and solar power. If our administration is serious about reducing our nation's emission output (and providing much-needed jobs in the
25 process), why does it fail to remove the roadblocks that unnecessarily bar our way? For instance, the Environmental Protection Agency, surely meaning for the best but also clearly misguided, enacts policies that punish states for doing exactly what the agency
30 is supposed to foster: investing in clean and reliable power—which I assert is nuclear power.

The EPA's preferred treatment of wind and solar energy is counterproductive. The advantages of nuclear energy aside, wind and solar power are simply
35 not reliable enough to be more than an ancillary asset. Solar power is only available when the sun shines, and the same kind of dependence obviously curtails wind power. What happens during downtimes? Is our nation supposed to stop and wait for the clouds
40 to part and for the wind to pick up again? Statistically speaking, any such facilities will only generate power one third of the time. Why not instead build a plant that never stops?

Passage 2

2015 might be a year to remember in the hot
45 debate between nuclear energy and alternative energy sources. One of the key arguments of the pro-nuclear camp—the sun does not shine 24 hours a day—is obsolete as of now. Utility-grade batteries are newly arriving on the market that will decisively change the
50 face of this discussion in a number of ways.

These batteries are scalable up to capacities that will allow them to store sufficient energy to make up for the loss of nighttime hours. Given enough solar panel real estate and batteries, solar utilities
55 will not have to worry about peak energy demand outstripping supply and having to buy electricity from other utilities at a higher price to make up for the loss. These advantages analogously apply to windmills that can now store unused energy to compensate for lulls.
60 Another essential facet of these batteries is their price. In a free market, price heavily influences adoption, and several studies indicate that making a capital investment in these batteries might actually result in a slight reduction on the end
65 user's electric bill. And while solar power coupled with these batteries will certainly be cheaper than new electric power (electric power coming from a newly constructed nuclear plant), wind power could possibly be offered at such prices that competing
70 nuclear utilities might have a hard time selling their electricity at all.

Nuclear proponents often cite emission standards and greenhouse gas emissions as reasons to construct more plants. Granted, more plants replacing coal-
75 firing facilities would reduce the burden on our environment. But even disregarding cost, the sheer amount of time it would take to construct these plants and get them hooked up to the grid also needs to be considered. We cannot afford to wait for years.
80 Windmills and solar panels, on the other hand, can go online immediately and help decrease greenhouse gas emissions at once.

Finally, let us not forget safety. Although safety standards for nuclear power plants have risen, they
85 are not applicable to every single nuclear power plant (especially the older ones). And as the Fukushima tragedy has hopefully taught us, even a miniscule risk is unacceptable if the consequences are such.

42

The author of Passage 1 indicates that solar and wind energy facilities trail nuclear power plants in terms of

A) uptime.
B) construction time.
C) safety.
D) innovation.

43

As used in line 30, "foster" most nearly means

A) harbor.
B) raise.
C) advance.
D) foment.

44

As used in line 50, "face" most nearly means

A) pretense.
B) nature.
C) dignity.
D) countenance.

45

The author of Passage 2 uses the word "actually" in line 64 in order to

A) suggest that capital investments are usually reflected in higher prices.
B) explicate the idea that free markets are driven by product prices.
C) emphasize the moderate nature of the possible fee reduction.
D) indicate that the mentioned savings are not a matter of certainty.

46

In lines 74-76 ("Granted . . . environment"), the author of Passage 2 mostly

A) acknowledges that an option might not represent the worst possibility.
B) concedes that building more nuclear power plants is a good idea.
C) implies that coal-firing plants hurt the environment the most.
D) mocks the rhetoric that nuclear proponents are wont to use.

47

Which choice best describes how the author of Passage 1 would probably respond to lines 79-82, Passage 2 ("We . . . once")?

A) He would question the assertion that alternative power generation can be added within a short amount of time.
B) He would agree that an immediate switch away from fossil fuels should be the highest priority for lawmakers.
C) He would assert that non-nuclear power generation is not up to the task of providing sufficient, clean power for the nation.
D) He would add to this that since nuclear power generates only 19%, this leaves enough room for wind and solar growth.

48

Which choice provides the best evidence for the answer to the previous question?

A) Lines 8-10 ("Another . . . country")
B) Lines 10-13 ("While . . . plants")
C) Lines 32-33 ("The EPA's . . . counterproductive")
D) Lines 36-38 ("Solar . . . wind power")

49

The author of Passage 2 would most likely regard the questions in lines 38-43, Passage 1 ("What . . . stops?") as

A) newly dated.
B) decisive.
C) completely unrelated.
D) histrionic.

50

Which choice provides the best evidence for the answer to the previous question?

A) Lines 46-48 ("One of . . . now")
B) Lines 51-53 ("These . . . hours")
C) Lines 58-59 ("These . . . lulls")
D) Lines 86-88 ("And as . . . such")

51

Which of the following choices best summarizes the relationship between the two passages?

A) Passage 2 challenges the reliability of the evidence brought forth in Passage 1.
B) Passage 2 provides facts that further corroborate the position held in Passage 1.
C) Passage 2 generalizes on a specific trend outlined in Passage 1.
D) Passage 2 questions the validity of the main criticism stated in Passage 1.

52

Both passages primarily seek to

A) evaluate the environmental impact and safety of nuclear power.
B) condone the direction that policy-makers are taking.
C) argue for a specific technology by criticizing alternatives.
D) explain the relationship between market forces and energy policy.

STOP

Do not move on to the next section if you finish early.

You may review your answers in this section only.

Answer Keys & Performance Breakdown

1	(B)	Summary	19	(C)	Local	37	(C)	Vocabulary
2	(A)	Local	20	(D)	Graph	38	(A)	Local
3	(C)	Local	21	(C)	Graph	39	(B)	Local
4	(B)	Synthesize	22	(C)	Style	40	(D)	Evidence
5	(D)	Local	23	(C)	Local	41	(A)	Context
6	(C)	Local	24	(A)	Vocabulary	42	(A)	Local
7	(C)	Context	25	(C)	Local	43	(C)	Vocabulary
8	(C)	Vocabulary	26	(B)	Evidence	44	(B)	Vocabulary
9	(A)	Local	27	(C)	Local	45	(A)	Context
10	(D)	Evidence	28	(B)	Local	46	(A)	Local
11	(D)	Summary	29	(D)	Evidence	47	(C)	Synthesize
12	(C)	Local	30	(B)	Graph	48	(D)	Evidence
13	(A)	Context	31	(C)	Graph	49	(A)	Synthesize
14	(B)	Local	32	(C)	Summary	50	(A)	Evidence
15	(C)	Evidence	33	(A)	Context	51	(D)	Synthesize
16	(B)	Vocabulary	34	(B)	Local	52	(C)	Synthesize
17	(C)	Evidence	35	(C)	Local			
18	(D)	Vocabulary	36	(B)	Evidence			

■ Write down the number of correct answers for each question type.

Question Types	Number of Correct Answers
Local	/ 18
Style	/ 1
Vocabulary	/ 7
Evidence	/ 9
Context	/ 5
Organization	0 / 0
Summary	/ 3
Stance	0 / 0
Synthesize	/ 5
Graph	/ 4
Total	**/ 52**

Answer Explanations

Questions 1-10

1. (B) — Summary

B is the best choice because the youth (the protagonist) mainly wonders if his comrades are secretly afraid of battle, or if they really look forward to it as many of them claim. He wishes he could ask them directly. The long conversation in the latter part again shows the youth's fixation on bravery versus cowardice.

A is incorrect because the passage focuses on the feelings and doubts of one soldier. C is incorrect because a lack of courage is never admitted to in the passage, and no such communities have formed. D is incorrect because the passage does not describe "dire odds" that could be faced with bravado.

2. (A) — Local

A is the best choice because he fears he might be "derided" by the "unconfessed" (those who did not confess their fears).

B is incorrect because to "implicate" means to "entangle" or to "incriminate." He is not concerned about others' well-being at this point. C is incorrect because formulating his concerns is not mentioned as a problem. D is incorrect because "never" is not supported.

3. (C) — Local

C is the best choice because line 21 mentions "courage unseen," so being blind refers to his inability to see their courage.

A is incorrect because it is the opposite of what the passage states. B is incorrect because passage states that in spite of the long time they have spent together, there were things he might not know. This is different from bias, or color. D is incorrect because it does not refer to the comrades in question.

4. (B) — Synthesize

The "men" in line 20 are those who might have more courage than he was aware of (see explanation for question 3) while the "men" in line 28 say they are eager to join battle and are suspected to be liars (line 31).

B is the best choice.

A is incorrect because reliability in battle is not mentioned. C is incorrect because maturity and naivety are not compared. D is incorrect because it mixes up bravery and fear for the respective parties.

5. (D) — Local

D is the best choice because within these lines, he curses the cows and flings implements, which implies frustration or rage.

A, B, and C are incorrect because none of these are supported by the specified lines.

6. (C) — Local

The "present point of view" is in opposition to his former dislike of farm life. Now, he would give anything to return to that time. In other words, the time he used to hate looks much more appealing in retrospect.

C is the best choice.

A, B, and D are incorrect because none of them mention that something previously hated looks better in retrospect.

7. (C) — Context

The "brass buttons" in the sentence is mentioned as the amount he would sacrifice to return to previous, happier times. He would sacrifice all of the brass buttons in America which stands for a huge amount.

C is the best choice.

A is incorrect because the brass buttons do not signify whether a wish is possible. B is incorrect because he feels longing, not excitement. D is incorrect because the brass buttons are not related to the wisdom of others.

8. (C) — Vocabulary

C is the best choice because in the sentence, Wilson's voice had an exultant ring. Therefore, "ring" describes the pitch or quality of his voice (which was exultant).

A is obviously incorrect. B refers to the sound of metal on metal. D is incorrect because it means to "echo."

9. (A) — Local

A is the best choice because of lines 86-87 (see next question). The youth turns bitter after Wilson

Answer Explanations

repeatedly and confidently emphasizes how they will beat the enemy in the next engagement. The youth is still struggling with his own feeling towards battle and suspects other soldiers are as afraid as he is.

B is incorrect because the passage does not indicate the youth is bothered by the loudness per se. C is incorrect because Wilson is not shown to be egoistic. D is incorrect because Wilson is not sanctimonious either.

10. (D) — Evidence

D is the best choice because his question directly addresses the question of bravery.

C is not the best evidence because, while it is sarcastic, it does not address the question of bravery as directly.

A is incorrect because it does not show the youth's reaction to Wilson's bravado. B is incorrect because the youth does not address Wilson's bravado.

Questions 11-21

11. (D) — Summary

The author notes a preponderance of males among evil leaders. The question becomes whether this is because women do not have the same opportunities to do evil, or whether men are inherently worse human beings. Statistics and studies are cited supporting that women do have fewer opportunities to attain leadership positions (necessary to do evil), but that men are intrinsically different from women as well. These differences facilitate evil behavior and the rise to higher positions. Therefore, men predominate both because of unequal opportunities and inherent differences.

D is the best choice.

A is incorrect because the passage does not advocate support for female CEOs. B is incorrect because nothing such is recommended. C is incorrect because "differences" are supported, not debunked.

12. (C) — Local

The question asks for the "rationale" (reason) for looking up recent examples, so lines 12-13 ("since . . . opportunity") are of interest which say that "this might shed light on the question of equal opportunity."

C is the best choice because the lines imply that the question of equal opportunity might have changed in recent times as compared to "history" (lines 3-4).

A and B are incorrect because they are unrelated to equal opportunity. D is incorrect because ease of research is not implied in context.

13. (A) — Context

A is the best choice because the paragraph in essence asks whether women have the opportunity to commit evil as opposed to whether men are simply different from women. This is a restatement of the questions found in lines 6-9 ("Do . . . outcome").

B is incorrect because the paragraph actually says that current times "are reflective of what history books tell us." C is incorrect because the paragraph does not question, it merely inquires. D is incorrect because the paragraph does not lead into historic occurrences.

14. (B) — Local

B is the best choice because of lines 34-36 (see next question).

A is incorrect because no such number is mentioned in the context of women and equal opportunities. C is incorrect because it is not mentioned in this context. D is incorrect because "dramatic pace" is not supported.

15. (C) — Evidence

C is the best choice because the lines state that it will take a long time before women attain 20% of the top leadership positions. Since "comparable" implies around 50%, C definitely supports the previous answer.

A, B, and D are incorrect because none of them show that women will not have as many opportunities as men any time soon.

16. (B) — Vocabulary

In the sentence, "makeup" stands in contrast to "perception." In context, these two concepts stand for the question of whether emancipation or inherent differences between men and women are the root cause (refer to lines 24-29 and see topic in explanation for question 11). Therefore, "makeup" stands for inherent differences. Since "makeup" can also mean "personality," B is the best choice.

A is obviously incorrect. C is incorrect because it means "structure" or "composition." D is incorrect because it describes an outward aspect.

17. (C)
Evidence

C is the best choice because the lines state that there is a link between "these tendencies" (men display more manipulative behavior and yearning for admiration) and "corporate promotions." Thus, men are promoted more because they possess more negative traits.

A, B, and D are incorrect because none of them support that society is the way it is because men are worse human beings.

18. (D)
Vocabulary

In line 9, an outcome is *favored*. In line 57, a path "favors" the ambitious and cunning people.

D is the best choice because it fits in both cases.

A is incorrect because it fits in line 9, but not in line 57. (Facilitating a person does not fit in context.) B is incorrect because it means "pay respect to." C is incorrect because it means "give permission" or "impose a penalty on."

19. (C)
Local

C is the best choice because the preceding sentence mentions that "the existence of inherently gender-based differences in disposition came as a surprise." This shows that he has not been able to discern gender-based differences.

A and D are incorrect because the "personal environment" refers to intrinsic differences between men and women. B is not supported because the only statement made is that the author did not perceive a difference between men and women.

20. (D)
Graph

D is the best choice because both statements are supported.

A is incorrect because the figure does not indicate what female CEOs themselves think. B is incorrect because they are not given more credit for ethical behavior. C is incorrect because women are seen as less egoistical (concerned with personal advancement).

21. (C)
Graph

C is the best choice because the passage states that men are more manipulative and tend to desire more admiration from others. This collides with the data in the figure which says that males are perceived as having better morals.

A is incorrect because the passage does not state women cannot become CEOs. B is incorrect because the passage mentions no such perspective. D is incorrect because it cannot be said to be an "excellent illustration." (Morality should be higher for women in that case.)

Questions 22-31

22. (C)
Style

C is the best choice because both phrases in essence mean that the majority knows and agrees about something. That something is that blue and yellow make green. This is then contrasted against Newton (line 7) who found that this is not true for colors of the spectrum. Therefore, this common knowledge that blue and yellow make green is qualified by Newton's findings.

A is incorrect because a fact is not built upon. Rather, the paragraph states that a common understanding is sometimes wrong. B is incorrect because the phrases do not show sarcasm. D is incorrect because the phrases do not show doubt or uncertainty.

23. (C)
Local

C is the best choice because in lines 6-7, the secondary color green is stated to be a mixture of two other colors. Newton, however, found that the green of the spectrum is not a mixture since it cannot be separated. Thus, the green of the spectrum is not a secondary color, which suggests that primary colors cannot be separated.

A is incorrect because the passage does not imply that only primary colors are visible. B is incorrect because it describes secondary colors. D is incorrect because the context focuses on the division of colors, not their presence in the spectrum.

24. (A)
Vocabulary

A is the best choice because the sentence describes the color of a spinning disc made up of yellow and blue which showed mostly gray and "inclining" to yellow or blue. Thus, "inclining" here means that the color, to a small degree, showed yellow or blue, which makes "tending" correct.

B is incorrect because it means "inciting" or "eliciting." C is incorrect because it means "slanting" or "inclining" (referring to angles and alignment). D is incorrect

Answer Explanations

because it means "convincing" or "influencing."

25. (C) — Local

C is the best choice because of lines 45-49 (see next question).

A is incorrect because the passage states that the experiment brought a conclusive result (no green). B is incorrect because obsolescence is not mentioned. D is incorrect because even though Forbes conducted similar experiments to Plateau, the passage does not indicate that this in itself is seen in a negative light by the author. ("Unoriginal" is pejorative.)

26. (B) — Evidence

B is the best choice because the lines describe the author's experiment where he, like Forbes, concludes that mixing blue and yellow light does not show green. Thus, he would characterize Forbes' experiment and results as correct or "legitimate."

A, C, and D are incorrect because none of them show that the author would characterize Forbes' experiment as legitimate.

27. (C) — Local

C is the best choice because Königsberg found that mixing two powders, we receive only light which has escaped absorption (lines 32-33), that this light acted on both blue and yellow particles (lines 36-37), and that this light is green since the blue stops (absorbs) the red, yellow, and orange, and yellow stops (absorbs) the blue and violet (lines 37-39). This is in accordance with C.

A is incorrect because the "latter" (mixing light) does not result in green ("this phenomenon" in line 25 refers to the results in the previous paragraph). B is incorrect because the "former" (mixing powders) does not only emit light that is not absorbed (check lines 35-36). D is incorrect because "all the light flowing from each color" refers to mixing light, not powders.

28. (B) — Local

B is the best choice because of lines 50-55 (see next question).

A is incorrect because it is not mentioned in the passage. C is incorrect because though Forbes' experiment might have been based on Plateau's, this was not mentioned as a requirement or obligation. D is incorrect because differing motivations were not mentioned.

29. (D) — Evidence

D is the best choice because the lines state that the author chose certain powders since others were difficult to mix even though they gave curious results. He prioritized ease of mixing.

A, B, and C are incorrect because none of them show that the author believes that experiments should be conducted in a practical manner.

30. (B) — Graph

B is the best choice because in the table, "E" stands for emerald-green and it does have the highest value in five consecutive data rows (starting in the third row from the top).

A is incorrect because emerald-green does not increase from Y_3 to Y_4. C is incorrect because it refers to mixing light, not powders. D is incorrect because the fact stated after "No" does not mean the rest of the data in the table does not support the author's statement.

31. (C) — Graph

C is the best choice because according to the statement in C, the value of ultramarine has to decrease every time yellow increases (since yellow absorbs ultramarine). This is the case.

A is incorrect because adding yellow can decrease the brightness ($B_8 \rightarrow B_7 Y_1$) as well as increase it (every other case). B is incorrect because if it were yellow's "quality" or characteristic to suppress vermillion, the latter's value would decrease with increasing yellow. The opposite is the case. D is incorrect because in the last two data rows, vermillion is equal or greater than emerald-green.

Questions 32-41

32. (C) — Summary

The passage first states that the source of crime and misery in New York is overcrowding (because of the way the city is enclosed by water). It then states that lack of living space and corruption result in higher and higher living expenses which put pressure on the laboring classes.

C is the best choice. ("Other social problems" refers to

crime and misery.)

A is incorrect because no comparisons are made to other cities. B is incorrect because "low rent prices" is not mentioned. D is incorrect because segregated living arrangements are not mentioned as a cause for friction among social classes.

33. (A) — Context

A is the best choice because the specified part of the sentence explains why the form of the city drives up land prices. Most dwellings being on a narrow island between two water-fronts indicates a lack of space which explains high land prices.

B is incorrect because even though "elongated" makes sense, description of the form is not the function of the specified words. C is incorrect because migration into the city is not mentioned. D is incorrect because lack of space, not water access, is indicated as a reason for high prices.

34. (B) — Local

B is the best choice because the same sentence specifies what the blessings are: "separate homes for each family."

A is incorrect because luxury is not suggested in context. C is incorrect because nothing indicates that separate homes are an "impractical fantasy." D is incorrect because cities that cover a large area are not the blessing itself. Rather, they are a factor that would make that blessing possible.

35. (C) — Local

C is the best choice because of lines 28-31 (see next question).

A is incorrect because the passage makes no such assertion. The fact that workers dislike living beyond a ferry does not necessarily mean that better transportation would change this fact. B is incorrect because the passage does not indicate that political corruption is something that has begun recently. D is incorrect because the passage only mentions that space is shared to economize and divide expense. This does not imply that most of the pressure is gone.

36. (B) — Evidence

B is the best choice because the lines state that the poor do not like to live beyond a ferry and that space will continue to be very expensive in New York. This implies that workers could take a ferry and live further away. Since high rent prices are a result of overcrowding, workers who decide not to take a ferry are part of the reason living space is expensive.

A, C, and D are incorrect because none of them show that workers are also part of the reason why rent prices are high.

37. (C) — Vocabulary

C is the best choice because the sentence states that a high population density is the reason that space will continue very "dear" in New York. Also, the context of this sentence discusses the cost of renting living space. Thus, "dear" has to mean "very expensive" or "steep."

A is incorrect because it means "confidential" or "loving." B is incorrect because it means "cherished" or "admired." D is incorrect because it means "esteemed" or "honored."

38. (A) — Local

A is the best choice. The sentence in which the specified phrase appears starts with "thus," so it can be seen as resulting from the previous sentence. The previous sentence says that the axioms of political economy are seldom understood by the masses. This implies that the "thoughtful man" is one who does understand the axioms (as opposed to the masses).

B is incorrect because eagerness to work for the government is not implied. C is incorrect because righting wrongs is not implied. D is incorrect because the "thoughtful man" is aware of economic circumstances which is not the same as causing plight.

39. (B) — Local

B is the best choice because of lines 45-49 (see next question).

A is incorrect because the passage only mentions that laborers mostly do not know about axioms of political economy, which is not the same as not knowing that you are going through hard times. C is incorrect because no such move is recommended or suggested. D is incorrect because the passage does not mention that laborers are forbidden from entering certain parts of the city.

40. (D) — Evidence

D is the best choice because the lines state that public losses and wastefulness are paid for by laborers

Answer Explanations

through increased rents and that "they never know" (line 48).

A, B, and C are incorrect because none of them show that the laborers do not know that they are shortchanged.

41. (A) — Context

A is the best choice because the paragraph details how several wards are very crowded. This supports the previous sentence (lines 61-63) which states that more people have to move together to save money.

B is incorrect because no improvement is reported in the paragraph. C is incorrect because no theory appears in context. D is incorrect because no limits or lines are explained.

Questions 42-52

42. (A) — Local

A is the best choice because of lines 36-38 and lines 40-43.

B is incorrect because construction times are not mentioned in Passage 1. C is incorrect because Passage 1 does not imply nuclear power is *safer*. (It merely claims it is safe.) D is incorrect because Passage 1 does not indicate that nuclear plants are more innovative.

43. (C) — Vocabulary

C is the best choice because the sentence says that an agency is supposed to "foster" policies such as investing in clean and reliable power.

A is incorrect because it means "shelter." B is incorrect because it means "nurture." D is incorrect because it means "instigate" or "provoke."

44. (B) — Vocabulary

B is the best choice because the sentence says that the "face" of a discussion will be changed. "Nature" or "characteristic" is therefore correct.

A is incorrect because it means "falsehood" or "charade." C is incorrect because it means "decorum" or "honor." D is incorrect because it is too literal.

45. (A) — Context

A is the best choice because within the sentence, the word implies surprise or an exception. Therefore, the reduction on the end user's electric bill is something unexpected. (Usually, higher prices would be expected.)

B is incorrect because the word in question does not explain this. C is incorrect because the word in question does not indicate by how much the price will fall. D is incorrect because "actually" does not indicate a level of certainty.

46. (A) — Local

A is the best choice because the sentence implies that nuclear plants (an option) are preferable to coal-firing plants (worse than nuclear plants) in terms of environmental impact.

B is incorrect because the author only concedes nuclear plants are better than coal power plants, which is not the same as recommending the construction of more nuclear plants. C is incorrect because "the most" is not supported. D is incorrect because nothing indicates that nuclear proponents would usually say this.

47. (C) — Synthesize

Lines 79-82 state that wind and solar power can contribute to reduced greenhouse gases immediately.

The author of Passage 1 is negatively disposed towards wind and solar because they do not produce enough energy, which is partly due to up- and downtimes.

C is the best choice.

A is incorrect because Passage 1 does not discuss construction times. B and D are incorrect because the author of Passage 1 asserts nuclear is the only way to go.

48. (D) — Evidence

D is the best choice because it supports the notion that wind and solar do not produce sufficient power.

A, B, and C are incorrect because none of them support this notion.

49. (A) — Synthesize

The specified questions basically imply that wind and solar power are not desirable because they suffer regular downtimes. Passage 2 asserts that batteries that have recently arrived on market render this argument obsolete because they can make up for the downtimes.

A is the best choice. ("Dated" means "obsolete.")

B is incorrect because it would mean Passage 2 agrees with Passage 1. C is incorrect because according to Passage 2, batteries decisively change the aspect of the discussion touched on by the specified questions. So the questions cannot be completely unrelated. D is incorrect because "histrionic" means "overly dramatic." Passage 2 does not characterize the opposition as histrionic.

50. (A) Evidence

A is the best choice because it mentions downtimes of solar facilities and that this argument is now obsolete.

B, C, and D are incorrect because they do not show that the author of Passage 2 would find the specified questions mentioned "newly dated."

51. (D) Synthesize

Passage 1 complains about the lack of support for nuclear power. It claims nuclear is superior to solar and wind power because the latter do not produce enough power, which is in part due to inherent downtimes (no sun or no wind). Passage 2 claims that batteries will more than offset the problem of downtimes with solar and wind facilities. It also claims that nuclear power is more expensive and plants take longer to construct.

D is the best choice.

A is incorrect because Passage 2 does not challenge evidence brought forth. B is incorrect because Passage 2 does not corroborate the position of Passage 1. C is incorrect because it does not generalize or place the discussion in a broader context.

52. (C) Synthesize

C is the best choice (see explanation for previous question).

A is incorrect because even though both environmental impact and safety are mentioned, their evaluation is not the main focus of the passages. B is incorrect because Passage 1 complains about current policies. D is incorrect because only Passage 2 mentions "market forces (price)."

SAT.Hackers.ac

Hackers New SAT Reading: 10 Practice Tests

TEST 2

Answer Keys & Performance Breakdown

Answer Explanations

Reading Test

65 MINUTES, 52 QUESTIONS

Mark your answers to the questions in Section 1 in the answer sheet provided.

DIRECTIONS

For each of the passages below, there are 10 or 11 questions. Choose the best answer for each of the questions after you have finished reading the passage. The answers to the questions should be based on the information that is stated or implied in the text and any associated graphics.

Questions 1-10 are based on the following passage.

This passage is adapted from Arthur Conan Doyle, "Sherlock Holmes: A Study in Scarlet." Originally published in 1887. The narrator has recently moved in with a mysterious new roommate and has so far restrained his curiosity as to his roommate's studies and profession.

It was upon the 4th of March, as I have good reason to remember, that I rose somewhat earlier than usual, and found that Sherlock Holmes had not yet finished his breakfast. The landlady had become so accustomed to my late habits that my place had not been laid nor my coffee prepared. With the unreasonable petulance of mankind I rang the bell and gave a curt intimation that I was ready. Then I picked up a magazine from the table and attempted to while away the time with it, while my companion munched silently at his toast. One of the articles had a pencil mark at the heading, and I naturally began to run my eye through it.

Its somewhat ambitious title was "The Book of Life," and it attempted to show how much an observant man might learn by an accurate and systematic examination of all that came in his way. It struck me as being a remarkable mixture of shrewdness and of absurdity. The reasoning was close and intense, but the deductions appeared to me to be far-fetched and exaggerated. The writer claimed by a momentary expression, a twitch of a muscle or a glance of an eye, to fathom a man's inmost thoughts. Deceit, according to him, was an impossibility in the case of one trained to observation and analysis. His conclusions were as infallible as so many propositions of Euclid. So startling would his results appear to the uninitiated that until they learned the processes by which he had arrived at them they might well consider him as a necromancer.

"From a drop of water," said the writer, "a logician could infer the possibility of an Atlantic or a Niagara without having seen or heard of one or the other. So all life is a great chain, the nature of which is known whenever we are shown a single link of it. Like all other arts, the Science of Deduction and Analysis is one which can only be acquired by long and patient study nor is life long enough to allow any mortal to attain the highest possible perfection in it. Before turning to those moral and mental aspects of the matter which present the greatest difficulties, let the enquirer begin by mastering more elementary problems. Let him, on meeting a fellow-mortal, learn at a glance to distinguish the history of the man, and the trade or profession to which he belongs. Puerile as such an exercise may seem, it sharpens the faculties of observation, and teaches one where to look and what to look for. By a man's finger nails, by his coat-sleeve, by his boot, by his trouser knees, by the callosities of his forefinger and thumb, by his expression, by his shirt cuffs—by each of these things a man's calling is plainly revealed. That all united should fail to enlighten the competent enquirer in any case is almost inconceivable."

"What ineffable twaddle!" I cried, slapping the magazine down on the table, "I never read such rubbish in my life."

"What is it?" asked Sherlock Holmes.

"Why, this article," I said, pointing at it with my egg spoon as I sat down to my breakfast. "I see that you have read it since you have marked it. I don't deny that it is smartly written. It irritates me though. It is evidently the theory of some arm-chair lounger who evolves all these neat little paradoxes in the seclusion of his own study. It is not practical. I should like to see him clapped down in a third class carriage on the Underground, and asked to give the trades of all his fellow-travellers. I would lay a thousand to one against him."

70 "You would lose your money," Sherlock Holmes remarked calmly. "As for the article I wrote it myself."

1

In context, the passage suggests that the narrator's actions in lines 7-8 are most like those of

A) a sulking child.
B) a tardy client.
C) an offended customer.
D) a reticent father.

2

In lines 14-15, the narrator suggests that the title of the article

A) refers to observational powers.
B) spontaneously caught his interest.
C) might be judged as grandiose.
D) is pretentious and misleading.

3

As used in line 19, "close" most nearly means

A) intimate.
B) adjacent.
C) precise.
D) literal.

4

The author most likely mentions "callosities" in line 49 to provide an example of

A) implements that hone observation.
B) the effects of a callow way of thought.
C) the signs of a hard-working person.
D) clues that betray a person's vocation.

5

Lines 52-54 ("That . . . inconceivable") suggest that the writer believes

A) cooperation will virtually guarantee the enquirer the answers he seeks.
B) an aggregate of information will lead to a virtually predetermined outcome.
C) enlightenment has to be predicated upon the vocations of those present.
D) only capable enquirers qualify for the Study of Deduction.

6

The passage indicates that the narrator regards the author of "The Book of Life" as

A) a writer who lacks exposure to reality.
B) a scientist whose work is deemed magic.
C) an adept observer impervious to trickery.
D) a charlatan given to cagey prevarication.

7

Which choice provides the best evidence for the answer to the previous question?

A) Lines 19-21 ("The reasoning . . . exaggerated")
B) Lines 24-25 ("Deceit . . . analysis")
C) Lines 27-30 ("So startling . . . necromancer")
D) Lines 62-65 ("It is . . . study")

8

What does the narrator mainly do in lines 62-65 ("It is . . . study")?

A) He accuses the article's writer of never having actually witnessed the subject of his research.
B) He concedes a point before launching an attack regarding the writer's lack of realism.
C) He implies that the article's writer proposes a theory that is merely academic in nature.
D) He airs his belief that a sedentary lifestyle will ultimately result in absurd conclusions.

9

As used in line 67, "give" most nearly means

A) award.
B) proffer.
C) announce.
D) cede.

10

Holmes' retort in line 70 and the preceding statement both

A) discuss Holmes' aptitude at performing a certain task.
B) assert sufficient confidence to bet against high stakes.
C) exude certainty in the accuracy of their positions.
D) reveal the exasperation of the respective speakers.

Questions 11-21 are based on the following passage and supplementary material.

This passage is adapted from Vice President Spiro T. Agnew's address on TV News Coverage in 1969.

At least 40 million Americans every night, it's estimated, watch the network news. Seven million of them view A.B.C., the remainder being divided between N.B.C. and C.B.S. According to Harris polls
[5] and other studies, for millions of Americans the networks are the sole source of national and world news. In Will Rogers' observation, what you knew was what you read in the newspaper. Today for growing millions of Americans, it's what they see and hear on
[10] their television sets.

Now how is this network news determined? A small group of men, numbering perhaps no more than a dozen anchormen, commentators, and executive producers, settle upon the 20 minutes or so
[15] of film and commentary that's to reach the public.

This selection is made from the 90 to 180 minutes that may be available. Their powers of choice are broad. They decide what 40 to 50 million Americans will learn of the day's events in the nation and in the
[20] world. We cannot measure this power and influence by the traditional democratic standards, for these men can create national issues overnight. They can make or break by their coverage and commentary a moratorium on the war. They can elevate men from
[25] obscurity to national prominence within a week. They can reward some politicians with national exposure and ignore others.

For millions of Americans, the network reporter who covers a continuing issue—like the ABM or civil
[30] rights—becomes, in effect, the presiding judge in a national trial by jury.

It must be recognized that the networks have made important contributions to the national knowledge—through news, documentaries,
[35] and specials. They have often used their power constructively and creatively to awaken the public conscience to critical problems. The networks made hunger and black lung disease national issues overnight. The TV networks have done what no other
[40] medium could have done in terms of dramatizing the horrors of war. The networks have tackled our most difficult social problems with a directness and an immediacy that's the gift of their medium.

They focus the nation's attention on its
[45] environmental abuses—on pollution in the Great Lakes and the threatened ecology of the Everglades.

But it was also the networks that elevated Stokely Carmichael[1] and George Lincoln Rockwell[2] from obscurity to national prominence.
[50] Nor is their power confined to the substantive. A raised eyebrow, an inflection of the voice, a caustic remark dropped in the middle of a broadcast can raise doubts in a million minds about the veracity of a public official or the wisdom of a Government
[55] policy. One Federal Communications Commissioner considers the powers of the networks equal to that of local, state, and Federal Governments all combined. Certainly it represents a concentration of power over American public opinion unknown in history.

[60] Now what do Americans know of the men who wield this power? Of the men who produce and direct the network news, the nation knows practically nothing. Of the commentators, most Americans know little other than that they reflect an urbane and
[65] assured presence, seemingly well-informed on every important matter. We do know that to a man these commentators and producers live and work in the geographical and intellectual confines of Washington, D.C., or New York City, the latter of which James
[70] Reston terms "the most unrepresentative community in the entire United States."

---

[1] a prominent figure in the civil rights and Black Power movements

[2] a major figure in the neo-Nazi movement in the United States, also known as the "American Hitler"

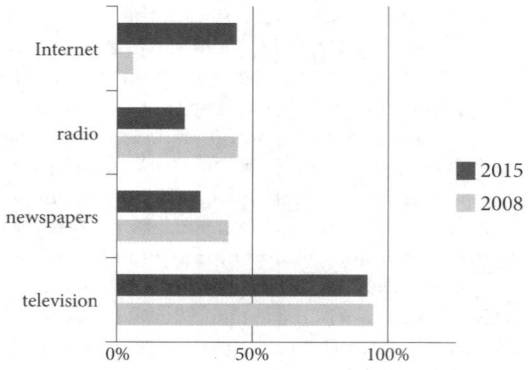

Figure 1
News Channels People State They Use Regularly in Region C

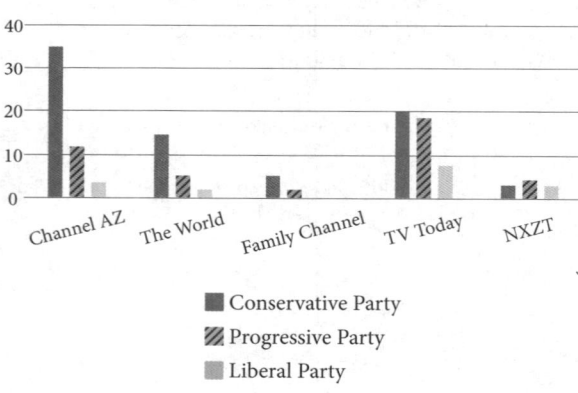

Figure 2
Number of Appearances of Different Political Parties on Popular TV Channels in Region C

11

Agnew's primary purpose is to

A) discuss the aptness of a medium's transparency and reach.
B) propose solutions to what he perceives to be a problem.
C) chronicle the rise of a new power in American society.
D) present the struggle between the government and news networks.

12

The "dozen" in line 13 is most similar to

A) "the network reporter" (line 28)
B) "One Federal Communications Commissioner" (line 55)
C) "men" (line 60)
D) "James Reston" (lines 69-70)

13

As used in line 25, "obscurity" most nearly means

A) nonentity.
B) darkness.
C) ambiguity.
D) fuzziness.

14

Which choice best supports the author's point that television networks deserve a measure of approval?

A) Lines 11-15 ("Now . . . public")
B) Lines 20-24 ("We . . . war")
C) Lines 24-27 ("They . . . others")
D) Lines 35-37 ("They . . . problems")

15

The passage suggests that Agnew regards Carmichael's and Rockwell's rise to national prominence (lines 47-49) with

A) satisfaction.
B) apathy.
C) incredulity.
D) disapproval.

16

In lines 50-55 ("Nor . . . policy"), Agnew implies that newscasters are capable of

A) mocking government officials without fear of punitive reprisal.
B) swaying public opinion even when they stray from the topic being discussed.
C) using non-verbal communication to sway the opinion of the public.
D) using their influence to countermand decisions of the U.S. government.

17

Agnew would probably agree with which of the following statements?

A) News networks represent a significant cornerstone of American freedom and democracy.
B) The fact that televised news is generally taken seriously is a potential problem.
C) The alarming amount of power news networks wield is more than offset by their lack of transparency.
D) America is controlled by a small group of influencers about whom little is known.

18

The passage most strongly suggests that TV news coverage is mainly problematic due to

A) contradicting messages on different news networks.
B) the displacement of newspapers as determiners of opinion.
C) its disproportionate ability to influence public opinion.
D) its failure to focus on issues that the public should learn about.

19

Which choice provides the best evidence for the answer to the previous question?

A) Lines 7-10 ("In Will . . . sets")
B) Lines 44-49 ("They focus . . . prominence")
C) Lines 55-59 ("One . . . history")
D) Lines 66-71 ("We do . . . States")

20

Figure 1 suggests which of the following about news media between 2008 and 2015?

A) Newspapers have lost their hegemonic position to television and the Internet.
B) The Internet has gained in popularity because of its multimedia aspect.
C) Newspapers and radio are more and more perceived as old-fashioned.
D) The most and least dominant media have moved closer together.

21

Which of the following concepts from the passage is best supported by the data in Figure 2?

A) News networks can grant or withhold national exposure at will.
B) A small group of men arbitrarily decides what Americans get to see.
C) Not enough is known about the motives of those who select news.
D) TV networks have the power to showcase critical issues to the public.

Questions 22-31 are based on the following passages.

These passages discuss the controversial use of DDT, a chemical compound known for its insecticidal qualities in the fight against malaria, a disease transmitted by mosquito bites.

Passage 1

During World War II, DDT gained prominence due to its insecticidal potency—it was the killer of choice against mosquitos. Allied forces relied on it as a vector[1] control agent in the fight against
5   diseases. With its help, they mostly drove typhus out of Europe and fended off malaria in the Pacific theater of operations. After the war, DDT was widely adopted by farmers as a pesticide, and it contributed to the ousting of the latter disease in the Western
10 world. In spite of these substantial contributions, environmental concerns that gained ground in the 1960s laid the groundwork for the agent's demise, and by the late 1980s, most developed countries had placed bans on its agricultural usage.
15 To be sure, these restrictions are based on valid reasons. Even though studies are inconclusive as to whether DDT causes significant harm to humans, its effects on wildlife are well-documented. Such theories were first voiced in Rachel Carson's 1962 book *Silent*
20 *Spring*. The publication proposed that chemicals such as DDT might be passed up the food chain from prey to predator thus implying that a seemingly harmless, low-intensity application over a wide area might *bioaccumulate* into high doses in the bellies of
25 relatively few apex predators.
    Indeed, North America and Europe witnessed a drastic decline in populations of local birds of prey that had ingested DDT through their marine quarry. The chemical's metabolized form causes a drastic
30 thinning of eggshells which in turn harms the birds' reproductive success rates. The bans that went into effect decades ago have a telling effect: said species are bouncing back to healthy levels.
    Nonetheless, DDT's importance in the fight
35 against malaria cannot be overstated. British politician Dick Taverne did not exaggerate when he stated that "DDT is the single most effective agent ever developed for saving human life." Malaria has ever been with humankind, possibly claiming half of
40 all human lives throughout history. It has been our companion on every continent—Chinese records of this fever plaguing humans date back over 4,000 years. Even in the United States, malaria infections numbered 15,000 annually until the National Malaria
45 Eradication Program effectively eradicated the disease through the use of DDT.
    The fight continues in many countries today. Renato Gusmao of the Pan American Health Organization's anti-malaria force "cannot envision the
50 possibility of rolling back malaria without the power of DDT." Other measures are "an auxiliary. In tropical Africa, if you don't use DDT, forget it."

Passage 2

African countries, due to a resurgence of malaria outbreaks, have once again approved the use of DDT.
55 Proponents of its use will quote the number of human lives DDT saves every day by killing mosquitos. The numbers are confounding: according to USAID[2], malaria causes around 584,000 deaths every year. The Ugandan Minister of Health justified the decision by
60 asking "How many people must die of malaria while these debates continue? If DDT can save lives, why not use it as we wait for the alternatives?" In light of the sheer number of lives at stake, is it not paramount to save lives first and shelve discussions regarding
65 negative health effects until a better alternative becomes viable?
    While it is true that DDT saves lives, it is also true that there are side effects that must not be ignored. Proponents like to gloss over the damage DDT inflicts
70 on exposed humans. For instance, certain studies indicate a link to diabetes while other research points to detrimental effects on reproduction and increased child mortality. Still other studies link use of the chemical to cases of cancer.
75 In addition to direct damage through exposure, the use of DDT has a track record of causing unwanted ramifications. In a globally observed phenomenon, cats succumbed due to indoor spraying which caused an explosion of the local rodent
80 populations. In Asian countries as well as in America, the damages caused by rats overrunning crop fields offset the "protection" that DDT provided. In another case, the successful extermination of one malaria-bearing mosquito species allowed for an increase of
85 the human population which in turn necessitated more crop fields at the expense of grazing land. The resulting decrease in cattle caused other mosquitos to start biting humans instead of bovines which resulted in another onslaught of malaria cases.
90 Advocates of DDT will say that *not* using DDT is an outrage. However, there are a number of effective alternatives available and in use today. These include nets treated with insecticide and the administering of

drug treatments. Studies conducted in a number of
95 Asian countries have shown that, given sufficiently
informed and trained personnel, alternatives to DDT
are not only highly efficient, they can also be more
cost-effective. In the end, the question is not whether
alternatives are viable but whether administrations
100 will go the extra mile to implement steps that save
lives while also protecting the long-term health of
their citizens.

1 a transmitter of infections into another organism

2 the U.S. government agency tasked to assist foreign countries in the fight against poverty

22

Within Passage 1, the main purpose of including information about DDT's effect on predators such as birds of prey is to

A) exonerate the decision to completely ban DDT in Western countries.
B) present information that supports the author's central argument regarding DDT.
C) acknowledge a circumscribed set of issues brought forth by the use of DDT.
D) establish that the detrimental side effects of DDT have been completely reversed.

23

As used in line 39, "claiming" most nearly means

A) needing.
B) collecting.
C) extinguishing.
D) declaring.

24

Passage 1 suggests that DDT should be valued primarily for its

A) ability to kill vectors of various kinds.
B) substantiated efficacy in fighting malaria.
C) propensity to bioaccumulate in top-level predators.
D) contributions to the advance of modern agriculture.

25

Which choice provides the best evidence for the answer to the previous question?

A) Lines 1-3 ("During . . . mosquitos")
B) Lines 11-14 ("environmental . . . usage")
C) Lines 35-38 ("British . . . life")
D) Lines 43-46 ("malaria . . . DDT")

26

The author of Passage 2 suggests that the statement by the Ugandan Minister of Health (lines 58-59) should be viewed as

A) the obvious way of dealing with the current malaria crisis.
B) overly simplistic since saving lives is not the whole picture.
C) phrased in a manner that intentionally misleads the audience.
D) an understandable reaction to the staggering malaria death toll.

27

As used in line 62, "light" most nearly means

A) awareness.
B) education.
C) luminescence.
D) attitude.

28

Within the context of Passage 2, what function does the discussion of the "successful extermination" in lines 83-89 mainly serve?

A) It supports the notion that a chosen solution might not be the best.
B) It explores unforeseen benefits that arise thanks to the application of DDT.
C) It provides the strongest reason why alternatives to DDT have gained traction.
D) It examines the consequences of an incomplete DDT application in the field.

29

Which statement best describes the relationship between the passages?

A) Passage 2 advocates a course that diverges from that proposed in Passage 1.
B) Passage 2 challenges the veracity of the facts offered in Passage 1.
C) Passage 2 presents first-hand experiences that Passage 1 describes from a historical point of view.
D) Passage 2 draws new conclusions based on the evidence presented in Passage 1.

30

Which choice provides the best evidence that the author of Passage 2 would probably disagree with the studies mentioned in lines 16-17, Passage 1?

A) Lines 67-68 ("While . . . ignored")
B) Lines 70-73 ("For instance . . . mortality")
C) Lines 77-80 ("In a . . . populations")
D) Lines 91-94 ("However . . . treatments")

31

Would the author of Passage 2 agree with the claim attributed to Renato Gusmao in lines 49-52, Passage 1?

A) Yes, because the sheer number of malaria victims demands a quick and effective solution.
B) Yes, because African experts and DDT proponents agree it should be used until alternatives are viable.
C) No, because most African countries have adopted alternatives due to their cost-efficiency.
D) No, because malaria can be fought efficiently using alternatives that are available right now.

Questions 32-41 are based on the following passage.

This passage discusses dialects.

Get on a train that will take you far away, maybe one that will take you from one part of your country to another. Regardless of the country, chances are that
Line after a while, the passengers boarding the train will
5 start to sound *off*. The way they speak, their intonation, and sometimes their diction will change to such a degree that these alterations grow into an obstacle to smooth communication. I once overheard a young boy telling his mother that the train conductor was
10 "speaking wrong," and from her grin I could tell she did not disagree. Personally though, I believe that to be a malapropism. Personally, I believe this would have been a fine chance for the mother to bring up a river.

Imagine a river, a typical river. No matter the
15 surrounding climate or remaining topography, let it be a single stream of water that conveys water from a point of origin to the ocean. Let that river then fan out into a delta of smaller streams that empty into the ocean. Before it fans out, it is undoubtedly
20 a river, but even after it fans out into several branches, it is still conveying water from point A to point B. Regardless of which particular stretch of the river you might happen to inspect, it will serve exactly the same function of transporting that precious blue.

25 Just like a river changes shape and branches out, language changes shape and branches out. Over time and with distance, it will change and evolve. If you follow the English language (itself a confluence of streams of completely different origins) and consider
30 the fact that the language spoken in London, though orthographically identical, might sound very different from the language spoken in other parts of the same island, the image of a river fanning out will come to life. If you zoom out drastically, you can conjure up
35 the main river splitting into several streams as the language changes quite remarkably with geographic distance as you get to Australia, Africa, or America. And even within those latter regions, local dialects like capillaries reveal that change in action—baby
40 steps (think small increments in time and distance) in the evolution of language right before our eyes!

What is important to keep in mind is that at each of those fine subdivisions, the local mutation of the original language serves the same purpose as
45 the "original": communication, whether orally or in written form. What is important to consider is that those speaking the local dialect feel that their way of

using language is natural and normal though it might differ from Queen's English. But does that clear up the
50 question of whether or not calling dialects wrong is right?

More than 2,000 years ago, Julius Caesar conquered what is France today. Subsequently, the Roman Empire occupied the region, and through
55 the establishment of their own administrative system introduced Latin to the previously Celtic-speaking population. Social promotion was dependent on learning the language of the victors, and over time, the use of Latin spread as it went hand in hand with
60 the acquisition of countless jobs and positions. The Latin influenced and spoken by Roman clerks and bilingual Celts gradually developed a flavor distinct from that of "classical Latin."

Back then, a Roman dignitary assigned to Gaul
65 holdings would have no doubt complained about the wrong and vulgar-sounding Latin in use. By today, that same process of evolution and change has turned this bastardized version of Latin into what is known as French, a completely legitimate language from our
70 point of view.

Disparaging dialects is denying the evolution of language. Dialects embody progress in progress (though nowadays it is greatly hampered by literacy, broadcast media, and a greater cultural cohesion),
75 and it is thanks to this progress that we get to be glad we do not speak as Shakespeare wrote.

32

Over the course of the passage, the main focus shifts from

A) explaining the origins of dialects to their waning significance.
B) placing dialects in context to defending their legitimacy.
C) reservations about modern dialects to praise for dialects of the antique.
D) establishing a metaphor for dialects to defending its significance.

33

In the context of the passage, the author mentions that "passengers boarding the train will start to sound off" (lines 4-5) in order to convey an experience that

A) reveals the difficulties inherent in interregional communication.
B) might be misjudged unless seen in broad context.
C) can only be experienced under certain conditions.
D) has had a singular impact on the author's outlook.

34

When applied to language, the "delta" mentioned in line 18 represents an instance of

A) isolation.
B) diversification.
C) dissension.
D) cleavage.

35

Lines 27-34 ("If you . . . life") emphasize which of the following about the English language?

A) Its geographical origin can be traced to the city of London.
B) Its pronunciation varies widely from region to region.
C) Its constituent languages can be heard in local dialects.
D) Its common orthography has helped it spread across England.

36

Which choice best supports the claim that time is not the only factor that brings change to a language?

A) Lines 22-24 ("Regardless . . . blue")
B) Lines 47-49 ("those . . . English")
C) Lines 53-57 ("the Roman . . . population")
D) Lines 66-69 ("By today . . . French")

37

In paragraph 5 (lines 52-63), "Latin" is primarily characterized as

A) a sign of successful subjugation.
B) an aspect of coexistence.
C) a prerequisite for civilization.
D) a replacement for Celtic.

38

As used in line 62, "flavor" most nearly means

A) character.
B) aroma.
C) feeling.
D) taste.

39

Which of the following best summarizes the main point of lines 64-70?

A) Roman officials often displayed a haughty attitude towards colonists.
B) Time and perspective greatly color our disposition to language.
C) Most languages today were at one point mocked or derided.
D) The French language left indelible traces on Roman Latin.

40

Within the context of the whole passage, "literacy, broadcast media, and a greater cultural cohesion" (lines 73-74) are brought up as factors that

A) embody the advances of modern civilization.
B) result from continuous development of language.
C) reveal the inexorable nature of diversification.
D) inhibit an ordinary process languages undergo.

41

The author most likely mentions Shakespeare in the last sentence in order to

A) suggest that Shakespeare's language would now be considered old-fashioned.
B) illustrate a high point in the evolution of the English language.
C) provide an example of literature which has held up the progress of dialects.
D) emphasize our ignorance regarding spoken English when he was alive.

Questions 42-52 are based on the following passage and supplementary material.

This passage deals with ambergris, a whale product.

To understand the drive behind the whaling industry that has contributed to an appalling decline in global whale populations, one needs to look no further than the substantial bounty that results from catching a whale. Considering the range and sheer amount of products that a single carcass yields, it is no surprise many of the giants' species have been flagged as endangered. Primarily, whales were hunted and killed for their oil and meat. The former used to illuminate the majority of domestic homes in oil lamps before the advent of mineral oils while the latter, being suitable for consumption, is indeed being consumed in large quantities in certain parts of the world. One whale product, however, cannot be harvested in such a direct fashion. Only a tiny fraction of sperm whales produce a substance called ambergris which, due to its elusive nature, is a highly coveted commodity.

Derived from Latin, ambergris literally means grey amber. Though the substance has been known since ancient times, theories regarding its origins which are widely endorsed today were established only in the twentieth century. Scientists suggest that the substance is produced by a biliary secretion within a sperm whale's gastrointestinal tract to facilitate the passing of solid and sharp objects such as squid beaks that the animal has ingested. In the absence of this process, the flow of ingested material within the intestines would likely be blocked. The result of this secretion which forms around intruding objects, ambergris, usually exits the whale along with its feces. A number of scientists suspect that accumulations too massive to pass through the intestines are expelled through the whale's mouth, which has led some to refer to this substance as whale vomit. It has been estimated that only roughly one in a hundred sperm whales produces ambergris, which separates it from other, more easily obtainable whale products and elevates it into the class of remarkably rare resources.

Ambergris is a solid substance which is slightly plastic to the touch. One might compare that plasticity to that of wax in that it is firm yet pliable. Its surface is black or grey in color; it has been described as highly nodular with squid beaks or other membranous material originating from the whale's prey visibly embedded within it. Whereas smaller pieces of ambergris, also called 'rognons,' are roughly egg-shaped, larger occurrences have been found to adhere to a distinct shape. Larger boulders of this substance are thicker on one end than on the other. The thick end features a depression whereas the thin end is tapered—a result of the flow of digested material against and around the boulder within the rectum. A single boulder of ambergris can weigh in excess of 400 kilograms.

The reason this whale excretion is so sought after lies, along with its notable scarcity, in its properties and its subsequent uses. Freshly harvested, ambergris emits a fecal and pungent odor. On the other hand, mature ambergris has been noted for its delicious and subtle scent of a sweet and earthy nature that puts one in mind of sandalwood or tobacco. Over the centuries, people have attributed an array of qualities to it. For instance, in Egypt, it was once used as incense whereas nowadays, people there use it for scenting tobacco. When the Black Plague harrowed Europe, people believed it would prevent contamination, its fragrance dispelling the stench in the air which was believed to transmit the disease. Ambergris has seen use as food flavoring, medicine, and it has even been used as an aphrodisiac. But its main application has ever been its role as a fixative for perfumes. Its heavy molecules naturally bind to molecules found in fragrances. Added to a perfume, it will enhance the longevity of the perfume's fragrance by reducing the rate at which it evaporates and adding stability to its more volatile ingredients. Connoisseurs often rave about the subtly marine, natural fragrance of ambergris which complements the other notes of a perfume.

While perfumes based on ambergris are still in limited production, its prohibitive price makes them rare indeed. Natural alternatives such as sandalwood, musk, or bergamot orange are usually chosen as fixatives instead. In addition, synthetic compounds that emulate ambergris' desirable properties have been developed. Being able to synthesize products like Ambroxan holds great commercial value what with the limited availability of its natural counterpart. These substitutes apparently fail to impart quite the same flair as ambergris, as aficionados often lament the fact that perfumes containing real ambergris have become few and far between.

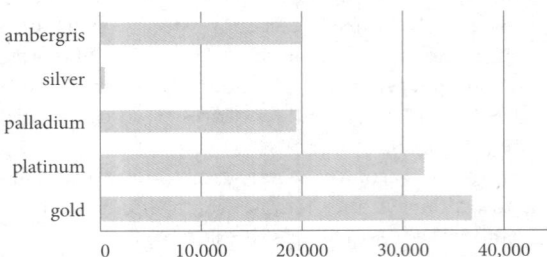

Price per Kilogram in $US (as of 2015)

42

The passage primarily serves to

A) call for additional research on ambergris.
B) account for the desirability of ambergris.
C) argue against the use of ambergris.
D) describe the physical properties of ambergris.

43

The passage suggests that coming across a boulder of ambergris on the beach would be an event best described as

A) celebrated.
B) serendipitous.
C) prosaic.
D) insipid.

44

The author mentions "solid and sharp objects" (line 25) in order to

A) establish the stimulus that sets off a process.
B) hint at the food sources of sperm whales.
C) explain the makeup of the whale's secretion.
D) pay tribute to the resilience of sperm whales.

45

The passage suggests that the "secretion . . . forms around intruding objects" (line 29) because it

A) is harmful to the whale and needs to be expelled from its body.
B) actually becomes a coveted commodity called ambergris.
C) facilitates the excretion of intruding objects into the ocean.
D) will dislodge objects that block the whale's intestines.

46

As used in line 40, "plastic" most nearly means

A) supple.
B) synthetic.
C) amenable.
D) chemical.

47

Which of the following summarizes the main point of lines 45-54 ("Whereas . . . kilograms")?

A) Larger boulders of ambergris are not as common as smaller 'rognons.'
B) The size of a piece of ambergris dictates its overall shape.
C) Larger boulders usually break up into smaller 'rognons' over time.
D) Ambergris is characterized by a bumpy surface and round shapes.

48

As presented in paragraph 4, the author believes that ambergris possesses which of the following properties?

A) Spicy flavor and delicious smell
B) Curative powers and pleasant fragrance
C) Subtle scent and bonding qualities
D) Ability to prevent contaminations

49

As used in line 78, "notes" most nearly means

A) cadences.
B) observations.
C) marks.
D) aromas.

50

Within the context of the final paragraph, the final sentence of the passage primarily functions to

A) question the assertion that Ambroxan will be commercially viable.
B) downplay the drawbacks of ambergris substitutes.
C) reveal an aspect of substitutes through enthusiasts' opinions.
D) imply that perfume makers are trying to shortchange consumers.

51

According to the figure, which of the following pairings would yield the highest price for a gram of each?

A) Palladium and gold
B) Platinum and silver
C) Ambergris and platinum
D) Platinum and palladium

52

The author would most likely consider the information in the figure to be

A) unreliable since the scarcity of ambergris prevents consistent pricing.
B) compelling evidence for the extraordinary hunger for ambergris.
C) unrealistic since synthetic compounds have deflated the value of ambergris.
D) significant for its comparison of ambergris to precious metals.

STOP

Do not move on to the next section if you finish early.
You may review your answers in this section only.

Answer Keys & Performance Breakdown

1	(A)	Context	19	(C)	Evidence	37	(B)	Local
2	(C)	Local	20	(D)	Graph	38	(A)	Vocabulary
3	(C)	Vocabulary	21	(A)	Graph	39	(B)	Local
4	(D)	Context	22	(C)	Context	40	(D)	Summary
5	(B)	Local	23	(C)	Vocabulary	41	(A)	Context
6	(A)	Local	24	(B)	Summary	42	(B)	Summary
7	(D)	Evidence	25	(D)	Evidence	43	(B)	Local
8	(C)	Local	26	(B)	Local	44	(A)	Context
9	(C)	Vocabulary	27	(A)	Vocabulary	45	(C)	Local
10	(C)	Local	28	(A)	Context	46	(A)	Vocabulary
11	(A)	Summary	29	(A)	Synthesize	47	(B)	Local
12	(C)	Synthesize	30	(B)	Synthesize	48	(C)	Local
13	(A)	Vocabulary	31	(D)	Synthesize	49	(D)	Vocabulary
14	(D)	Evidence	32	(B)	Organization	50	(C)	Context
15	(D)	Local	33	(B)	Summary	51	(A)	Graph
16	(C)	Local	34	(B)	Local	52	(B)	Graph
17	(B)	Summary	35	(B)	Local			
18	(C)	Local	36	(B)	Evidence			

■ Write down the number of correct answers for each question type.

Question Types	Number of Correct Answers
Local	/ 17
Style	0 / 0
Vocabulary	/ 8
Evidence	/ 5
Context	/ 7
Organization	/ 1
Summary	/ 6
Stance	0 / 0
Synthesize	/ 4
Graph	/ 4
Total	**/ 52**

Answer Explanations

Questions 1-10

1. (A) — Context

A is the best choice because he rang the bell and gave an intimation with "unreasonable petulance" (illogical sulking). This behavior is unreasonable because the narrator got up earlier than usual, so the landlady, used to him getting up late, could not have known he would want breakfast at this time.

B is incorrect because it means that the client is too late (which does not fit his petulant behavior). C is incorrect because though he seemed annoyed, the sentence also states that his annoyed behavior was "unreasonable" which differs from being "offended." D is incorrect because nothing like "father" is hinted at.

2. (C) — Local

C is the best choice because "ambitious" can also mean "grandiose."

A is incorrect because the title does not refer to observational powers. (The "observant man" is referred to in the article, not the title.) B is incorrect because spontaneity is not suggested. D is incorrect because the specified line does not imply that the title is "misleading" or "deceptive."

3. (C) — Vocabulary

C is the best choice because in the sentence, "close" refers to "reasoning" (logical thinking). Thus, "precise" is correct.

A is incorrect because it means "friendly" or "private." B is incorrect because it is too literal, meaning "next to." D is incorrect because it means "word for word."

4. (D) — Context

In context, "callosities" is one element in a list of traits, and "by each of these things a man's calling is plainly revealed" (lines 51-52).

D is the best choice because "calling" means "job" or "vocation" in this context.

A is incorrect because "callosities" is not "implements" or "tools." B is incorrect because "callow" means immature whereas "callosity" refers to thickened and hardened skin. C is incorrect because even though C factually makes sense, characterizing hard-working persons is not the point of this context.

5. (B) — Local

B is the best choice because the lines state that it is almost unthinkable that all united (an aggregate of information) should fail to enlighten the enquirer (will not lead to a realization). In other words, it is almost certain that this aggregate of information will lead someone to a realization.

A is incorrect because "cooperation" is not mentioned. C is incorrect because no "vocations" or "jobs" are mentioned as a condition. D is incorrect because no necessary qualifications pertaining to the enquirers are suggested in the lines.

6. (A) — Local

A is the best choice because of lines 62-65 (see next question).

B is incorrect. Though line 30 mentions that the author of the article might be considered a "necromancer" (magic wielder), this is part of the article itself, not the opinion of the narrator. C is incorrect for the same reason (check lines 24-25). D is incorrect because even though lines 18-21 support "cagey," they do not suggest that the narrator believes the article's author to be a liar.

7. (D) — Evidence

D is the best choice because the lines state that the narrator believes the author of the article is "some arm-chair lounger" (person who stays at home) who evolves all these neat little paradoxes in the seclusion of his own study. ("Seclusion" implies he is alone and does not meet other people.)

A, B, and C are incorrect because none of them support that the author of the article lacks exposure to reality.

8. (C) — Local

The sentence states that someone develops little paradoxes in the seclusion of their study. "Seclusion" implies "isolation" or "retirement" which means that this person is not part of the rest of the world.

C is the best choice because "academic" means "theoretical" or "conjectural." (This person merely speculates about things without having seen or experienced them.)

TEST 2 63

Answer Explanations

A is incorrect because "never having actually witnessed" is not supported (extreme statement). B is incorrect because "concedes" means in favor of the opposition. D is incorrect because "sedentary" means "sitting" which is too literal.

9. (C) Vocabulary

C is the best choice because the narrator would like the "arm-chair lounger" (who does not really know reality) to sit on the subway and "give" the trades of his fellow-travelers. Therefore, he wants him to "say" or "announce" what other people do for a living.

A is incorrect because it means to "give a prize." B is incorrect because it means to "suggest" or "offer." D is incorrect because it means to "abandon" or "surrender."

10. (C) Local

The preceding statement states that the narrator would bet a thousand to one which indicates supreme confidence. Holmes' retort "You would lose your money" also sounds certain.

C is the best choice.

A is incorrect because the preceding statement does not refer to Holmes. B is incorrect because it only applies to the preceding statement. D is incorrect because "exasperation" means "annoyance" which at least for Holmes is not true.

Questions 11-21

11. (A) Summary

Agnew states that millions watch news every night, but that only a few men decide what is on the news which gives them immense power: they can at will focus the nation's attention on certain issues or leave others out of the news altogether. In addition, the way news is presented carries tremendous influence. Agnew then emphasizes that very little is known about these powerful men.

A is the best choice. ("Reach" means "influence.")

B is incorrect because no solutions are proposed. C is incorrect because Agnew does not simply chronicle, he asserts that there is a problem. D is incorrect because no struggle is mentioned.

12. (C) Synthesize

C is the best choice because the "dozen" refers to the men who decide what will be on the news, which is the same persons as the "men" because it says that these men "produce and direct the network news" (lines 61-62).

A, B, and D are incorrect because none of them refer to decision-makers in news networks like the "dozen."

13. (A) Vocabulary

A is the best choice because in the sentence, "obscurity" is contrasted to "national prominence" (fame). Thus, "obscurity" means being unknown, like "nonentity."

B is incorrect because it is too literal. C and D are incorrect because none of them indicate the opposite of "fame."

14. (D) Evidence

D is the best choice because the lines state that television networks "have often used their power constructively and creatively to awaken the public conscience to critical problems." This definitely deserves approval.

A, B and C are incorrect because none of them show that television networks deserve approval.

15. (D) Local

D is the best choice because Carmichael's and Rockwell's rise is contrasted to the news networks' focus on environmental abuses. Agnew conceded that such coverage benefits society (previous paragraph). Therefore, it can be inferred that Agnew disapproves of the focus on Carmichael's and Rockwell's rise to prominence (line 47: "But it was also the networks").

A is incorrect because it means "gratification" or "contentment." B is incorrect because it means "indifference." C is incorrect because it means "disbelief" or "amazement."

16. (C) Local

C is the best choice because "a raised eyebrow, an inflection of the voice (non-verbal cues) . . . can raise doubts in a million minds" (which supports swaying public opinion).

A is incorrect because neither "mock" nor "fear of punitive reprisal" is implied in the specified lines. B is incorrect because straying from the topic is not suggested in the specified lines. D is incorrect because "raise doubts" and "countermand" (annul, cancel) are different.

17. (B) — Summary

The main point (refer to question 11 explanation) is that a small number of people decide what is on the news and thus wield tremendous influence. The fact that little is known about these people is problematic.

B is the best choice because it fits with the main point.

A is incorrect because Agnew does not state this. C is incorrect because it implies that one negative trait is offset by another negative trait, which does not make sense. D is incorrect because "control" is too strong (much stronger than being influential).

18. (C) — Local

C is the best choice because of lines 55-59 (see next question).

A is incorrect because news networks contradicting each other is not mentioned. B is incorrect because even though this was mentioned (lines 7-10), this in itself is not characterized as problematic. (The problem is the way news is selected.) D is incorrect because failure to focus is not described as the main issue. Also, "failure" implies "lack of capacity" whereas the passage asserts that news networks have the ability to select news at will.

19. (C) — Evidence

C is the best choice because the lines state that the news networks wield as much influence as all of the government organs combined (disproportionate). This is further described as a "concentration of power over American public opinion unknown in history."

A, B, and D are incorrect because none of them support that networks wield a disproportionate amount of power to influence public opinion.

20. (D) — Graph

D is the best choice because in 2008, television had the highest percentage and the Internet the lowest. The former has decreased and the latter increased, so they have moved closer together.

A is incorrect because newspapers were not dominant in 2008. B is incorrect because the figure has no data about the reasons underlying the increase in Internet consumption. C is incorrect because the figure has no data concerning how different media are perceived.

21. (A) — Graph

Figure 2 shows that most TV channels give more airtime to the conservative party than to the other parties. This fits the main idea of the passage which states that news networks are free to decide what people will see on the news.

A is the best choice.

B is incorrect because "small group of men" is not supported by Figure 2. C is incorrect because the figure shows no information about how much is known of "those who select news." D is incorrect because the figure only shows which parties receive how much exposure. There is no information on "critical issues."

Questions 22-31

22. (C) — Context

The specified information states that DDT application resulted in loss of wildlife since DDT would travel up the food chain and end up in apex predators. The bans on DDT proved telling because the affected species recovered as a result. Before and after the specified part (paragraphs 2 and 3), the author emphasizes DDT's importance and efficacy in fighting malaria by killing mosquitos (main idea of Passage 1).

C is the best choice.

A is incorrect because no complete ban was mentioned. This also goes against the main thrust of the author of Passage 1. B is incorrect because the specified information does not support the central argument. D is incorrect because "completely" is not supported and because it does not show the purpose of paragraphs 2 and 3 within the passage.

23. (C) — Vocabulary

C is the best choice because the sentence states that malaria possibly claimed half of all human lives throughout history. Thus, "claiming" means "exterminating" or "taking away."

A is obviously incorrect. B is incorrect because it means to "accumulate." D is incorrect because it means to "make known" or to "announce."

Answer Explanations

24. (B) — Summary

B is the best choice because of lines 5-7, and because of lines 43-46 (see next question).

A is incorrect because the passage primarily talks about using DDT against malaria (and therefore killing mosquitos) as opposed to using it against a broad array of insects. C is incorrect because it describes a negative side effect. D is incorrect because even though "agriculture" is mentioned, the passage primarily focuses on combating malaria.

25. (D) — Evidence

D is the best choice because it gives evidence that DDT was used to eradicate malaria in the U.S.

A, B, and C are incorrect because none of them substantiate the fact that DDT was used effectively against malaria.

26. (B) — Local

B is the best choice because of lines 67-70. After quoting the Minister of Health, the author of Passage 2 continues by asking if saving lives using DDT for now is not the best choice which is answered in paragraph 2. The answer is basically that DDT saves lives, but there are side effects to its use such as human health implications that must be considered. This suggests that only thinking about saving lives using DDT is simplistic and not the whole picture.

A is incorrect because the author of Passage 2 speaks against the use of DDT. C is incorrect because the author of Passage 2 does not imply that the Minister is trying to mislead the audience. D is incorrect because the author of Passage 2 does not state this in their answer.

27. (A) — Vocabulary

A is the best choice because the phrase "in light of (something)" as used in the sentence means "considering (something)" or "taking (something) into account." Thus, "awareness" is correct.

B is incorrect because it means "instruction in knowledge." C is incorrect because it is too literal. D is incorrect because it means "stance" or "outlook."

28. (A) — Context

The specified lines tell of a case where the use of DDT resulted in unintended, negative side effects. This story supports the notion of the paragraph as a whole that "the use of DDT has a track record of causing unwanted ramifications" (lines 76-77).

A is the best choice. (DDT might not be the best solution.)

B is incorrect because "unforeseen benefits" does not occur in context. C is incorrect because nothing supports that this is the strongest (most compelling) reason for the use of alternatives to DDT. D is incorrect because nothing suggests that the DDT application was incomplete.

29. (A) — Synthesize

Passage 1 emphasizes that DDT is proven, efficient, and in fact crucial to combating malaria. Passage 2 states that DDT's negative side effects make alternatives more desirable, and it adds that alternatives are available and cost-effective.

A is the best choice.

B is incorrect because Passage 2 does not question the facts stated in Passage 1 but the conclusion that DDT is important and crucial for fighting malaria. C is incorrect because "first-hand experiences" is not supported. Passage 2 does not indicate that the author is recounting things they have experienced in person. D is incorrect because the conclusions in Passage 2 are not based on evidence presented in Passage 1.

30. (B) — Synthesize

The studies mentioned in lines 16-17 are inconclusive as to whether DDT causes significant harm to humans. This means it is unclear whether DDT is detrimental to humans.

B is the best choice because the lines cite a study which shows a link between DDT and diabetes, reproduction problems, and child mortality.

A mentions side effects, but does not specifically bring up human health. C and D are incorrect because none of them show that the author of Passage 2 would disagree with the specified studies.

31. (D) — Synthesize

Gusmao states that DDT is crucial for fighting malaria in Africa. Without it, malaria cannot be defeated.

D is the best choice because Passage 2 advocates the use of alternatives to DDT which are effective and available (main idea for Passage 2).

A and B are incorrect because Passage 2 would

disagree. C is incorrect because most African countries having adopted alternatives is not supported. Also, "cost-efficiency" is not mentioned as the underlying motive for the adoption of such alternatives.

Questions 32-41

32. (B) — Organization

B is the best choice because dialects are first explained in the context of how languages evolve and change over time and distance (paragraphs 3 and 4) after which the passage states that today's dialect might become tomorrow's language (lines 66-70).

A is incorrect because the author does not indicate that the significance of dialects is waning. C is incorrect because the author does not imply modern dialects are objectionable. D is incorrect because the significance of the metaphor (river) is not defended.

33. (B) — Summary

B is the best choice because sounding *off* refers to dialects which in the example of the train caused mild amusement in a mother and child who thought that the dialect sounded wrong. However, the main idea of the passage is that dialects are actually the steps a language takes as it evolves and progresses over time and distance; i.e., the author would see a dialect as part of an advance, not as "speaking wrong."

A is incorrect because it is not the focus of the passage. C is incorrect because the author implies this will happen anywhere (line 3). D is incorrect because "singular impact" is not supported by the passage.

34. (B) — Local

A delta is the region of a river where one river fans out into several smaller streams. Thus, it is a metaphor for one language splitting up into several smaller languages (dialects).

B is the best choice. (One becomes many.)

A is incorrect because a delta does not imply being alone and cut off. C is incorrect because "dissension" implies disagreement. D is incorrect because it means a "sharp division" or "split."

35. (B) — Local

B is the best choice because of lines 31-33. A is incorrect because the passage does not mention London as the origin of English. C is incorrect because "constituent languages" is not mentioned in the specified lines. D is incorrect because it is not stated that English spread thanks to orthography.

36. (B) — Evidence

B is the best choice. A factor besides time which underlies language change is asked for. B shows that local dialects differ from Standard English. This means that different locations (which is different from time) are mentioned as a factor for language change.

A, C, and D are incorrect because none of them show that a factor besides time underlies language change.

37. (B) — Local

The paragraph states that after Rome conquered France, Latin was introduced as part of the Roman administration. Latin became a prerequisite for social promotion and the attainment of many jobs and positions.

B is the best choice.

A is incorrect because the passage does not present Latin as a mark of Roman oppression. C is incorrect because "social promotion" and "civilization" are not the same. D is incorrect because it implies that Roman took the place of or supplanted Celtic. Instead, the passage states that both languages were used.

38. (A) — Vocabulary

A is the best choice because the sentence says that the Latin in France developed a flavor distinct from "classical Latin." "Character" is the correct choice in describing the changed aspect or nature of a language.

B is incorrect because it implies smell. C is incorrect because it means "idea," "impression," or "ambience." D is incorrect because it means "gustation." (It is too literal.)

39. (B) — Local

The paragraph in essence states that a contemporary Roman would have disliked the vulgar-sounding Latin spoken in France. Today, we regard the result of this dialect, French, as a legitimate language.

B is the best choice.

A is incorrect because the point of the paragraph is change in perspective. C is incorrect because the

Answer Explanations

statement is not supported by the information in the specified lines. D is incorrect because no such thing is stated in the specified lines.

40. (D) *Summary*

The main point of the passage is that languages, just like rivers, naturally fan out and change over time and distance, and that this process creates new languages.

D is the best choice because the passage states that the literacy, media, and cultural cohesion hamper dialects in progress.

A is incorrect because it does not match the focus of the passage. B is incorrect because "result from" does not equal "hamper" or "hinder." C is incorrect because the quoted phenomena do not "reveal" or "illustrate" diversification, but rather hinder it.

41. (A) *Context*

A is the best choice because it states that we can be glad or happy that our spoken language is unlike the language that Shakespeare used to write. Therefore, we would not like using Shakespeare's language. Since Shakespeare wrote his works a long time ago, "old-fashioned" is supported.

B is incorrect because Shakespeare is used as a negative example while B mentions him as a "high point" which is positive. C is incorrect because no example of literature is mentioned. D is incorrect because Shakespeare is mentioned as a juxtaposition to today's language, not to point out our lack of knowledge regarding the past.

Questions 42-52

42. (B) *Summary*

The passage states that ambergris is a very rare and highly sought-after whale commodity. It describes its formation and its outer appearance. After that, diverse ways ambergris is used are listed to explain why ambergris is a highly desired substance. Finally, alternatives to and synthetic replacements for ambergris are mentioned.

B is the best choice.

A is incorrect because additional research is not recommended in the passage. C is incorrect because it is never stated. D is incorrect because the description of its properties serves to account for the desirability of ambergris (the focus of the passage).

43. (B) *Local*

B is the best choice because ambergris is rare and highly coveted.

A is incorrect because it means "famous" or "acclaimed." C is incorrect because it means "mundane" or "banal." D is incorrect because it means "dull" or "tasteless."

44. (A) *Context*

In context, the passage states that ambergris is produced by a secretion to facilitate the passing of solid and sharp objects that the animal has ingested. Thus, solid and sharp objects are the trigger that cause ambergris to be produced.

A is the best choice.

B is incorrect because the context does not describe feeding habits or preferences. C is incorrect because the "solid and sharp objects" do not describe what the whale's secretion is made of. D is incorrect because recovery from illness or injury are not the focus of the context.

45. (C) *Local*

The reason for line 29 can be found in lines 26-28 (since line 28 starts with "The result of this secretion . . ."). Lines 26-28 state that in the absence of this process (secretion to facilitate the passing of solid and sharp objects), the flow of ingested material within the intestines would be blocked. In other words, thanks to this process (secretion), the flow of material in the intestines is not blocked.

C is the best choice.

A is incorrect because the "secretion" is not harmful but helpful. B is incorrect because it is not mentioned as a reason for the secretion (even though the secretion does become ambergris). D is incorrect because "dislodge" is not supported.

46. (A) *Vocabulary*

A is the best choice because the sentence says "plastic to the touch" and the next sentence says that the plasticity is comparable to "that of wax." It is "firm yet pliable." Thus, "plastic" means "malleable" or "pliable" which can also be expressed by "supple."

B is incorrect because it means "artificial." C is incorrect because it means "willing" or "cooperative."

D is incorrect because it means "relating to chemistry" or "synthetic."

47. (B) *Local*

In the specified lines, the passage states that smaller pieces are roughly egg-shaped whereas larger pieces have a distinct shape (thicker on one end with a depression).

B is the best choice.

A is incorrect because the passage does not state which is more commonplace. C is incorrect because such fragmentation is not mentioned. D is incorrect because this information was not presented in the specified lines.

48. (C) *Local*

C is the best choice because of line 60 (subtle scent) and lines 71-72 (bonding qualities).

A is incorrect because "spicy flavor" is not mentioned. B is incorrect because "curative powers" is not mentioned as something the author believes personally (lines 68-69). D is incorrect because this is something "people" believed. The passage does not indicate that the author agrees (lines 65-68).

49. (D) *Vocabulary*

D is the best choice because "notes" refers to the fragrance of a perfume.

A is incorrect because it means "rhythm" or "inflection" and is used with music. B is incorrect because it means "attention" or "examination." C is incorrect because it means "characteristic" or "criterion" or "goal."

50. (C) *Context*

C is the best choice because according to the final sentence, substitutes do not have the same effect as ambergris which is lamented by aficionados (enthusiasts).

A is incorrect because the paragraph mentions Ambroxan holds great commercial value since ambergris is rare. (This suggests that even with its reduced impact, it will be viable.) B is incorrect because the last sentence "mentions" rather than downplays drawbacks. D is incorrect because "shortchange" means to "cheat." The last sentence implies no such intention.

51. (A) *Graph*

Between C and D, C commands a higher price (ambergris > palladium). Between A and C, A commands a higher price because the gap between gold and platinum (in favor of A) is visibly higher than the gap between ambergris and palladium (in favor of C).

A is the best choice.

52. (B) *Graph*

The figure only tells us that ambergris commands a price that is comparable to precious metal prices. This fits the main idea that ambergris is a rare and highly coveted commodity.

B is the best choice.

A is incorrect because neither the figure nor the passage supports this. C is incorrect because the passage does not support this statement. D is incorrect because the passage does not mention precious metals.

SAT.Hackers.ac

Hackers New SAT Reading: 10 Practice Tests

TEST 3

Answer Keys & Performance Breakdown
Answer Explanations

Reading Test
65 MINUTES, 52 QUESTIONS

Mark your answers to the questions in Section 1 in the answer sheet provided.

DIRECTIONS

For each of the passages below, there are 10 or 11 questions. Choose the best answer for each of the questions after you have finished reading the passage. The answers to the questions should be based on the information that is stated or implied in the text and any associated graphics.

Questions 1-10 are based on the following passage.

This passage is adapted from J. Meade Falkner, "Moonfleet." Originally published in 1898. The narrator, John, has been sitting on a tombstone in the churchyard, which he finds comfortable for looking out to sea—an activity he enjoys.

It must have been past four o'clock in the afternoon, and I was for returning to tea at my aunt's, when underneath the stone on which I sat I heard
Line a rumbling and crumbling, and on jumping off saw
5 that the crack in the ground had still further widened, just where it came up to the tomb, and that the dry earth had so shrunk and settled that there was a hole in the ground a foot or more across. Now this hole reached under the big stone that formed one side of
10 the tomb, and falling on my hands and knees and looking down it, I perceived that there was under the monument a larger cavity, into which the hole opened. I believe there never was a boy yet who saw a hole in the ground, or a cave in a hill, or much more
15 an underground passage, but longed incontinently to be into it and discover whither it led. So it was with me; and seeing that the earth had fallen enough into the hole to open a way under the stone, I slipped myself in feet foremost, dropped down on to a heap
20 of fallen mould, and found that I could stand upright under the monument itself. . . .

. . . [T]he hole into which I had crept was only the mouth of a passage, which sloped gently down in the direction of the church. My heart fell to thumping
25 with eagerness and surprise, for I thought I had made a wonderful discovery, and that this hidden way would certainly lead to great things, perhaps even to Blackbeard's hoard; for ever since Mr. Glennie's tale I had constantly before my eyes a vision of the diamond
30 and the wealth it was to bring me. The passage was two paces broad, as high as a tall man, and cut through the soil, without bricks or any other lining; and what surprised me most was that it did not seem deserted nor mouldy and cobwebbed, as one would expect such
35 a place to be, but rather a well-used thoroughfare; for I could see the soft clay floor was trodden with the prints of many boots, and marked with a trail as if some heavy thing had been dragged over it.

So I set out down the passage, reaching out my
40 hand before me lest I should run against anything in the dark, and sliding my feet slowly to avoid pitfalls in the floor. But before I had gone half a dozen paces, the darkness grew so black that I was frightened, and so far from going on was glad to turn sharp about, and
45 see the glimmer of light that came in through the hole under the tomb. Then a horror of the darkness seized me, and before I well knew what I was about I found myself wriggling my body up under the tombstone on to the churchyard grass, and was once more in the low
50 evening sunlight and the soft sweet air. . . .

My aunt gave me but a sorry greeting when I came into the kitchen, for I was late and hot. She never said much when displeased, but had a way of saying nothing, which was much worse; and would
55 only reply yes or no, and that after an interval, to anything that was asked of her. . . .

You may guess that I said nothing of what I had seen, but made up my mind that as soon as my aunt's back was turned I would get a candle and tinder-box,
60 and return to the churchyard. The sun was down before Aunt Jane gave thanks for what we had received, and then turning to me, she said in a cold and measured voice:

'John, I have observed that you are often out
65 and about of nights, sometimes as late as half-past seven or eight. Now, it is not seemly for young folk to be abroad after dark, and I do not choose that my

nephew should be called a gad-about. "What's bred in the bone will come out in the flesh," and 'twas with
70 such loafing that your father began his wild ways, and afterwards led my poor sister such a life as never was, till the mercy of Providence took him away.'

1

The passage serves primarily to describe a young man's

A) resentment towards his aunt.
B) excitement due to a discovery.
C) escape from his painful reality.
D) curiosity about a certain event.

2

The passage implies that the narrator views his decision to enter the hole as

A) foolhardy.
B) predictable.
C) deplorable.
D) appropriate.

3

Which choice provides the best evidence for the answer to the previous question?

A) Lines 13-16 ("I believe . . . led")
B) Lines 25-28 ("for I . . . hoard")
C) Lines 42-44 ("before . . . about")
D) Lines 47-50 ("I found . . . air")

4

In lines 39-42, the narrator could best be described as

A) horrified.
B) deliberate.
C) wily.
D) pessimistic.

5

The passage indicates that John returned to the "evening sunlight and the soft sweet air" (line 50) because

A) he knew he was already late for tea with his aunt.
B) he planned to return with something to light his way.
C) the absolute and complete darkness caused him to panic.
D) he grew so frightened that his body unwittingly took over.

6

The main point of lines 32-38 ("and what . . . over it") is that to John, the underground passage

A) appeared ancient and abandoned.
B) exuded a dark, threatening air.
C) showed remarkable signs of traffic.
D) looked more dilapidated than expected.

7

According to the passage, John's "heart fell to thumping" (line 24) because

A) the place reminded him of a tale he had heard.
B) he was anxious to leave the dark underground.
C) he was the first to make this great discovery.
D) he knew this to be the location of a treasure hoard.

CONTINUE

8

As used in line 51, "sorry" most nearly means

A) remorseful.
B) melancholy.
C) callous.
D) pitiful.

9

The passage indicates that Aunt Jane believes which of the following about John?

A) John is grateful his father has passed away since he was the cause of his mother's suffering.
B) He is more likely to listen if she exercises restraint than if she openly shows her disgruntlement.
C) John is naturally predisposed to displaying the wayward behavior she dislikes.
D) John will ignore her admonition and disregard propriety by sneaking out after dark.

10

Which choice provides the best evidence for the answer to the previous question?

A) Lines 52-55 ("She never . . . no")
B) Lines 58-60 ("but made . . . churchyard")
C) Lines 60-63 ("The sun . . . voice")
D) Lines 66-69 ("it is . . . flesh")

Questions 11-21 are based on the following passages.

These passages discuss intelligent design, a theory that challenges the theory of Darwinian evolution.

Passage 1

Something that never fails to amaze me when the issue of intelligent design is brought up is the term pseudoscience. Intelligent design is science—
a scientific theory that implements the scientific
5 method. It seems ironic that scientists would fail to grasp this simple truth. It is perhaps this very lack of comprehension which also manifests itself in their adherence to Neo-Darwinism, overwhelming evidence delineating its flaws notwithstanding.
10 As I just stated, intelligent design is the name given to a branch of scientific research. It observes, posits hypotheses, tests against these through experiments and from the results, draws conclusions. The aim is to ascertain design underlying nature, to
15 show whether some intelligent agent rather than a random, undirected process like natural selection has sculpted us living beings and our surroundings.
For instance, intelligent design has examined features of irreducible complexity in nature. This
20 refers to adaptations in living beings whose every part is required towards its function. To put it differently, irreducibly complex adaptations are perfectly modeled for a certain need and cannot be the result of random mutation. Through experiments on the biological
25 structures in question, design proponents have concluded that these are indeed irreducibly complex, and we can conclude that they are indeed designed.
Proponents of Darwinism impugn the integrity of intelligent design as valid science by claiming it is
30 nothing but creationism in a different guise. These claims are as obstreperous as they are groundless—no wonder if one considers the unsubstantiated nature of their "scientific" convictions. Creationism obviously centers on religious texts and tries to explain the
35 world as we see it on that basis whereas intelligent design focuses on empirical observations and deduces from them scientific truths.
If my fellow scientists would deign to do the same, they would be unable to ignore the host of
40 problems with evolution according to Darwin. Take a look at the fossil record. If natural selection was correct, we ought to be able to find the fossilized remains of progressive stages of adaptation. Instead, we have mostly come across radically new body
45 plans that appeared seemingly out of the blue.

Fossils showing intermediate, transitional stages of adaptation constitute rare exceptions. Another issue that needs to be mentioned is cellular complexity. Our cells perform phenomenal feats such as error-checking
50 and duplicating our DNA which, in the opinion of many scientists, random Darwinian evolution cannot account for.

Passage 2
The Discovery Institute (DI) is the driving force behind the intelligent design (ID) movement. ID,
55 far from being a science, aims to assert Christian and theistic values in place of a purely scientific perspective on the world. The Discovery Institute's purpose thus is to reestablish a strong link between church and state, and to propagate its religious beliefs
60 using the public education system. It seeks to achieve this, however, while trying to beguile the public into accepting its self-proclaimed status as a legitimate science.

One of its strategies lies in its attempt to
65 falsely depict the theory of evolution, which diametrically contradicts ID, as a "theory in crisis." By misrepresenting the degree to which design poses a challenge to accepted science, they open the door to strategies that demand teachers "teach the
70 controversy" in classrooms. At the same time, design proponents, instead of meeting scientists head-on in debates, prefer to spread their message in educational settings where they will face schoolchildren instead of schooled scientists who are prepared to rebut their
75 claims.

In order to establish itself as a legitimate branch of science as opposed to being shelved as a religious view, ID first had to cut all visible ties to creationism. Creationism seeks to prove that the Book of Genesis
80 in the Bible truly depicts the creation of the earth while rejecting the scientific data that supports the actual formation of our planet and the ensuing evolution of life. This view has been overwhelmingly rejected by the scientific community as being
85 religious rather than scientific, and teaching it in public classrooms has been proscribed by the U.S. Supreme Court.

Thus, a new image was needed to establish credibility, and it was proposed to expunge the
90 terms associated with creationism from the group's vocabulary. For instance, "creation science" was replaced by "intelligent design." In fact, any word pointing toward the root "creation" was systematically purged and henceforth referred to as "intelligent
95 design."

Even in its current incarnation, unsurprisingly, ID was found to be creationist and thus religious in motivation by the District Court for the Middle District of Pennsylvania in 2005.

11

The general topic of both passages is the

A) origin of a new branch of science.
B) the validity of a claim made by a group.
C) impact of legal courts on intelligent design.
D) flawed nature of an established theory.

12

In lines 5-6 ("It seems . . . truth"), the author of Passage 1 describes certain people as

A) dense.
B) obstinate.
C) complicated.
D) recalcitrant.

13

Passage 1 most strongly suggests that the error-checking and duplication of DNA is

A) the foremost issue casting doubt on the theory of evolution.
B) a complex task that Darwinian evolution cannot account for.
C) a trait that has been uncovered thanks to intelligent design.
D) controversial even among intelligent design scientists.

14

Which choice provides the best evidence for the answer to the previous question?

A) Lines 11-13 ("It observes . . . conclusions")
B) Lines 21-24 ("To put . . . mutation")
C) Lines 28-30 ("Proponents . . . guise")
D) Lines 38-40 ("If my . . . Darwin")

15

The first paragraph of Passage 2 suggests that the author of Passage 2 primarily views the Discovery Institute as

A) artful.
B) fanatic.
C) cavalier.
D) charitable.

16

The quotation marks around the phrase "teach the controversy" in lines 69-70 serve to

A) emphasize the author's distress since the theory of evolution is in crisis.
B) nod at the fact that intelligent design proponents avoid scientists in discussion.
C) suggest that teachers are not prepared to handle this kind of content in class.
D) point out the author's skepticism regarding the usage of the phrase.

17

As described in the third and fourth paragraphs of Passage 2 (lines 76-95), the actions of intelligent design are most akin to a person who

A) conceals parts of his life in order to find greater acceptance.
B) changes his name in order to escape unjustified prosecution.
C) abandons his family after they helped him rise to fame and power.
D) denies knowing his friend due to differing opinions on an issue.

18

The author of Passage 2 would most likely characterize the "overwhelming evidence" (lines 8-9, Passage 1) as

A) a dearth of intelligence.
B) fabrication of facts.
C) falsification of data.
D) a misunderstanding of beliefs.

19

Which choice provides the best evidence for the answer to the previous question?

A) Lines 60-63 ("It seeks . . . science")
B) Lines 64-66 ("One of . . . crisis")
C) Lines 73-75 ("they will . . . claims")
D) Lines 76-78 ("In order . . . creationism")

20

The author of Passage 1 would most likely respond to the account regarding a "new image" (line 88, Passage 2) by arguing that

A) creationism actually lives on under the new identity of intelligent design.
B) the alleged connection to creationism is nothing but unwarranted slander.
C) intelligent design is a true science regardless of its questionable origins.
D) these bothersome claims cannot be explained by evolutionary theories.

21

The authors of both passages would most likely agree that

A) there are biological structures that point to the existence of a creator.
B) intelligent design endeavors to be accepted as a legitimate science.
C) intelligent design styles itself a science merely to advance its religious agenda.
D) intelligent design should be taught in classrooms like any other science.

Questions 22-32 are based on the following passage and supplementary material.

This passage discusses research efforts directed at reducing the effects of climate changing factors.

What merely seemed like one far off, future possibility in the 1980s has today turned into a hot topic for debate: is our climate changing? If the polar
Line ice caps start melting at accelerated rates and release
5 more water into the oceans, how will this affect our coastal regions and cities? And while global warming is a controversial issue, the existence of which is sometimes denied or, if admitted to, often attributed to natural climate cycles rather than anthropogenic
10 activities, to many scientists, there is no question about the existence or origin of this phenomenon: worldwide carbon emissions that mainly arise from the burning of fossil fuels.
   Although alternative energy sources are often
15 cited as a possible way to reduce the carbon footprint of our race, it seems unlikely that alternative energy sources will replace our fossil-based fuels. Among the obstacles for solar or wind energy are high cost and low energy yields per square foot. Nuclear energy
20 also presents an array of issues what with fears of large-scale accidents and the as yet imperfectly solved problem of fuel rod disposal. In order to stem the tonnage of carbon dioxide entering the atmosphere and thus ameliorate the earth's greenhouse effect,
25 carbon sequestration, also referred to as carbon capture, is considered by many as a more realistic measure.
   Carbon sequestration in essence describes methods of capturing carbon dioxide and safely storing it long term to prevent it from entering and
30 thus acting upon the atmosphere. If implemented on a large enough scale, carbon capture could play a significant part in cushioning the blow of our activities on global climate. There are a number of different ways this solution could be put into place.
35   One logical approach, tagged geosequestration, starts out at stationary points of carbon emissions such as power plants. Carbon dioxide is caught right around the combustion of the fuel before it has a chance to escape into the air. It needs to then
40 be safely transported to a subterranean storage area away from the atmosphere where it will finally be deposited. Underground geologic reservoirs such as aquifers have been proposed as possible repositories for long term storage, but there are challenges that
45 need to be addressed before this plan can be put into motion. Worldwide emissions of CO_2 are measured in gigatons (that means nine zeroes) per year, which calls for more research pertaining to sustainable high-volume injection rates and the maximum amount of
50 CO_2 a given subsurface structure can accommodate.
   Another possibility is plant sequestration which takes advantage of naturally occurring photosynthesis to capture CO_2 directly from the atmosphere and act as a carbon sink. Through managed revegetation
55 and forestation programs, this natural process could be boosted for an amount of time. What makes this a transient measure, however, is that plants at some point reach their full growth potential and thus start binding less CO_2. What ultimately will become of the
60 plant material is an additional item of uncertainty.
   Along with underground caching and the use of fauna, soil is an interesting storage option. The enormous potential of soil to hold carbon has led to research into possibly enhancing this quality. A fruit
65 of such efforts is biochar, made from heating organic waste products such as crop residue, manure, or wood chips in dedicated oxygen-poor environments to generate electricity. During this process, the carbon ends up in the "waste" product called biochar instead
70 of the atmosphere. Biochar is chemically stable and its carbon is bound in the soil for significant periods of time.

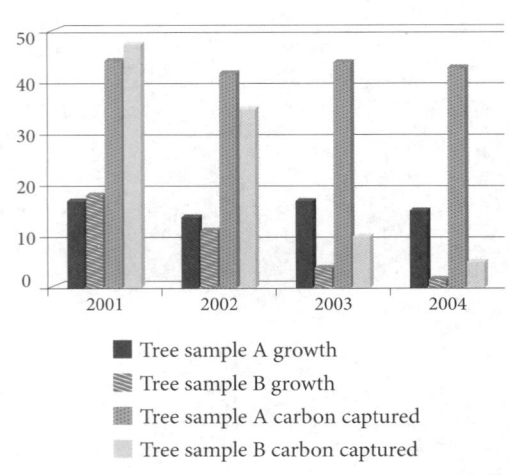

Tree Growth Rates in Relation to Carbon Capture Strength for Two Sample Groups of Trees

■ Tree sample A growth
▨ Tree sample B growth
▦ Tree sample A carbon captured
▢ Tree sample B carbon captured

22

The primary purpose of the passage is to

A) single out the culprit for our changing climate.
B) introduce a way to curb the impact of human activities.
C) offer ways to reverse anthropogenic damage using sequestration.
D) argue for using alternative energy to curb carbon emissions.

23

The author mentions that "Nuclear energy also presents an array of issues" (lines 19-20) in order to

A) support the notion that certain energy sources do not represent a feasible solution.
B) point out that disasters are the reason why its proliferation progresses slowly.
C) illustrate how cost and problematic energy yields inhibit alternative fuel development.
D) indicate that problems surrounding it cannot be completely resolved.

24

The passage most strongly suggests that on the whole, the effect carbon sequestration would have on our carbon output could best be described as

A) temporary.
B) mitigating.
C) decisive.
D) negligible.

25

Which choice provides the best evidence for the answer to the previous question?

A) Lines 30-33 ("If implemented . . . climate")
B) Lines 46-49 ("Worldwide . . . rates")
C) Lines 56-59 ("What makes . . . CO_2")
D) Lines 62-64 ("The enormous . . . quality")

26

The statement in lines 30-31 ("If implemented . . . scale") serves mainly to

A) point out difficulties in executing a plan.
B) describe the likely outcome of a procedure.
C) impose a condition on a plan's success.
D) reinforce the notion of substantial benefits.

27

Those who consider the attribution mentioned in lines 8-9 as correct would most likely consider the concept of geosequestration as described in lines 35-39 to be

A) pointless since human activities are not at fault.
B) a commendable solution to a controversial issue.
C) evidence for natural causes of climate change.
D) a laudable way of capturing carbon and storing it.

28

The passage mostly suggests that the author views geosequestration as

A) preferable to plant sequestration.
B) immensely dangerous.
C) costly but necessary.
D) difficult but feasible.

29

Which choice provides the best evidence for the answer to the previous question?

A) Lines 37-39 ("Carbon . . . air")
B) Lines 39-42 ("It needs . . . deposited")
C) Lines 42-46 ("Underground . . . motion")
D) Lines 46-50 ("Worldwide . . . accommodate")

30

What does the author imply about "The enormous potential of soil to hold carbon" (lines 62-63)?

A) It makes soil the optimal vessel for capturing carbon.
B) It lies idle without research that will unlock its great capacities.
C) It ought to be considered only after geo- and plant sequestration.
D) It is not being used to its full potential unless further studied.

31

Which idea is supported by the passage and by the information in the graph?

A) What will become of carbon in fully grown trees remains an uncertainty.
B) Plants naturally capture CO_2 from their environment as they photosynthesize.
C) Plants' efficiency in capturing carbon decreases with growth rates.
D) Only certain trees can be used as permanent carbon sinks because they do not stop growing.

32

The graph suggests which of the following about plant-based carbon capture in the indicated period of time?

A) The majority of trees underwent a steady decrease in growth rates over time.
B) The only increase in growth rates occurs between 2002 and 2003.
C) The tree samples as a whole captured more carbon in 2003 than in the previous year.
D) The amount of carbon captured by the combined groups never exceeds 50.

Questions 33-42 are based on the following passage and supplementary material.

This passage is adapted from Booker T. Washington, "The Future of the American Negro." Originally published in 1899. It discusses the future of African Americans.

   I remember not long ago, when about five hundred coloured people sailed from the port of Savannah bound for Liberia, that the news was
Line flashed all over the country, "The Negro has made
  5 up his mind to return to his own country," and that, "in this was the solution of the race problem in the South." But these short-sighted people forgot the fact that before breakfast that morning about five hundred more Negro children were born in the South alone....
 10   Somebody else conceived the idea of colonising the coloured people, of getting territory where nobody lived, putting the coloured people there, and letting them be a nation all by themselves. There are two objections to that. First, you would have to build
 15 one wall to keep the coloured people in, and another wall to keep the white people out. If you were to build ten walls around Africa to-day you could not keep the white people out, especially as long as there was a hope of finding gold there.
 20   I have always had the highest respect for those of our race who, in trying to find a solution for our Southern problem, advised a return of the race to Africa, and because of my respect for those who have thus advised, especially Bishop Henry M. Turner, I
 25 have tried to make a careful and unbiased study of the question, during a recent sojourn in Europe, to see what opportunities presented themselves in Africa for self-development and self-government.
   I am free to say that I see no way out of the
 30 Negro's present condition in the South by returning to Africa. Aside from other insurmountable obstacles, there is no place in Africa for him to go where his condition would be improved. All Europe—especially England, France, and Germany—has been running
 35 a mad race for the last twenty years, to see which could gobble up the greater part of Africa; and there is practically nothing left. Old King Cetewayo put it pretty well when he said, "First come missionary, then come rum, then come traders, then come army" and
 40 Cecil Rhodes has expressed the prevailing sentiment more recently in these words, "I would rather have land than 'niggers.'" And Cecil Rhodes is directly responsible for the killing of thousands of black natives in South Africa, that he might secure their land.
 45   In a talk with Henry M. Stanley, the explorer, he told me that he knew no place in Africa where the

Negroes of the United States might go to advantage; but I want to be more specific. Let us see how Africa has been divided, and then decide whether there is
50 a place left for us. On the Mediterranean coast of Africa, Morocco is an independent State, Algeria is a French possession, Tunis is a French protectorate, Tripoli is a province of the Ottoman Empire, Egypt is a province of Turkey. On the Atlantic coast,
55 Sahara is a French protectorate, Adrar is claimed by Spain, Senegambia is a French trading settlement, Gambia is a British crown colony, Sierra Leone is a British crown colony. Liberia is a republic of freed Negroes, Gold Coast and Ashanti are British
60 colonies and British protectorates, Togoland is a German protectorate, Dahomey is a kingdom subject to French influence, Slave Coast is a British colony and British protectorate, Niger Coast is a British protectorate, the Cameroons are trading settlements
65 protected by Germany, French Congo is a French protectorate, Congo Free State is an international African Association, Angola and Benguela are Portuguese protectorates, and the inland countries are controlled as follows: The Niger States, Masina, etc.,
70 are under French protection; Land Gandu is under British protection, administered by the Royal Haussan Niger Company. . . .

All this shows pretty conclusively that a return to Africa for the Negro is out of the question, even
75 provided that a majority of the Negroes wished to go back, which they do not. The adjustment of the relations of the two races must take place here; and it is taking place slowly, but surely. As the Negro is educated to make homes and to respect himself, the
80 white man will in turn respect him.

Control of African Territory in 1912

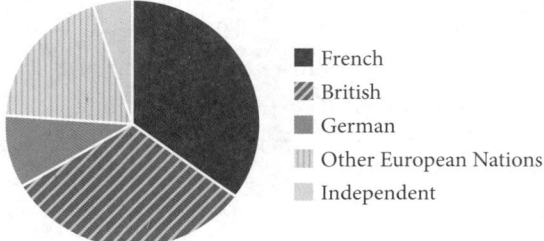

- French
- British
- German
- Other European Nations
- Independent

33

The primary purpose of the passage is to

A) outline major powers on a continent.
B) defend the champions of a proposition.
C) offer ways to improve a relationship.
D) assess a solution that was put forward.

34

According to the author, certain people are "short-sighted" (line 7) because

A) they do not care about birthrates in the South.
B) the solution put forward is as yet untested.
C) they wrongly assume that a group has decreased.
D) colonizing African Americans is a questionable plan.

35

The author probably mentions the prospect of finding gold in Africa in order to

A) characterize the unique lure of a continent.
B) concede that going to Africa is worth considering.
C) explain why a proposed plan will not work.
D) criticize the greedy nature of white people.

CONTINUE

36

Which of the following best describes the author's attitude toward people who "advised a return of the race to Africa" (lines 22-23)?

A) Veiled skepticism
B) Respectful neutrality
C) Profound esteem
D) Deserved animosity

37

The author studied the question of whether returning to Africa is feasible by

A) emigrating to Africa to evaluate the benefits that a colony would offer.
B) securing land in Africa alongside the European powers.
C) applying the lessons of European civilization to an envisioned colony.
D) pondering the viability of creating a nation on a trip to Europe.

38

What does Old King Cetewayo's quote in lines 38-39 imply in context?

A) European powers use bribes unless they can enforce their will.
B) The process of colonization tends to follow a broad pattern.
C) Thanks to Europe, Africa has gained in religion, commerce, and security.
D) Without missionaries paving the way, colonization is not feasible.

39

What does the author mainly do in lines 45-72?

A) Explain a continent's topography
B) Justify a planned exodus to Africa
C) Point out the rich diversity of an area
D) Expound on an authority's findings

40

The passage as a whole suggests that the author would view the persons who "sailed from the port of Savannah bound for Liberia" (lines 2-3) as

A) ungrateful hypocrites who desert their brethren in hopes of a better life.
B) a misguided group that will not find better conditions in Africa.
C) avid explorers who will find a solution to the problems of African Americans.
D) part of a solution that deserves the widespread approval it received.

41

Which of the following options is best supported by the passage and the information in the chart?

A) The competition among European nations to claim as much land as possible cannot continue much longer.
B) Returning to Africa is not a viable solution for African Americans since European nations occupy all of it.
C) British and French pursuit of gold has been especially ruthless, which has driven the expansion of their territories.
D) French colonies are among the oldest in Africa which explains why France controls a great part of Africa.

42

Which choice provides the best evidence for the answer to the previous question?

A) Lines 16-19 ("If . . . there")
B) Lines 33-37 ("All . . . left")
C) Lines 45-50 ("In a . . . for us")
D) Lines 50-56 ("On the . . . settlement")

Questions 43-52 are based on the following passage.

This passage is adapted from Albert Einstein, "Relativity: The Special and General Theory," published in 1920.

Lightning has struck the rails on our railway embankment at two places *A* and *B* far distant from each other. I make the additional assertion that these
Line two lightning flashes occurred simultaneously. If I ask
5 you whether there is sense in this statement, you will answer my question with a decided "Yes." But if I now approach you with the request to explain to me the sense of the statement more precisely, you find after some consideration that the answer to this question is
10 not so easy as it appears at first sight.

After some time perhaps the following answer would occur to you: "The significance of the statement is clear in itself and needs no further explanation; of course it would require some
15 consideration if I were to be commissioned to determine by observations whether in the actual case the two events took place simultaneously or not." I cannot be satisfied with this answer for the following reason. Supposing that as a result of ingenious
20 considerations an able meteorologist were to discover that the lightning must always strike the places *A* and *B* simultaneously, then we should be faced with the task of testing whether or not this theoretical result is in accordance with the reality. We encounter the same
25 difficulty with all physical statements in which the conception "simultaneous" plays a part. The concept does not exist for the physicist until he has the possibility of discovering whether or not it is fulfilled in an actual case. We thus require a definition of
30 simultaneity such that this definition supplies us with the method by means of which, in the present case, he can decide by experiment whether or not both the lightning strokes occurred simultaneously. As long as this requirement is not satisfied, I allow myself to be
35 deceived as a physicist (and of course the same applies if I am not a physicist), when I imagine that I am able to attach a meaning to the statement of simultaneity. (I would ask the reader not to proceed farther until he is fully convinced on this point.)
40 After thinking the matter over for some time you then offer the following suggestion with which to test simultaneity. By measuring along the rails, the connecting line *AB* should be measured up and an observer placed at the mid-point *M* of the distance
45 *AB*. This observer should be supplied with an arrangement (e.g. two mirrors inclined at 90°) which allows him visually to observe both places *A* and *B* at the same time. If the observer perceives the two flashes of lightning at the same time, then they are
50 simultaneous.

I am very pleased with this suggestion, but for all that I cannot regard the matter as quite settled, because I feel constrained to raise the following objection:
55 "Your definition would certainly be right, if only I knew that the light by means of which the observer at *M* perceives the lightning flashes travels along the length $A \rightarrow M$ with the same velocity as along the length $B \rightarrow M$. But an examination of this supposition
60 would only be possible if we already had at our disposal the means of measuring time. It would thus appear as though we were moving here in a logical circle."

43

The primary purpose of the passage is to

A) evaluate whether two events took place at the same time.

B) present a deceptively simple but sound experiment.

C) show that the simple appearance of a question is misleading.

D) assert that certain phenomena cannot be perceived by the naked eye.

44

Which of the following best summarizes lines 19-26 ("Supposing . . . part") of the passage?

A) It is always harder to come up with experiments to validate a theory than with the theory itself.

B) Any hypothesis that claims simultaneity might or might not correspond to the physical reality.

C) Even brilliant hypotheses cannot be correct unless they are proven correct in an experiment.

D) The very concept of simultaneity makes proving whether a theory coincides with reality more difficult.

45

The author suggests that he believes which of the following about the work of a physicist?

A) Its findings benefit many other disciplines.
B) A concept is meaningless without validation.
C) It mostly revolves around the speed of light.
D) It requires that we question the depth of our knowledge.

46

Which choice provides the best evidence for the answer to the previous question?

A) Lines 6-10 ("But if . . . sight")
B) Lines 19-24 ("Supposing . . . reality")
C) Lines 33-37 ("As long . . . simultaneity")
D) Lines 59-63 ("But an . . . circle")

47

Which of the following does the remark in lines 38-39 suggest about the author's belief regarding "this point"?

A) The reader has never pondered it before.
B) Without it, the reader cannot understand what follows.
C) It is a logical requirement for his next point.
D) It might seem unconvincing due to the nature of experiments.

48

The passage identifies all of the following as significant factors for setting up an experiment to test for simultaneity EXCEPT

A) a method of calculating time.
B) the exact distance between points A and B.
C) a means to observe two points from one position.
D) finding the mid-point M.

49

The author would characterize the suggested setup for the experiment as

A) appropriate.
B) inspired.
C) unconventional.
D) misguided.

50

Which choice provides the best evidence for the answer to the previous question?

A) Lines 29-33 ("We thus . . . simultaneously")
B) Lines 51-54 ("I am . . . objection")
C) Lines 55-59 ("Your . . . $B \to M$")
D) Lines 59-63 ("But an . . . circle")

51

The sentence in lines 51-54 ("I am . . . objection") mainly serves to

A) indicate that the author is displeased with a certain idea.
B) supply the solution to an ongoing question.
C) summarize the author's train of thought up to this point.
D) introduce the concept of speed as a part of a problem.

52

As used in line 53, "constrained" most nearly means

A) impelled.
B) inhibited.
C) incarcerated.
D) necessitated.

STOP

Do not move on to the next section if you finish early.

You may review your answers in this section only.

Answer Keys & Performance Breakdown

1	(B)	Summary	19	(B)	Evidence	37	(D)	Local
2	(B)	Local	20	(B)	Synthesize	38	(B)	Context
3	(A)	Evidence	21	(B)	Synthesize	39	(D)	Local
4	(B)	Local	22	(B)	Summary	40	(B)	Summary
5	(D)	Local	23	(A)	Context	41	(A)	Graph
6	(C)	Local	24	(B)	Local	42	(B)	Evidence
7	(A)	Local	25	(A)	Evidence	43	(C)	Summary
8	(D)	Vocabulary	26	(C)	Context	44	(B)	Local
9	(C)	Local	27	(A)	Synthesize	45	(B)	Local
10	(D)	Evidence	28	(D)	Local	46	(C)	Evidence
11	(B)	Synthesize	29	(C)	Evidence	47	(C)	Local
12	(A)	Local	30	(D)	Local	48	(B)	Local
13	(B)	Local	31	(C)	Graph	49	(A)	Local
14	(B)	Evidence	32	(B)	Graph	50	(C)	Evidence
15	(A)	Local	33	(D)	Summary	51	(D)	Context
16	(D)	Context	34	(C)	Local	52	(A)	Vocabulary
17	(A)	Local	35	(C)	Context			
18	(B)	Synthesize	36	(C)	Local			

■ Write down the number of correct answers for each question type.

Question Types	Number of Correct Answers
Local	/ 22
Style	0 / 0
Vocabulary	/ 2
Evidence	/ 9
Context	/ 6
Organization	0 / 0
Summary	/ 5
Stance	0 / 0
Synthesize	/ 5
Graph	/ 3
Total	**/ 52**

Answer Explanations

Questions 1-10

1. (B) *Summary*

B is the best choice because in the beginning, John willingly enters the hole in the ground and excitedly thinks of pirate treasure before returning to his aunt's where he already plans to return to the hole at night to explore it further.

A is incorrect because no resentment toward the aunt is actually mentioned. His feelings towards her are also not the focus of the passage. C is incorrect because the passage does not indicate that reality is painful to John. D is incorrect because even though John is curious, the object of the curiosity is the hole in the ground, not a certain event.

2. (B) *Local*

B is the best choice because of lines 13-16 (see next question).

A is incorrect because "foolhardy" means reckless or foolishly rash. The passage does not imply that John thinks this way. C is incorrect because though he grows frightened at the darkness in the hole, he does not see his decision as "deplorable." Indeed, he plans to be back to explore more as soon as he can. D is incorrect because "appropriate" means suitable for a certain purpose or occasion, which is not implied in the passage.

3. (A) *Evidence*

A is the best choice because the lines state that "there never was a boy yet who . . . but longed . . . to be into it"; i.e., every single boy who sees a hole in the ground longs to go inside and discover whither it leads. If every boy longs to do the same, that longing can be described as predictable.

B, C, and D are incorrect because none of them support that John believed his action to be predictable.

4. (B) *Local*

B is the best choice because the lines show him to be cautious in the dark to avoid running against anything and to avoid pitfalls. Therefore, "deliberate" as in "careful" or "considered" is correct.

A is incorrect because the lines do not mention great fright. C is incorrect because being careful and being cunning are not the same. D is incorrect because pessimism indicates expecting a negative outcome. John is merely careful.

5. (D) *Local*

D is the best choice because the passage states that a horror of the darkness seized him and he was outside before he knew what he was about, which supports "unwittingly."

A is incorrect because it is not mentioned as a reason for his return to the surface. B is incorrect because this was not mentioned as a reason for leaving the hole. C is incorrect because the darkness was not absolute: a glimmer of light was still visible.

6. (C) *Local*

C is the best choice because what surprised John most was that it was "a well-used thoroughfare" with boot prints and drag marks.

A is incorrect because of lines 33-34 (it did not seem deserted nor mouldy). B is incorrect because "dark, threatening" is not supported in these lines. D is incorrect because the opposite is stated in the passage.

7. (A) *Local*

A is the best choice because he believes the underground passage might even lead to Blackbeard's hoard which he had heard of in Mr. Glennie's tale (lines 27-30).

B is incorrect because the thumping heart signifies eagerness and excitement. C is incorrect because though it was a great discovery, the passage does not state he was the first to make it. D is incorrect because he thought it was a possibility, but he did not know with certainty that it would be there.

8. (D) *Vocabulary*

D is the best choice because in the sentence, the aunt gives John "but a sorry greeting" because he was late. Therefore, "sorry" indicates the lack of friendliness in the aunt's greeting, and "pitiful" is correct.

A is incorrect because it means that the aunt feels she did something wrong. B is incorrect because it indicates sadness as opposed to annoyance. C is incorrect because it means "heartless" or "indifferent."

Answer Explanations

"Callous" is too strong in context.

9. (C) *Local*

C is the best choice because of lines 66-69 (see next question).

A is incorrect because the aunt does not mention John's feelings while discussing his father's death. B is incorrect because even though she uses a cold and measured voice, she does spell out in detail the kind of behavior she dislikes. Also, the passage does not mention her reason for exercising a certain measure of restraint. D is incorrect because the passage does not indicate that she knows of his plans.

10. (D) *Evidence*

D is the best choice because the lines state that she would dislike for John to be a gad-about. She then implies that John has inherited this disposition from his father by saying "What's bred in the bone will come out in the flesh."

A, B, and C are incorrect because none of them state that John has inherited traits that his aunt dislikes.

Questions 11-21

11. (B) *Synthesize*

B is the best choice because Passage 1 emphasizes that intelligent design's claim to be a science is well-founded and true while Passage 2 attacks that very notion by asserting that the Discovery Institute that promotes intelligent design is really a religious organization.

A is incorrect because Passage 1 does not focus on ID's origins, and Passage 2 does not consider ID a science. C is incorrect because only Passage 2 mentions legal courts. D is incorrect because only Passage 1 focuses on the flawed nature of an established theory (Darwinism).

12. (A) *Local*

A is the best choice because the lines state that scientists fail to grasp a simple truth. This means they lack understanding. Thus, "dense" as in "obtuse" is correct.

B is incorrect because it means "stubborn." C is incorrect because "complicated" is not suggested. D is incorrect because "defiance" is not suggested.

13. (B) *Local*

B is the best choice because of lines 48-52 and lines 21-24 (see next question).

A is incorrect because of the word "foremost" which is not supported by the passage. C is incorrect because the passage does not indicate how the feature in question was discovered. D is incorrect because no debate or controversy within the ranks of the ID movement was mentioned.

14. (B) *Evidence*

B is the best choice because the lines state that irreducibly complex adaptations are perfectly modeled and thus cannot be the result of random mutation. This ties in well with the description of error-checking and duplicating DNA using the phrases "phenomenal feats" and "cellular complexity."

A, C, and D are incorrect because none of them deny random mutation due to complexity.

15. (A) *Local*

A is the best choice because the specified paragraph mainly focuses on the fact that the ID movement tries to propagate religious beliefs while beguiling the public into accepting its status as a legitimate science. In other words, the paragraph states that ID is a religious movement, but its members want people to believe that it is a science. Therefore, "artful" as in "deceitful" is correct.

B is incorrect because extreme zeal is not mentioned. C is incorrect because "cavalier" either means "haughty" or "offhand." D is incorrect because charity is not suggested.

16. (D) *Context*

D is the best choice because the previous sentence states that evolution is falsely portrayed as a "theory in crisis." (There is no real crisis.) Similarly, "teach the controversy" suggests there is no real controversy. Thus, "skepticism" is correct.

A is incorrect because the author does not believe the crisis is real. B is incorrect because avoiding scientists in discussions is a separate strategy from misrepresenting Darwinism as threatened by ID. C is incorrect because the quotation marks serve to suggest that there is no controversy.

17. (A) — Local

A is the best choice because paragraphs 3 and 4 describe how ID hid its ties to creationism to establish credibility as a science. Creationism had been overwhelmingly rejected by the scientific community for its religious aspect.

B is incorrect because Passage 2 does not indicate that the prosecution or censure that creationism underwent was unjustified. C is incorrect because abandoning (to not take care of) does not equal hiding (to conceal). D is incorrect because differing opinions would mean that ID and creationism have different opinions, but Passage 2 indicates that ID and creationism are actually the same.

18. (B) — Synthesize

B is the best choice because of lines 64-66 (see next question).

A is incorrect because the author of Passage 2 does not accuse ID of being unintelligent. C is incorrect because "falsification of data" is not supported by Passage 2. D is incorrect because the author of Passage 2 believes the actions of the ID movement to be deliberate (lines 64-66).

19. (B) — Evidence

B is the best choice because lines 7-9 state that there is overwhelming evidence showing the flaws of Darwinism. Lines 64-66 state that the ID movement falsely depicts the theory of evolution as a "theory in crisis." This supports "fabrication of facts."

A, C, and D are incorrect because none of them show that the author of Passage 2 sees the "overwhelming evidence" as mentioned in lines 8-9 as a fabrication of facts.

20. (B) — Synthesize

B is the best choice because the "new image" represents the author of Passage 2's claim that ID is creationism under a different name. To this, the author of Passage 1 would not agree since he claims ID is a true science, and he would call this claim "obstreperous" and "groundless."

A is incorrect because the author of Passage 1 would disagree. The author of Passage 2 would think this way. C is incorrect because the author of Passage 1 does not acknowledge that ID comes from questionable origins. D is incorrect because what cannot be explained by evolutionary theories is irreducible complexity (wrong context).

21. (B) — Synthesize

B is the best choice because the author of Passage 1 states that ID is a legitimate science while the author of Passage 2 emphasizes that ID tries hard to disguise its religious motivations to appear as a legitimate science.

A is incorrect because only the author of Passage 1 would agree. C is incorrect because only the author of Passage 2 would agree. D is incorrect because only the author of Passage 1 would agree.

Questions 22-32

22. (B) — Summary

B is the best choice because according to the passage, carbon emissions are caused by human activities. The passage focuses on explaining the concept of carbon capture or carbon sequestration which serves to prevent carbon from entering the atmosphere.

A is incorrect because placing blame is not the focus of the passage. C is incorrect because sequestration does not "reverse" damage. It only mitigates it. D is incorrect because alternative energy sources are mentioned as a minor detail: since alternative energy is not viable, the author proposes carbon capture as a more realistic measure.

23. (A) — Context

A is the best choice because right before this sentence, the author mentions that solar and wind power are faced with obstacles. Before that, the author mentions that alternative energy sources are not likely to replace fossil-based fuels. Therefore, "certain energy sources" refers to alternative energy sources, and the issues and obstacles are mentioned to show that alternative energy is not feasible.

B is incorrect because the context does not focus on the proliferation of nuclear energy. C is incorrect because energy yields and cost refer to solar and wind energy while nuclear energy has its own set of separate issues. D is incorrect because the purpose of mentioning nuclear energy is to support the fact that alternative energies in general are not feasible. Also, D is contradicted by "as yet" in line 21.

Answer Explanations

24. (B) — Local

B is the best choice because of lines 30-33 (see next question).

A is incorrect because the question asks for carbon sequestration in general whereas "temporary" only refers to plant sequestration. C is incorrect because "decisive" implies that thanks to carbon sequestration, a turning point has been reached or a momentous change is facilitated. This is not supported by the passage. D is incorrect because "negligible" means that carbon sequestration is practically useless.

25. (A) — Evidence

A is the best choice because the lines state that carbon sequestration could cushion, or mitigate, the effect of human activities on our global climate.

B, C, and D are incorrect because none of them state that carbon sequestration could have a mitigating effect on our carbon output.

26. (C) — Context

C is the best choice because the following clause shows a result that is made possible if the condition is satisfied.

A is incorrect because the statement itself does not mention difficulty. A large scale does not necessarily result in difficulty. B is incorrect because the statement in question refers to a condition, not an outcome. Also, "likely" is not supported. D is incorrect because the condition to a plan has to be seen as a price, an effort, or some kind of *investment* which is different from a benefit.

27. (A) — Synthesize

A is the best choice because the "attribution" refers to attributing global warming to natural climate cycles and not to human activity. If one believes humans are not at fault for the changing climate, stemming the carbon output of human activities (geosequestration) becomes pointless.

B is incorrect because those who believe in the attribution would believe it is meaningless, not commendable. C is incorrect because capturing human-generated carbon cannot be evidence that climate change is not caused by humans. D is incorrect for the same reason as B.

28. (D) — Local

D is the best choice because of lines 42-46 (see next question).

A is incorrect because geosequestration and plant sequestration are not compared in terms of which one is preferable. B is incorrect because "immensely" is too strong. Lines 39-40 call for safe transportation, but this does not warrant the use of the word "immensely." C is incorrect because money is not mentioned in the context of geosequestration.

29. (C) — Evidence

C is the best choice because the lines state that certain sites have been "proposed as possible repositories for long term storage (feasible), but there are challenges that need to be addressed (difficult)." The latter part also implies that the challenges *can* be addressed.

A, B, and D are incorrect because none of them characterize geosequestration as difficult but feasible.

30. (D) — Local

D is the best choice because the passage states there is research into enhancing the potential of soil to hold carbon. This means that before it is studied further (researched), its potential of holding carbon is lower than after it is studied. Therefore, soil is definitely not used to its full potential.

A is incorrect because "optimal" means the best. No comparisons to other vessels are made. B is incorrect because the passage does not state that soil does not capture any carbon (idle) before it is researched. C is incorrect because no priorities or such rankings are mentioned in the passage.

31. (C) — Graph

C is the best choice because the passage also discusses plants capturing carbon and states that plants reach their full growth potential and therefore start binding less carbon (lines 57-59). Tree sample B's growth rate decreases over time, and along with it does its carbon capture strength which matches the statement in the passage.

A is incorrect because no such information is offered in the graph. B is incorrect because the graph correlates growth and carbon capture, not photosynthesis. D is incorrect because the passage mentions that plant sequestration is a transient measure (thus implying they cannot be used permanently), and the graph does not offer enough information to support the claim that tree sample A will *never* stop growing.

32. (B) — Graph

B is the best choice because for both tree samples, growth rates decrease with each year except for tree sample A between 2002 and 2003.

A is incorrect because only tree sample B's growth rates steadily decrease. Whether or not this constitutes the majority of trees is not indicated in the graph. C is incorrect because tree sample B lost a considerably larger amount of carbon capture strength in 2003 than the slight gain that tree sample A saw in that year. D is incorrect because in order to get the combined carbon capture strength of both tree samples, one has to add together the capture strength values for tree samples A and B. These sums exceed 50 in every year except for 2004.

Questions 33-42

33. (D) — Summary

D is the best choice because Washington mentions the idea of African Americans going back to Africa. After mentioning that he studied this matter with great care out of respect for those who proposed it, he in essence states that going back to Africa is meaningless and that African Americans need to earn respect here in America. Thus, he assesses the solution (of going back to Africa).

A is incorrect because while these powers were mentioned, they were mentioned in order to support the *greater* idea that Africa does not represent a viable solution. B is incorrect because the champions of a proposition are neither attacked nor defended. C is incorrect because while improving the relationship between black and white people is mentioned as a goal, the passage *focuses* on the feasibility of returning to Africa.

34. (C) — Local

C is the best choice because "short-sighted" refers to the fact that people did not take into account birthrates when they believed that the departure of black people to Africa "was the solution of the race problem." They mistakenly believed that this departure meant fewer black people were left.

A is incorrect because not caring is different from not being aware. The passage states that they "forgot."

B is incorrect because "short-sighted" refers to oversight, not testing. D is incorrect because "short-sighted" criticizes those who forgot about birthrates, not those who came up with the idea of colonizing African Americans.

35. (C) — Context

C is the best choice because the mentioned "hope of finding gold" serves to support the impossibility of keeping white people out of Africa. Thus, the author mentions gold to explain why colonizing African Americans into empty territory is impossible.

A is incorrect because "unique" implies there is no gold to be found anywhere else. B is incorrect because the gold constitutes a reason not to even try going to Africa (since it will lure white people into the new colonies). D is incorrect because though it implies greed, the gold is not mentioned to support the idea of greed but rather to justify pessimism towards a plan.

36. (C) — Local

C is the best choice because of lines 20-24.

A is incorrect because hidden or concealed skepticism is not suggested in context. B is incorrect because "neutrality" applies to their plan, but not to the people. D is incorrect because nothing in the passage suggests hostility.

37. (D) — Local

D is the best choice because of lines 26-28 that state he was on a "sojourn in Europe (trip), to see what opportunities presented themselves in Africa for self-development and self-government (viability of creating a nation)."

A is incorrect because he was in Europe. B is incorrect because "securing land" is not mentioned in context of that study. C is incorrect because "applying the lessons of European civilization" is not mentioned in context.

38. (B) — Context

B is the best choice because the four stages Cetewayo mentions (missionary, rum, traders, army) refer to the gobbling up of Africa by European powers. In other words, he suggests that for each country, colonization happened in these four stages (a broad pattern).

A is incorrect because this implies that use of force might fail which was not mentioned. C is incorrect because the quote refers to colonization which

Answer Explanations

ultimately involved conquest by armed forces. This does not imply security gained by Africa. D is incorrect since the fact that something happens a certain way does not mean it has to necessarily happen this way.

39. (D) — Local

D is the best choice because in line 48, he mentions he wants "to be more specific" regarding the conclusion of the explorer Henry M. Stanley that Africa has no place for African Americans.

A is incorrect because "topography" means the layout of the land, not the explorer's conclusion that Africa offers no place for African Americans. B is incorrect because rather than justifying an exodus, he declares it futile. C is incorrect because, like A, it does not take into account the explorer's conclusion.

40. (B) — Summary

B is the best choice. The main idea of the passage is that going back to Africa would be futile for African Americans. Considering this futility, the author would view those who still choose to go back to Africa as misguided.

A is incorrect because the author deeply respects those who proposed the idea and he thus carefully studied the proposal. In his conclusion, nothing justifies calling those who go back "hypocrites." C is incorrect because the author does not see Africa as a solution. D is incorrect because he does not approve of the idea of returning to Africa.

41. (A) — Graph

A is the best choice because of lines 33-37 (see next question). Also, the chart shows that only a small fraction of Africa is independent in the year of 1912 which supports the statement.

B is incorrect because the chart shows that European nations do not occupy 100% of Africa. The passage does not specifically state this, either. C is incorrect because neither the passage not the chart specify whether France or Britain are more ruthless than other European nations in their pursuit of gold, or whether this was the cause of their territorial expansion. D is incorrect because no information is given regarding the age of colonies.

42. (B) — Evidence

B is the best choice because the lines state that Europeans nations are in a race to consume the greater part of Africa, and "there is practically nothing left."

A, C, and D are incorrect because none of them show that the competition among European nations to claim as much land as possible cannot continue much longer.

Questions 43-52

43. (C) — Summary

Einstein first states that the question regarding simultaneity is not as easily answered as it might seem. He then explains this by asserting that actual proof obtained through experiment is vital to assess the truth of the initial statement. In the latter half, he describes a proper way to test for simultaneity, but he then states that without a way to measure speed, even this experiment will not be meaningful.

C is the best choice.

A is incorrect because the passage does not try to answer this question. Rather, it discusses the difficulty of finding the answer. B is incorrect because the passage does not stress how very simple the setup of an experiment is. "Deceptively simple" implies that it is more useful than it would first appear, which is definitely not the focus of this passage. D is incorrect because the passage implies it is possible to visually check for concurrence.

44. (B) — Local

B is the best choice because lines 24-26 state that all physical statements that include the word "simultaneous" involve the same "difficulty." "Difficulty" (check the previous sentence) refers to testing whether a theoretical result corresponds to reality.

A is incorrect because no such comparison was made. C is incorrect because it only describes a subset of hypotheses (brilliant ones) whereas the passage asserts that this is true for all statements. D is incorrect because the passage does not imply that simultaneity raises the difficulty of finding proof.

45. (B) — Local

B is the best choice because of lines 33-37 (see next question).

A is incorrect because even supposing that physics benefits the field of meteorology (though this is just a hypothetical example which does not necessarily imply that physics actually benefits the latter field), no other disciplines are mentioned. C is incorrect because the passage does not indicate that the speed of light is central to physics. D is incorrect because the passage does not mention this requirement.

46. (C) Evidence

C is the best choice because the lines state that without experiment (this requirement), attaching a meaning to simultaneity (a concept) is akin to self-deception.

A, B, and D are incorrect because none of them show that a concept is meaningless without validation.

47. (C) Local

C is the best choice because the specified sentence asks the reader not to read the next point (proceed farther) *unless* they are convinced on this point. Thus, "requirement" makes sense.

A is incorrect because the sentence does not imply that this might be the first time the reader thinks on this. B is incorrect because the sentence deals with persuasion or belief which is not a requirement for comprehension. D is incorrect because the sentence does not concede that a point might lack persuasive power.

48. (B) Local

B is the best choice because the exact distance, or the precise amount of space, between two points was neither mentioned nor was it brought up as important in order to test for simultaneity.

A is mentioned in lines 59-61. C is mentioned in lines 45-48. D is mentioned in lines 42-45.

49. (A) Local

A is the best choice because of lines 55-59 (see next question).

B is incorrect because "pleased" (line 51) does not equal saying that something is "inspired" (resulting from divine or supernatural inspiration). C is incorrect because whether or not it is conventional is not mentioned in context. D is incorrect because the author thinks the setup is adequate.

50. (C) Evidence

C is the best choice because the lines state a "definition would certainly be right" which refers to the result of the experiment asked for in the previous question. The specified lines go on to say that this is predicated upon knowing the velocity of light (which is not part of the setup of the experiment).

B is not the best choice because though the author mentions he is pleased, this does not indicate that the setup of the experiment is adequate.

A and D are incorrect because none of them show that the author would characterize the experiment's setup as appropriate.

51. (D) Context

D is the best choice because within the specified lines, the author focuses on an objection that he has which he subsequently mentions in lines 55-59 (the velocity of light).

A is incorrect because it is in opposition to the specified sentence. B is incorrect because no solution is offered. C is incorrect because no summary of previous thoughts is supplied.

52. (A) Vocabulary

A is the best choice because within the sentence, the author feels "constrained" to make an objection. Thus, he feels "forced" to or "impelled" to make an objection.

B is incorrect because it means "hindered" or "restricted." C is incorrect because it means "imprisoned" or "confined." D is incorrect because it means "made necessary" or "entailed" which does not work grammatically.

SAT.Hackers.ac

Hackers New SAT Reading: 10 Practice Tests

TEST 4

Answer Keys & Performance Breakdown
Answer Explanations

1

Reading Test
65 MINUTES, 52 QUESTIONS

Mark your answers to the questions in Section 1 in the answer sheet provided.

DIRECTIONS

For each of the passages below, there are 10 or 11 questions. Choose the best answer for each of the questions after you have finished reading the passage. The answers to the questions should be based on the information that is stated or implied in the text and any associated graphics.

Questions 1-10 are based on the following passage.

This passage is adapted from a novel and describes a third generation Japanese-American visiting his ancestral homeland for the first time.

"You'll get a tan just standing here." I followed Dad's eyes and looked around the cluster of commercial buildings blotting out the sky in every
Line direction. Or rather, what I had to assume were
5 buildings behind those outlandishly big floodlight-strength neon walls that screamed brand names at your eyes—mostly in their proud red and white. But then again, back home, we did use a lot of red, white, and blue. Back home, though, it would take 50 of my
10 towns pitching in to even reach the ballpark of the light output on just this intersection.
   I was about to agree when Dad grabbed my arm. "Green!" he barked, and dragged me and Mom off across the intersection. A flood of pedestrians
15 inundated the asphalt from every direction at once. We were riding one of those crests, and I was sure the waves must crash just like football players, and spill onto the street in disarray . . .
   Visibility was down to inches. Countless bodies
20 expertly slid by left and right. The swish of clothes brushing past. Almost no physical contact. No eye contact, and no communication to facilitate. And suddenly, we were through. I started breathing again.
   "That was insane!" I managed to say. "I mean . . .
25 that was more people just crossed the road than you'll see in the entire mall downtown!"
   Mom laughed. "Remember when your aunt came to visit and asked us to take her downtown when we already were?"
30   "And you were so offended," Dad added with a look that managed to convey the words he didn't say.

   The question kind of made sense now that I was standing in this endless orderly chaos of humans going every which way; every store front brighter
35 than Holy Eve, each building looming larger than J.C. Penney.
   "Well, Dad and I are gonna go shopping and give you some time to explore. I know you hate being out with your parents. It's . . . uncool, *ne*? See you back
40 here in an hour."
   Mom saw the look on my face. "Oh, you'll be okay," she promised. And with that, they turned around and were gone. I mean seriously gone. Ten seconds, and they were gobbled up by the crowd and
45 good luck trying to pick them out.
   I felt utterly lost. I wasn't used to everyone looking like, well, looking like me. I edged up against a display window to escape the currents and just get it together. The chatter of schoolgirls passing me by
50 sounded as Martian as that of the businessmen. I turned around and looked at the display. The clothes looked pretty much like the ones they sold in the States, but the signs and labels were all covered in this angular gibberish that only my grandparents could read, and
55 the numbers didn't make sense. 20,000 for a coat?
   Was that how Grandma felt when she first landed in the States? How did she manage to get by? Find a job? Make friends? Or survive, for that matter? I thought about that wizened old woman, and it
60 suddenly occurred to me I had never really talked to her. *Well, she doesn't speak English!*
   I looked around, and a familiar sign caught my eye: an American island in this ocean of Japan.
   "Thank God," I muttered to myself and started
65 walking.

1

1

The passage mainly revolves around

A) the narrator's inability to adapt to new situations.
B) Japan's sheer foreignness as experienced by the narrator.
C) the narrator's parents trying to reacquaint their son with Japan.
D) the empathy that arises out of the narrator's visit to Japan.

2

The sentence in lines 16-18 ("We were . . . disarray") indicates that

A) the pedestrians were in complete disarray.
B) the ocean reminded the narrator of sports.
C) the narrator was walking in the front lines.
D) the narrator felt annoyance towards Japan.

3

In context, lines 19-22 ("Visibility . . . facilitate") mostly convey an impression of

A) a choreographed dance.
B) unexpected efficiency.
C) complete relief.
D) urban anonymity.

4

In context, the father's communication in lines 30-31 suggests which of the following about the narrator?

A) His hometown is actually much bigger than his aunt's request suggested.
B) He feels justified because his aunt purposely ridiculed his hometown.
C) He was overly defensive of his hometown due to his own ignorance.
D) He feels ashamed for having overreacted to his aunt's request.

5

Which of the following best summarizes the narrator's thoughts in lines 32-36?

A) He grasps the idea that diverse origins can result in diverse perspectives.
B) He recants his idea that his home country is superior to Japan.
C) He relishes the differences between Japan and the USA.
D) He condemns Japanese ostentatiousness and profligacy.

6

The "angular gibberish" in lines 53-54 most likely refers to

A) signs and labels.
B) prices.
C) Japanese writing.
D) people chattering.

7

Which of the following best characterizes the thoughts in lines 56-61?

A) A complete change of heart
B) Indignation at his parents
C) A sincere bout of empathy
D) An epiphany regarding his origins

CONTINUE

8

What does the narrator mainly do when he mentions that his grandmother "*doesn't speak English*" (line 61)?

A) He justifies a neglect.
B) He consoles himself.
C) He dismisses a rationale.
D) He attacks a shortcoming.

9

The passage most likely mentions an "island in this ocean" (line 63) in order to

A) suggest that the narrator will be stranded with no escape.
B) emphasize the conspicuous nature of the sign.
C) describe the narrator's emotion by continuing a metaphor.
D) convey the relief the narrator felt at seeing familiar faces.

10

Which choice provides the best evidence for the answer to the previous question?

A) Lines 4-7 ("Or rather . . . eyes")
B) Lines 37-40 ("Well . . . hour")
C) Lines 46-49 ("I felt . . . together")
D) Lines 53-55 ("the signs . . . coat")

Questions 11-20 are based on the following passage.

This passage is adapted from Edward A. Johnson, "History of Negro Soldiers in the Spanish-American War, and Other Items of Interest." Originally published in 1899. In this excerpt, Theodore Roosevelt starts out by praising the courage of black soldiers in a battle that took place in 1898.

When Colonel Theodore Roosevelt returned from the command of the famous Rough Riders[1], he delivered a farewell address to his men, in which he made the following kind reference to the gallant
5 Negro soldiers:

"Now, I want to say just a word more to some of the men I see standing around not of your number. I refer to the colored regiments, who occupied the right and left flanks of us at Guasimas, the Ninth and Tenth
10 cavalry regiments. The Spaniards called them 'Smoked Yankees,' but we found them to be an excellent breed of Yankees. I am sure that I speak the sentiments of officers and men in the assemblage when I say that between you and the other cavalry regiments there
15 exists a tie which we trust will never be broken."

The foregoing compliments to the Negro soldiers by Colonel Roosevelt started up an avalanche of additional praise for them, out of which the fact came, that but for the Ninth and Tenth Cavalry (colored)
20 coming up at Las Guasimas, destroying the Spanish block house and driving the Spaniards off, when Roosevelt and his men had been caught in a trap, with a barbed-wire fence on one side and a precipice on the other, not only the brave Capron and Fish, but the
25 whole of his command would have been annihilated by the Spanish sharp-shooters, who were firing with smokeless powder under cover, and picking off the Rough Riders one by one, who could not see the Spaniards. To break the force of this unfavorable
30 comment on the Rough Riders, it is claimed that Colonel Roosevelt made the following criticism of the colored soldiers in general and of a few of them in particular, in an article written by him for the April Scribner; and a letter replying to the Colonel's
35 strictures, follows by Sergeant Holliday, who was an "eye-witness" to the incident:

Colonel Roosevelt's criticism was, in substance, that colored soldiers were of no avail without white officers; that when the white commissioned officers
40 are killed or disabled, colored non-commissioned officers could not be depended upon to keep up a charge already begun; that about a score of colored infantrymen, who had drifted into his command, weakened on the hill at San Juan under the galling

Spanish fire, and started to the rear, stating that
they intended finding their regiments, or to assist
the wounded; whereupon he drew his revolver and
ordered them to return to ranks and there remain,
and that he would shoot the first man who didn't obey
him; and that after that he had no further trouble.
   Colonel Roosevelt is sufficiently answered in the
following letter of Sergeant Holliday, and the point
especially made by many eye-witnesses (white) who
were engaged in that fight is, as related in Chapter V,
of this book, that the Negro troops made the charges
both at San Juan and El Caney after nearly all their
officers had been killed or wounded. Upon what
facts, therefore, does Colonel Roosevelt base his
conclusions that Negro soldiers will not fight without
commissioned officers, when the only real test of this
question happened around Santiago and showed just
the contrary of what he states? We prefer to take the
results at El Caney and San Juan as against Colonel
Roosevelt's imagination.

[1] The Rough Riders is the name of the 1st United States Volunteer Cavalry, Theodore Roosevelt's unit.

11

The author's primary purpose in the passage is to

A) honor a group.
B) vindicate a changed opinion.
C) evaluate a reaction.
D) denigrate undeserved praise.

12

Which choice provides the best evidence for the answer to the previous question?

A) Lines 12-15 ("I am . . . broken")
B) Lines 29-34 ("To break . . . Scribner")
C) Lines 34-36 ("a letter . . . incident")
D) Lines 51-53 ("Colonel . . . eye-witnesses")

13

In line 7, "your number" refers to

A) the size of his unit.
B) white soldiers.
C) black soldiers.
D) the Ninth and Tenth regiments.

14

The author indicates that "Las Guasimas" (line 20) was a place where

A) the Ninth and Tenth Cavalry were saved by the arrival of Roosevelt.
B) Roosevelt's actions resulted in unnecessary casualties.
C) black soldiers received due credit for their actions.
D) black soldiers distinguished themselves by assisting others.

15

The passage indicates that Roosevelt mainly "made the following criticism of the colored soldiers" (lines 31-32) because

A) recognition of the Ninth and Tenth Cavalry's efforts hurt the Rough Riders' reputation.
B) black soldiers refused to attack the enemy in the absence of white officers.
C) he felt that the Rough Riders' morale needed a boost after being saved by black soldiers.
D) in his opinion, his Rough Riders had received less commendation than they deserved.

16

As used in line 43, "drifted" most nearly means

A) chanced.
B) gallivanted.
C) strolled.
D) lingered.

17

The author's mention of the word "white" in line 53 implies the assumption that

A) certain ethnic groups inherently tended to prevaricate.
B) the testimony's credibility depended in part on the witness' skin color.
C) Roosevelt mistrusted the black soldiers under his command.
D) the evidence supporting the black soldiers' courage is irrefutable

18

Roosevelt claims that he drew his revolver while giving orders to black soldiers because

A) they were sullen and obstinate, and they refused to listen to verbal commands.
B) after setting a forceful example, he knew that no one would defy him.
C) he believed they were key in relieving his own beleaguered Rough Riders.
D) in the absence of leadership, they tended to abandon their line of duty.

19

The passage indicates that Sergeant Holliday would most likely characterize Roosevelt's conclusions as

A) compelling testimony regarding the discipline of black soldiers.
B) unsupported fabrications that contradict verified facts.
C) a delusional account that does little to hide the latter's racism.
D) accusations that cannot be rescinded for lack of factual support.

20

Which choice provides the best evidence for the answer to the previous question?

A) Lines 30-33 ("it is claimed . . . particular")
B) Lines 39-42 ("when . . . begun")
C) Lines 55-57 ("that the . . . wounded")
D) Lines 60-62 ("when the . . . states")

Questions 21-31 are based on the following passages.

Passage 1 is adapted from Percival Lowell, "Mars and Its Canals." Originally published in 1906. Passage 2 is adapted from Alfred Russel Wallace, "Is Mars Habitable?: A Critical Examination of Professor Percival Lowell's Book 'Mars and Its Canals,' with an Alternative Explanation." Originally published in 1907.

Passage 1

Now, it is not a little startling that the semblance of just such signs of intelligent interference with nature is what we discern on the face of Mars,—in
Line the canals and oases. So dominant in its mien is
5 the pencil-like directness of the canals as to be the trait that primarily strikes an unprejudiced observer who beholds this astounding system of lines under favorable definition for the first time, and its impressiveness only grows on him with study of the
10 phenomena.

That they suggested rule and compass, Schiaparelli said of them long ago, without committing himself as to what they were. In perception the great observer was, as usual, quite
15 right; and the better they are seen the more they justify the statement. Punctilious in their precision, they outdo in method all attempts of freehand drawing to copy them. Often has the writer tried to represent the regularity he saw, only to draw and
20 redraw his lines in vain. Nothing short of ruling them could have reproduced what the telescope revealed.

Strange as their depiction may look in the drawings, the originals look stranger still. Indeed, that they should look unnatural when properly
25 depicted is not unnatural if they are so in fact. For it is the geodetic[1] precision which the lines exhibit that instantly stamps them to consciousness as artificial. . . .

Suggestive of design as their initial appearance is, the idea of artificiality receives further sanction from
30 more careful consideration, even from a static point of view, on at least eight counts:
1. Their straightness;
2. Their individually uniform size;
3. Their extreme tenuity;
35 4. The dual character of some of them[2];
5. Their position with regard to the planet's fundamental features;
6. Their relation to the oases;
7. The character of these spots; and, finally,
40 8. The systematic networking by both canals and spots of the whole surface of the planet.

Now, no natural phenomena within our

knowledge show such regularity on such a scale upon any one of these eight counts, *a fortiori*[3] upon all. When one considers that these lines run for thousands of miles in an unswerving direction, as far relatively as from London to Bombay, and as far actually as from Boston to San Francisco, the inadequacy of natural explanation becomes glaring.

Passage 2

The special characteristics of the numerous lines which intersect the whole of the equatorial and temperate regions of Mars are, their straightness combined with their enormous length. It is this which has led Mr. Lowell to term them 'non-natural features.' Schiaparelli, in his earlier drawings, showed them curved and of comparatively great width. Later, he found them to be straight fine lines when seen under the best conditions, just as Mr. Lowell has always seen them in the pure atmosphere of his observatory....

Mr. Lowell urges, however, that their perfect straightness, their extreme tenuity, their uniformity throughout their whole length, the dual character of many of them, their relation to the 'oases' and the form and position of these round black spots, are all proofs of artificiality and are suggestive of design. And considering that some of them are actually as long as from Boston to San Francisco, and relatively to their globe as long as from London to Bombay, his objection that "no natural phenomena within our knowledge show such regularity on such a scale" seems, at first, a mighty one.

It is certainly true that we can point to nothing exactly like them either on the earth or on the moon, and these are the only two planetary bodies we are in a position to compare with Mars. Yet even these do, I think, afford us some hints towards an interpretation of the mysterious lines. But as our knowledge of the internal structure and past history even of our earth is still imperfect, that of the moon only conjectural, and that of Mars a perfect blank, it is not perhaps surprising that the surface-features of the latter do not correspond with those of either of the others.

The best clue to a natural interpretation of the strange features of the surface of Mars is that suggested by the American astronomer Mr. W. H. Pickering in *Popular Astronomy* (1904). Briefly it is, that both the 'canals' of Mars and the rifts as well as the luminous streaks on the moon are cracks in the volcanic crust, caused by internal stresses due to the action of the heated interior. These cracks he considers to be symmetrically arranged with regard to small 'craterlets' (Mr. Lowell's 'oases') because they have originated from them, just as the white streaks on the moon radiate from the larger craters as centres.

[1] Pertaining to calculating the shape and area of the earth or large portions of it. By extension, it refers to the geometry of curved surfaces.

[2] According to Lowell, some canals "parallel one another like twin rails of a railway track."

[3] used to express a conclusion for which there is stronger evidence than for a previously accepted one

21

In Passage 1, Lowell indicates that the mark of intelligent life on Mars' surface is readily apparent because of

A) the directness of Mars' canals.
B) the surface's similarity to Earth.
C) Schiaparelli's precise observations.
D) the nature of the surface's likenesses.

22

As used in line 4, "mien" most nearly means

A) appearance.
B) bearing.
C) demeanor.
D) aura.

23

Which of the following is implied about the "writer" mentioned in line 18, Passage 1?

A) He was a keen observer though he lacked in logic.
B) His conclusions were better than his drawings.
C) He failed to use a necessary implement.
D) He felt that his drawings looked unnatural.

24

As used in line 49, "glaring" most nearly means

A) brazen.
B) manifest.
C) garish.
D) excessive.

25

It can be inferred from Passage 2 that Wallace believed which of the following about Schiaparelli?

A) The acuity of his perception grew over time.
B) He fundamentally agreed with Lowell's theory.
C) He did not like to speculate on Mars' canals.
D) His ruled drawings are better than any freehand drawings.

26

How would Lowell most likely react to Pickering's statement in Passage 2 regarding the symmetrical arrangement of cracks?

A) With skepticism, because a number of factors suggest that this arrangement is caused by design.
B) With exasperation, because it is obvious and generally known that size of these cracks means they are artificial.
C) With disapproval, because phenomena on the moon cannot be used to explain occurrences on Mars.
D) With appreciation, because science needs to keep an open mind even if the evidence overwhelmingly suggests a different answer.

27

Which choice provides the best evidence for the answer to the previous question?

A) Lines 4-10 ("So . . . phenomena")
B) Lines 23-27 ("Indeed . . . artificial")
C) Lines 28-31 ("Suggestive . . . counts")
D) Lines 42-45 ("Now . . . all")

28

Wallace would most likely respond to the statement in lines 42-45, Passage 1 with which of the following?

A) Cautious disagreement
B) Sarcastic disdain
C) Complete agreement
D) Noncommittal equivocation

29

Which choice provides the best evidence for the answer to the previous question?

A) Lines 61-66 ("Mr. Lowell . . . design")
B) Lines 67-72 ("And considering . . . one")
C) Lines 73-76 ("It is . . . Mars")
D) Lines 78-83 ("But as . . . others")

30

Which choice best describes the relationship between the two passages?

A) Passage 2 argues for an alternative conclusion from the observations discussed in Passage 1.
B) Passage 2 presents evidence that refutes the proposal put forth in Passage 1.
C) Passage 2 elaborates on the central claim made by the author of Passage 1.
D) Passage 2 warns about problems that have been omitted by the author of Passage 1.

31

The authors of both passages would most likely agree on which of the following points?

A) Knowledge of the earth and the moon allow inferences regarding Mars.
B) The dual character of some of Mars' canals warrants additional research.
C) The appearance of Mars' surface has led to the opinion that it is unnatural.
D) The sheer scale of Mars' canals ultimately makes for a powerful argument.

Questions 32-42 are based on the following passage and supplementary material.

This passage is adapted from Barbara Jordan's Democratic National Convention Keynote Address in 1976.

   This is the question which must be answered in 1976: Are we to be one people bound together by common spirit, sharing in a common endeavor;
Line or will we become a divided nation? For all of its
 5 uncertainty, we cannot flee the future. We must not become the "New Puritans" and reject our society.
   We must address and master the future together. It can be done if we restore the belief that we share a sense of national community, that we share a common
10 national endeavor. It can be done.
   There is no executive order; there is no law that can require the American people to form a national community. This we must do as individuals, and if we do it as individuals, there is no President of the
15 United States who can veto that decision.
   As a first step, we must restore our belief in ourselves. We are a generous people, so why can't we be generous with each other? We need to take to heart the words spoken by Thomas Jefferson: "Let us
20 restore to social intercourse that harmony and that affection without which liberty and even life are but dreary things."
   A nation is formed by the willingness of each of us to share in the responsibility for upholding the
25 common good. A government is invigorated when each one of us is willing to participate in shaping the future of this nation. In this election year, we must define the "common good" and begin again to shape a common future. Let each person do his or her part.
30   If one citizen is unwilling to participate, all of us are going to suffer. For the American idea, though it is shared by all of us, is realized in each one of us.
   And now, what are those of us who are elected public officials supposed to do? We call ourselves
35 "public servants" but I'll tell you this: We as public servants must set an example for the rest of the nation. It is hypocritical for the public official to admonish and exhort the people to uphold the common good if we are derelict in upholding the
40 common good. More is required of public officials than slogans and handshakes and press releases. More is required. We must hold ourselves strictly accountable. We must provide the people with a vision of the future.
45   If we promise as public officials, we must deliver. If we as public officials propose, we must produce. If we say to the American people, "It is time for you to be sacrificial"—sacrifice. If the public official says that, we [public officials] must be the first to give. We
50 must be. And again, if we make mistakes, we must be willing to admit them. We have to do that. What we have to do is strike a balance between the idea that government should do everything and the idea, the belief, that government ought to do nothing. Strike
55 a balance.
   Let there be no illusions about the difficulty of forming this kind of a national community. It's tough, difficult, not easy. But a spirit of harmony will survive in America only if each of us remembers that we
60 share a common destiny; if each of us remembers, when self-interest and bitterness seem to prevail, that we share a common destiny. I have confidence that we can form this kind of national community. I have confidence that the Democratic Party can lead the
65 way. I have that confidence. We cannot improve on the system of government handed down to us by the founders of the Republic. There is no way to improve upon that. But what we can do is to find new ways to implement that system and realize our destiny.

How Many Policies Were Enacted by Government Compared to Public Support Behind Those Policies (Region A)

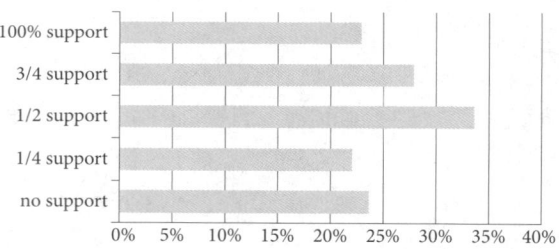

32

The stance Jordan takes in the passage is best described as that of

A) an analyst making predictions about the future.
B) a challenger trying to undermine tradition.
C) an advocate promoting necessary measures.
D) a witness documenting established positions.

33

Jordan most likely mentions that "there is no executive order" (line 11) in order to imply that

A) the dearth of laws regarding a national community needs to be rectified.
B) individuals value their freedom and would balk at its use.
C) the President's power over individuals has diminished.
D) a goal can only be obtained through individual agency.

34

Which choice provides the best evidence for the answer to the previous question?

A) Lines 2-4 ("Are we . . . nation")
B) Lines 27-29 ("In this . . . part")
C) Lines 45-48 ("If we . . . sacrifice")
D) Lines 58-60 ("But a . . . destiny")

35

As used in line 39, "derelict" most nearly means

A) dilapidated.
B) remiss.
C) neglected.
D) forsaken.

36

The passage implies that the role of elected officials is to

A) follow a code of conduct that lets them lead by example.
B) define the common good the public should aspire to.
C) become the voice that reminds the public of the common good.
D) expand upon the ideals of the Founding Fathers with new principles.

37

Which choice provides the best evidence for the answer to the previous question?

A) Lines 8-10 ("It can . . . endeavor")
B) Lines 27-29 ("In this . . . part")
C) Lines 45-49 ("If we . . . give")
D) Lines 51-55 ("What we . . . balance")

38

The statement in lines 51-54 ("What . . . nothing") most likely rests on which assumption?

A) It is impossible to say if an intrusive government is preferable to a passive kind of government.
B) The role that government should play has been the subject of scathing controversy.
C) Different schools of thought exist concerning the scale that government should assume.
D) A balanced approach to government intervention has been proven to be the most efficient.

39

The "New Puritans" (line 6) would most likely view the "self-interest and bitterness" mentioned in line 61 as

A) significant factors in deciding whether to seek out a new destiny.
B) less important than the shared goals that bind a nation together.
C) confirmation that human nature prevails regardless of time and place.
D) obstacles that bar the way to achieving national community.

40

Jordan characterizes the "system of government" (line 66) as

A) lacking communal spirit.
B) completely infallible.
C) magnificently formulated.
D) beholden to the people.

41

What statement is best supported by the data presented in the chart?

A) 100% public support for a policy has a smaller chance than 0% support.
B) The enactment of policies is inversely proportional to their public support.
C) Policies that evenly polarize public opinion have been implemented the least.
D) Most policies that were enacted were unanimously backed by the public.

42

Jordan would most likely consider the information in the chart to be

A) representative of the kind of government that she aims to establish.
B) indicative of the fact that government completely ignores the will of the public.
C) evidence for the need to establish goals that government and citizens share.
D) typical of a system in which the government accommodates the will of the majority.

Questions 43-52 are based on the following passage and supplementary material.

This passage discusses taste and our perception of it.

Our five senses allow us to perceive our surroundings, make judgments, and thus react to them. They are such an integral part of our constant
Line interaction with the environment that we need not
5 consciously think about their application; our probes are exploring, whether we will them to or not. An interesting aspect of this is that most of us think of them as working separately or in a fashion where, for instance, three senses will simply provide more
10 input than one. What is often overlooked, however, is that a combination of sensory signals can produce alterations instead of simple addition.

Taste provides a good example of this phenomenon. Taste buds in our mouth transmit
15 signals to our brain that are then interpreted as flavors. But why does a whiff from the kitchen alone lead to increased output by our salivary glands? How do we know what kind of food is being prepared and what it will probably taste like without even
20 employing our visual or gustatory senses? The answer is simple: we "taste" food with our noses as well, so smells alone can be very telling. Gustation and olfaction together account for the sensation we experience while eating food. The elimination of one
25 would thus change our perception. Holding one's nose while swallowing bitter medicine clearly demonstrates how, by eliminating one sense, you dull the other. Another such situation can easily be conjured up if you just remember how a common cold can impair
30 your appetite.

In addition to this "hardwired" connection, visual cues such as color also play a large role in how we perceive flavors. In contrast to odors, the association between color and food has been partially imparted
35 upon us by means of marketing efforts rather than our inherent instincts. While a lot of food items exhibit inherent coloration or color patterns that we have come to associate with certain flavors, many processed products owe their hues to human design.
40 These might have been willfully created or modified, but they are nonetheless associated with a certain taste, which reinforces our identification of one with the other. Tomato juice naturally looks red (though its excellent hue is often helped along), and Coca Cola
45 sparkles in its unchanging trademark brown—hard to attribute to mother nature, but nevertheless an undeniably strong association we have learned to form.

Intuitively, some might perceive this lack of
50 originality as bad for business. The adherence to tradition can be explained by the fact that, however much novelty can become a product sales driver, pairing consumable products with new hues is usually detrimental to sales. Certain flavors just go along
55 with certain colors; unexpected collisions between the two can result in confusion because our belief in this cause and effect relationship is strongly imbued within us. Imagine stepping onto an escalator that is not working. You surely know the momentary
60 sensation of being pushed *backwards*? In this sense, bluish-grey tomato juice would not be as palatable as red tomato juice, and Pepsi Cola famously failed to book a success when it attempted to sell colorless Pepsi, in spite of its identical taste.

The Effect of Consuming Certain Amounts of Fruit Juice on Its Ability to Stimulate Reactions in the Brain

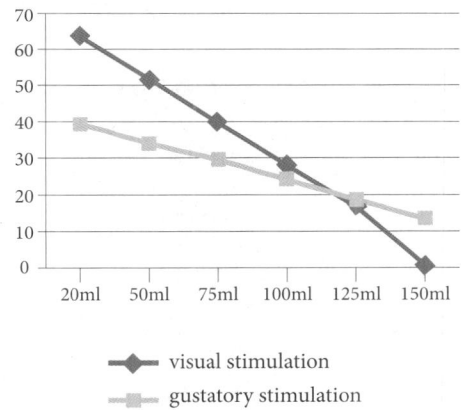

43

The primary purpose of the passage is to

A) explain that not all sensory associations occur purely naturally.
B) show that perception can be more than the mere sum of its parts.
C) refute the notion that taste can be experienced without smell.
D) assert that a lack of marketing innovation can benefit businesses.

44

The questions in lines 16-20 serve primarily to

A) point out an apparent inconsistency.
B) introduce a new topic for discussion.
C) emphasize the author's puzzlement.
D) suggest that taste is very subjective.

45

The passage indicates that a combination of signals can result in different flavor perception

A) owing to the fact that certain color-flavor combinations are surprising.
B) only when one of the signals is temporarily impaired.
C) as a result of learned associations rather than natural ones.
D) unless two or more senses register a stimulus simultaneously.

46

Which choice provides the best evidence for the answer to the previous question?

A) Lines 25-27 ("Holding . . . other")
B) Lines 33-36 ("In contrast . . . instincts")
C) Lines 50-54 ("The adherence . . . sales")
D) Lines 58-60 ("Imagine . . . *backwards*")

47

As used in line 46, "attribute to" most nearly means

A) blame on.
B) characterize as.
C) apply to.
D) trace to.

48

The passage indicates that tomato juice

A) is like Coca Cola in that both have arbitrarily designated colors.
B) does not necessarily owe its pleasant appearance to its innate qualities.
C) is different from Coca Cola in that tomato juice is never tampered with.
D) does not create taste associations as strong as Coca Cola does.

49

The author would most likely view the "lack of originality" mentioned in lines 49-50 as

A) necessitated by tradition.
B) an obvious outcome.
C) sound business sense.
D) an unfortunate decision.

50

Which of the following statements regarding the "bitter medicine" consumed "Holding one's nose" (lines 25-26) and the "colorless Pepsi" in lines 63-64 is true?

A) While the former situation makes for a positive deviation, the latter is possibly perceived as an unpleasant mismatch.
B) Both are examples of a changed perception in taste resulting from the elimination of an input that normally contributes.
C) The former focuses on impaired taste without olfaction while the latter is an example of enhanced tasting abilities.
D) Both instances show that contravening the inherently occurring association of taste with other senses can impact business.

51

Data in the graph indicates that gustatory stimulation is the farthest above visual stimulation at which amount?

A) 25ml
B) 100ml
C) 125ml
D) 150ml

52

Does the data in the graph support the author's notion that visual cues play a role in flavor perception?

A) Yes, because both visual stimulation and gustatory stimulation decrease with juice consumption.
B) Yes, because while both visual and gustatory stimulation decrease, visual stimulation decreases faster due to its artificial nature.
C) No, because both visual stimulation and gustatory stimulation decrease with juice consumption.
D) No, because while both visual and gustatory stimulation decrease, visual stimulation decreases faster due to its artificial nature.

STOP

Do not move on to the next section if you finish early.

You may review your answers in this section only.

Answer Keys & Performance Breakdown

1	(B)	Summary	19	(B)	Local	37	(C)	Evidence
2	(C)	Local	20	(D)	Evidence	38	(C)	Local
3	(B)	Context	21	(D)	Local	39	(A)	Synthesize
4	(C)	Context	22	(A)	Vocabulary	40	(C)	Local
5	(A)	Local	23	(C)	Local	41	(A)	Graph
6	(C)	Local	24	(B)	Vocabulary	42	(C)	Graph
7	(C)	Local	25	(A)	Local	43	(B)	Summary
8	(A)	Local	26	(A)	Synthesize	44	(A)	Context
9	(C)	Context	27	(D)	Evidence	45	(C)	Local
10	(C)	Evidence	28	(C)	Synthesize	46	(B)	Evidence
11	(C)	Summary	29	(C)	Evidence	47	(D)	Vocabulary
12	(D)	Evidence	30	(A)	Synthesize	48	(B)	Local
13	(B)	Local	31	(C)	Synthesize	49	(C)	Local
14	(D)	Local	32	(C)	Stance	50	(A)	Synthesize
15	(A)	Local	33	(D)	Local	51	(D)	Graph
16	(A)	Vocabulary	34	(D)	Evidence	52	(A)	Graph
17	(B)	Local	35	(B)	Vocabulary			
18	(D)	Local	36	(A)	Local			

■ Write down the number of correct answers for each question type.

Question Types	Number of Correct Answers
Local	/ 21
Style	0 / 0
Vocabulary	/ 5
Evidence	/ 8
Context	/ 4
Organization	0 / 0
Summary	/ 3
Stance	/ 1
Synthesize	/ 6
Graph	/ 4
Total	**/ 52**

Answer Explanations

Questions 1-10

1. (B) *Summary*

B is the best choice. The feeling of foreignness is emphasized in the beginning at the intersection and again after the parents leave the narrator to explore on his own.

A is incorrect because the passage does not show whether the narrator will be able to adapt, nor is it the focus. C is incorrect because such a motivation is not mentioned, and "reacquaint" does not make sense if it is the narrator's first time in Japan. D is incorrect because though a kind of empathy is mentioned, the narrator does not dwell on it.

2. (C) *Local*

C is the best choice because "riding one of those crests" implies that they were on the top of a wave of people.

A is incorrect because "disarray" as used in the passage merely refers to a possible outcome. B is incorrect because "the waves" does not refer to the ocean but is used as a way to describe people crossing the street. D is incorrect because nothing in the sentence supports "annoyance."

3. (B) *Context*

B is the best choice because right before line 19, the narrator was worried people would crash into each other and there would be chaos. However, people "expertly" passed each other without accident.

A is incorrect because "choreographed dance" implies that everyone follows some kind of preordained pattern which is not supported. C is incorrect because the specified part does not convey "relief." D is incorrect because the context focuses on the efficient crossing of a street, not people's familiarity with each other.

4. (C) *Context*

C is the best choice because the dad's statement is a response to the mother's remark, in essence stating that the aunt's failure to recognize the downtown area for what it was aggravated the narrator. Thus, the narrator is defensive of his hometown. Also, "ignorance" makes sense because after the dad's remark, the narrator admits it makes sense now (as opposed to previously when he felt offended).

A is incorrect because nothing in context suggests this. B is incorrect because there is nothing to support that the aunt "purposely" mocked his hometown. D is incorrect because nothing in context suggests "shame" or "remorse."

5. (A) *Local*

A is the best choice because "diverse origins" refers to living in the USA or Japan. His aunt's failure to recognize the narrator's downtown area now makes sense to him because he realizes downtown in Japan is very unlike his hometown (diverse perspectives).

B is incorrect because the narrator merely admits he understands his aunt's point of view. C is incorrect because the differences between countries are mentioned only to support the narrator's changed opinion. D is incorrect because this negative attitude is not mentioned.

6. (C) *Local*

C is the best choice because only his grandparents can read the "angular gibberish."

A is incorrect because signs and labels are the objects that contain the "angular gibberish." B is incorrect because "numbers" (line 55) is mentioned separately. D is incorrect because you do not read people's chatter.

7. (C) *Local*

C is the best choice because the narrator is trying to put himself into his grandmother's shoes. Just like his grandmother, he does not speak the language of his environment.

A is incorrect because he does not completely change his opinion about anything. He merely comes to a realization. B is incorrect because "indignation" is not suggested. D is incorrect because he does not suddenly realize anything about his own background.

8. (A) *Local*

A is the best choice because he justifies his own failure to talk to his grandmother.

B is incorrect because "consoles" implies sadness or disappointment which is not supported. C is incorrect because "rationale" does not fit here. If

Answer Explanations

anything, he dismisses his obligation to try to talk to his grandmother. D is incorrect because he does not blame his grandmother. Rather, he is justifying why he himself is not to blame.

9. (C) *Context*

C is the best choice because, as if coming across an island in the ocean, the narrator feels relief at coming across a familiar American sign within the alien Japanese ocean. The metaphor is a continuation of the water metaphor in line 16 and in line 48.

A is incorrect because nothing suggests the author will not be able to escape. B is incorrect because though the sign, being American, stands out, "island in this ocean" serves to suggest that it promises a place to escape the feeling of being in an alien environment. D is incorrect because of the word "faces."

10. (C) *Evidence*

C is the best choice because the lines mention "currents" he is trying to escape, which refers to a host of unknown people passing him by. This is akin to the ocean metaphor in the previous question.

A, B, and D are incorrect because none of them connect to the ocean metaphor.

Questions 11-20

11. (C) *Summary*

C is the best choice because Roosevelt first praises, then criticizes black soldiers since their heroic actions reflected badly on Roosevelt's unit. This change of mind is, in turn, criticized (i.e., evaluated) by Sergeant Holliday.

A is incorrect because the passage focuses on Roosevelt's change of mind rather than the valor of soldiers. B is incorrect because a changed opinion is criticized, not vindicated. D is incorrect because the passage does not state that praise (the praise of black soldiers) was undeserved. Rather, it indicates that the praise was deserved.

12. (D) *Evidence*

D is the best choice because the lines mention how Roosevelt is "sufficiently answered," thus tying together Roosevelt's criticism of black soldiers and indicating Holliday's response is of importance.

A is incorrect because it only mentions Roosevelt's initial praise of black soldiers. B is incorrect because it only shows how Roosevelt reacted to criticism of his unit. C is incorrect because it mentions a written exchange, but it does not make clear the importance of Holliday's response.

13. (B) *Local*

B is the best choice because Roosevelt refers to "colored" regiments in the next sentence using the third person.

A is incorrect because "your number" is used to address his listeners directly. C and D are incorrect because the author uses the third person when referring to "colored" regiments.

14. (D) *Local*

D is the best choice because the author states that without the help of the Ninth and Tenth Cavalry (colored), "the whole of his command would have been annihilated" (lines 24-25).

A is incorrect because rescuer and rescued are mixed up. B is incorrect because "unnecessary" is not supported. C is incorrect because the passage does not say that the Ninth and Tenth Cavalry received praise *at* Las Guasimas. Rather, Roosevelt gives them credit *due to* their actions there.

15. (A) *Local*

A is the best choice because of lines 29-30 which state that breaking the force of unfavorable comment on the Rough Riders was the motivation behind Roosevelt's criticism.

B is incorrect because it states the particulars of the criticism rather than the reason behind the criticism. C is incorrect because it implies that the Rough Riders' morale sank due to being rescued while the passage indicates that unfavorable comments were the cause. D is incorrect because it is not stated in the passage.

16. (A) *Vocabulary*

A is the best choice because soldiers "drifted" into Roosevelt's command after a failed attack. Therefore, to "chance" as in to "happen by chance" is correct since drifting implies aimless wandering.

B is incorrect because it indicates seeking pleasures or diversion. C is incorrect because it implies leisure and relaxation. D is incorrect because it means to remain.

17. (B) — Local

B is the best choice because "white" describes "eye-witnesses." In context, the eye-witnesses are mentioned in order to give credibility to the claim that black troops fought well which contradicts Roosevelt's statement. Thus, it becomes clear that "white" is used to lend more credibility to the "eye-witnesses."

A is incorrect because implying that ethnicity confers more credibility to one group does not logically mean that specific other groups tend to lie. C is incorrect because "white" is mentioned in the context of observers who recount the actions of black soldiers. D is incorrect because "irrefutable" is too absolute.

18. (D) — Local

D is the best choice because in line 47, it says "whereupon" which indicates that reason for drawing Roosevelt's weapon is stated in the preceding lines (lines 39-42 mention this choice).

A is incorrect because it is not mentioned. B is incorrect because no act of defiance is mentioned. C is incorrect because "Rough Riders in trouble" does not appear in this context.

19. (B) — Local

B is the best choice because of lines 60-62 (see next question).

A is incorrect because Holliday believes Roosevelt's testimony was factually incorrect rather than "compelling." C is incorrect because "delusional" implies unrealistic beliefs possibly due to mental illness. This is not supported in the passage. D is incorrect because it means that in essence, Roosevelt's accusations are true.

20. (D) — Evidence

D is the best choice because the lines state that there was only one event that answers the question of whether black soldiers will fight without white officers present, and that event shows that Roosevelt's criticism is incorrect.

A, B, and C are incorrect because none contain an evaluation of Roosevelt's conclusion.

Questions 21-31

21. (D) — Local

D is the best choice because the passage states in lines 23-25 that it is normal that drawings (likenesses) look unnatural if they are, in fact, unnatural. Thus, the fact that the drawings look unnatural shows that the surface of Mars is unnatural (shaped by intelligent life).

A is incorrect because "directness" is not mentioned as a reason that Mars looks unnatural. B is incorrect because the passage does not state Mars' surface is similar to that of Earth. C is incorrect because Schiaparelli's observations are not mentioned as a reason that Mars looks unnatural.

22. (A) — Vocabulary

A is the best choice because the sentence states that a directness is so dominant in its "mien" that it strikes an observer. Thus, "appearance" is correct.

B is incorrect because it means "relevance" or "conduct." C is incorrect because it means "behavior" or "manner." D is incorrect because it means "air" or "character."

23. (C) — Local

C is the best choice because lines 16-20 state that Schiaparelli's observations could not be copied freehand. Lines 20-21 state that nothing short of using a ruler (implement) could have reproduced the observations. Thus, the writer drew "in vain."

A is incorrect because it refers to Schiaparelli. Also, "lacked in logic" is not supported. B is incorrect because conclusions are not mentioned. D is incorrect because no such information is given about the writer.

24. (B) — Vocabulary

B is the best choice. The sentence states that due to the colossal size of certain features, the inadequacy of an explanation becomes "glaring." Thus, "obvious" or "manifest" is correct.

A is incorrect because it means "impudent" or "unashamed." C is incorrect because it means "gaudy" or "tasteless." D is incorrect because it means "disproportionate" or "exaggerated."

25. (A) — Local

A is the best choice because lines 55-60 state Schiaparelli's drawings changed later on and became

Answer Explanations

compatible to Lowell's observations, the latter of which were made "under the best conditions." Thus, it becomes clear that Schiaparelli's later drawings were more accurate depictions of Mars' surface.

B is incorrect because the passage does not suggest that Schiaparelli agreed with Lowell's theory (that Mars' lines are suggestive of design). C is incorrect because it is not mentioned by Passage 2. D is incorrect because it is not mentioned by Passage 2.

26. (A) — Synthesize

Pickering states that cracks (on the moon) are symmetrically arranged since they radiate outwards from craters. Thus, he suggests that the same applies to canals on Mars.

A is the best choice because of lines 42-45 (see next question).

B is incorrect because Lowell does not indicate that he believes the artificial nature of Mars' surface to be general knowledge. C is incorrect because Lowell makes no statement regarding the possibility of making inferences regarding Mars based on knowledge of the moon. D is incorrect because Lowell makes no such statement.

27. (D) — Evidence

D is the best choice because the lines state that "no natural phenomena within our knowledge show such regularity on such a scale upon any one of these eight counts, *a fortiori* upon all." These eight counts refer to factors that suggest Mars' surface is artificial.

A, B, and C are incorrect because none of them show that a number of factors suggest that a symmetrical arrangement is caused by design.

28. (C) — Synthesize

The specified lines state that no natural phenomena within our knowledge show such regularity on such a scale upon any one of these eight counts, a fortiori upon all. These "eight counts" refer to factors that suggest Mars' surface is artificial.

C is the best choice because of lines 73-76 (see next question).

A is incorrect because Wallace would agree. B is incorrect because Wallace does not display an attitude of sarcastic disdain in Passage 2. D is incorrect because Wallace does not equivocate. Rather, he agrees.

29. (C) — Evidence

C is the best choice because the lines state that it is certainly true that we can point to nothing exactly like them either on the earth or on the moon, and these are the only two planetary bodies we are in a position to compare with Mars.

A, B, and D are incorrect because none of them show that Wallace would agree that no natural phenomena within our knowledge show such regularity on such a scale upon any one of these eight counts.

30. (A) — Synthesize

Passage 1 argues that the appearance of the canals, their scale, and the absence of comparable features on Earth suggests that these canals are of an artificial nature. Passage 2 agrees with the description of the canals, but does not agree with the suggestion of artificiality. Rather, Passage 2 argues that a natural cause (symmetry caused by craters) is a better explanation.

A is the best choice.

B is incorrect because Passage 2 does not present evidence that refutes a proposal made in Passage 1. C is incorrect because Passage 2 does not elaborate on the central claim of Passage 1. Rather, it refutes the conclusion of Passage 1. D is incorrect because Passage 2 does not warn about any problems.

31. (C) — Synthesize

For a short summary of the passages, check the explanation for question 30.

C is the best choice because Lowell believes that Mars' surface is unnatural. Wallace also mentions Lowell and his belief.

A is incorrect because only Wallace would agree. B is incorrect because none of the authors argue that additional research is made necessary due to the dual character of canals. D is incorrect because only Lowell would agree. Wallace would ultimately disagree because he states that the given argument is "at first" a mighty one (line 72). Then he refutes this argument in the following paragraph.

Questions 32-42

32. (C) — Stance

C is the best choice because Jordan mainly emphasizes

the need to establish goals that everyone in the U.S. can get behind, and the need for politicians to lead towards these common goals by example (necessary measures).

A is incorrect because Jordan does not say what *will* happen, but what she thinks *ought* to happen in the sense of what would be best for the nation. B is incorrect because undermining tradition is never brought up. D is incorrect because Jordan is not merely speaking as a witness, but she is trying to effect change.

33. (D) Local
D is the best choice because "executive order" is explained as a law that can require people to do something, i.e., that can force people to do something. Since there is no such law (line 11), doing something must be done "as individuals" (line 13), or voluntarily. Thus, "only . . . through individual agency" is correct.

A is incorrect because Jordan does not state that she wants to establish more laws. B is incorrect because the passage does not imply how people would react to such a law if it existed. C is incorrect because there is no comparison of presidential powers at different points in time.

34. (D) Evidence
D is the best choice because the lines state that a goal (harmony) will only be achieved "if each of us remembers that we share a common destiny." The condition that each of us has to remember supports "individual agency" in the previous question.

A, B, and C are incorrect because none of them *stipulate* individual agency.

35. (B) Vocabulary
B is the best choice because Jordan mentions being "derelict in upholding the common good." Thus, she means failing to uphold the common good. "Remiss" means "negligent" or "careless," so it is a good match.

A is incorrect because it would mean that "we" (the persons upholding the common good) fall into ruin. C is similarly incorrect because it would mean that "we" did not receive care and attention. D is wrong in the same way as A and C.

36. (A) Local
A is the best choice because of lines 45-49 (see next question).

B is incorrect because Jordan states the common good should be established by every citizen, not just politicians (lines 27-29). C is incorrect because of lines 25-29. D is incorrect because expanding upon ideals of the Founding Fathers is not mentioned (lines 63-67).

37. (C) Evidence
C is the best choice because Jordan states that politicians need to do something themselves and do it first before asking it of the public.

A, B, and D are incorrect because none of them mention politicians leading by example.

38. (C) Local
C is the best choice because the lines state that a balance must be found between the idea that government should do everything, and another idea which is that government should do nothing. Since she mentions both as "the idea," it is clear that these are established positions. Therefore, "different schools of thought (two ideas) exist" is supported.

A is incorrect because no qualitative comparison takes place. B is incorrect because "scathing" is not supported. D is incorrect because balance has yet to be found. Also, the passage does not mention any evidence or results.

39. (A) Synthesize
A is the best choice because "New Puritans" refers to those who would flee an uncertain future and thus reject their society. Since "self-interest and bitterness" constitute averse conditions within a society, it must be concluded based on the information about "New Puritans" available in the passage that they would flee their society. Therefore, seeking out a new destiny is correct.

B, C, and D are incorrect because none of them reflect the "New Puritan" way of thinking as presented in the passage.

40. (C) Local
C is the best choice because Jordan states there is no way to improve upon the system of government (lines 67-68). This implies that it is so excellent that it cannot be made better. "Formulated" is also correct because it means "to express precisely"—which is what you do with abstract concepts such as government.

Answer Explanations

A is incorrect because it is not mentioned. B is incorrect because it is too extreme. It absolutely precludes any forms of error or the possibility that the U.S. will fail. D is incorrect because the context does not state that the system of government is indebted to the people.

41. (A)   Graph

A is the best choice because the bar that shows "no support" is longer than the bar that shows "100% support."

B is incorrect because it means all the bars grow shorter the higher the public support. C is incorrect because the chart does not indicate whether there were cases of even polarization. D is incorrect because that means most of the policies that were enacted were supported 100%, which is not supported by the chart.

42. (C)   Graph

C is the best choice because the information in the chart clearly shows that the level of support for policies does not signify when it comes to policy enactment. For instance, policies without support have a higher likelihood of being enacted than policies with 100% support. The government and the public obviously do not share the same goals. This fits the central idea of Jordan's speech where she advocates the use of common goals that everyone can get behind.

A is incorrect because Jordan wishes the opposite. B is incorrect because the chart shows that there is partial overlap between government policies and public support. D is incorrect because the chart does not support that the government is listening to the majority. (Less than 30% of policies supported by 3/4 and less than 25% of policies supported by 100% of the public were enacted.)

Questions 43-52

43. (B)   Summary

B is the best choice because the passage focuses on how the combination of sensory input can lead to alterations. For instance, olfaction influences gustation, and visual input also influences gustation.

A is incorrect because while mentioned, it is just a minor detail. C is incorrect because the passage does not refute the notion. It merely states that taste changes without smell. D is incorrect because while mentioned, it is just a minor detail.

44. (A)   Context

A is the best choice because the questions indicate that we can anticipate food even if it is out of sight using our noses alone. Enjoyment of food, however, is traditionally associated with taste buds in the mouth (stated in the previous sentence).

B is incorrect because rather than a new topic, the questions are elaboration of the same topic. C is incorrect because the author is not confused. Instead, he uses the questions to make a point. D is incorrect because subjectivity is not mentioned.

45. (C)   Local

C is the best choice because of lines 33-36 (see next question).

A is incorrect because surprising combinations are not mentioned in context. B is incorrect because temporary impairment of senses is not mentioned in context. D is incorrect because no such stipulation is made.

46. (B)   Evidence

B is the best choice because the lines state that visual and gustatory associations are due to "marketing efforts" rather than "inherent instincts," which means that promotion, packaging and other such marketing activities (acquired after birth) caused the association rather than our inborn traits.

A, C, and D are incorrect because none of them state that an association is learned rather than inborn.

47. (D)   Vocabulary

D is the best choice because the sentence states that the brown color of Coca Cola is hard to "attribute to" mother nature (which in context implies that its color is a result of human decision). Therefore, "attribute to" means "see as a result of" or "trace to."

A is incorrect because it means "accuse" or "condemn" which is too negative in context. B is incorrect because it means "distinguish" or "describe." C is incorrect because it means "belong to" or "deal with."

48. (B)   Local

B is the best choice because it says in lines 43-44 that its excellent hue is often "helped along" even though it "naturally" looks red as well. This indicates that the helping is not natural or "innate."

A is incorrect because the passage does not state that the color of tomato juice is arbitrary. C is incorrect because "never tampered" is not true. D is incorrect because no such comparison is made in the passage.

49. (C)　　　　　　　　　　　　　　　　Local

C is the best choice because the passage says that pairing consumable products with new hues (i.e., originality) is usually detrimental to sales. "Sound" means "sensible" or "valid" in this context.

A is incorrect because "tradition," rather than making it necessary, merely refers to "lack of originality." B is incorrect because "obvious" is not suggested. D is incorrect because it is opposite to what the passage states (see correct answer).

50. (A)　　　　　　　　　　　　　　　Synthesize

A is the best choice because holding one's nose will ameliorate the bitter taste of medicine while colorless Pepsi was said to be unsuccessful which supports "unpleasant mismatch."

B is incorrect because the elimination of an input that normally contributes only applies to holding one's nose. C is incorrect because of the word "enhanced." D is incorrect because the impact on business only applies to "colorless Pepsi."

51. (D)　　　　　　　　　　　　　　　　Graph

D is the best choice because gustatory stimulation is only above visual at 125ml and 150ml, and the difference between the two lines is greatest at 150ml.

A, B, and C are incorrect because all of the answer choices in this question are mutually exclusive.

52. (A)　　　　　　　　　　　　　　　　Graph

A is the best choice because the passage mentions that visual stimulation is connected to flavor perception (lines 17-22, lines 31-64), which is supported by the graph as stated in A.

B and D are incorrect because the rate of loss of stimulation is not a focus of the passage. C and D are incorrect because the passage states that there is a connection between our visual input and flavor perception, which is supported by the graph (both visual and gustatory stimulation decrease with juice consumption).

SAT.Hackers.ac

Hackers New SAT Reading: 10 Practice Tests

TEST 5

Answer Keys & Performance Breakdown

Answer Explanations

Reading Test

65 MINUTES, 52 QUESTIONS

Mark your answers to the questions in Section 1 in the answer sheet provided.

DIRECTIONS

For each of the passages below, there are 10 or 11 questions. Choose the best answer for each of the questions after you have finished reading the passage. The answers to the questions should be based on the information that is stated or implied in the text and any associated graphics.

Questions 1-10 are based on the following passage.

This passage is adapted from Jack London, "Children of the Frost: In the Forests of the North." Originally published in 1902. Professor Van Brunt is on an expedition exploring the Canadian Arctic.

The Barrens—well, they are the Barrens, the bad lands of the Arctic, the deserts of the Circle, the bleak and bitter home of the musk-ox and the lean plains
Line wolf. So Avery Van Brunt found them, treeless and
5 cheerless, sparsely clothed with moss and lichens, and altogether uninviting. At least so he found them till he penetrated to the white blank spaces on the map, and came upon undreamed-of rich spruce forests and unrecorded Eskimo tribes. It had been his intention,
10 (and his bid for fame), to break up these white blank spaces and diversify them with the black markings of mountain-chains, sinks and basins, and sinuous river courses; and it was with added delight that he came to speculate upon the possibilities of timber belts and
15 native villages.

Avery Van Brunt, or, in full distinction, Professor A. Van Brunt of the Geological Survey, was second in command of the expedition, and first in command of the sub-expedition which he had led on a side tour of
20 some half a thousand miles up one of the branches of the Thelon and which he was now leading into one of his unrecorded villages.... First of all men of his breed was he to enter this lone Northland village, and at the thought an exultancy came upon him, an exaltation,
25 and his followers noted that his leg-weariness fell from him and that he insensibly quickened the pace.

The village emptied itself, and a motley crowd trooped out to meet him, men in the forefront, with bows and spears clutched menacingly, and women
30 and children faltering timidly in the rear. Van Brunt lifted his right arm and made the universal peace sign, a sign which all peoples know, and the villagers answered in peace. But to his chagrin, a skin-clad man ran forward and thrust out his hand with a
35 familiar "Hello." He was a bearded man, with cheeks and brow bronzed to copper-brown, and in him Van Brunt knew his kind.

"Who are you?" he asked, gripping the extended hand. "Andrée?"
40 "Who's Andrée?" the man asked back.
Van Brunt looked at him more sharply. "By George, you've been here some time."
"Five years," the man answered, a dim flicker of pride in his eyes. "But come on, let's talk."
45 "Let them camp alongside of me," he answered Van Brunt's glance at his party. "Old Tantlatch will take care of them. Come on."

He swung off in a long stride, Van Brunt following at his heels through the village. In irregular
50 fashion, wherever the ground favored, the lodges of moose hide were pitched. Van Brunt ran his practised eye over them and calculated.

"Two hundred, not counting the young ones," he summed up.
55 The man nodded.... "Any tobacco?... A-h, thanks, and a pipe? Good. Now for a fire-stick and we'll see if the weed has lost its cunning."

He scratched the match with the painstaking care of the woodsman, cherished its young flame as
60 though there were never another in all the world, and drew in the first mouthful of smoke. This he retained meditatively for a time, and blew out through his pursed lips slowly and caressingly. Then his face seemed to soften as he leaned back, and a soft blur
65 to film his eyes. He sighed heavily, happily, with immeasurable content, and then said suddenly:

"God! But that tastes good!"

Van Brunt nodded sympathetically. "Five years, you say?"

"Five years." The man sighed again. "And you, I presume, wish to know about it, being naturally curious, and this a sufficiently strange situation, and all that. But it's not much. I came in from Edmonton after musk-ox, and like Pike and the rest of them, had my mischances, only I lost my party and outfit. Starvation, hardship, the regular tale, you know, sole survivor and all that, till I crawled into Tantlatch's, here, on hand and knee."

"Five years," Van Brunt murmured retrospectively, as though turning things over in his mind.

"Five years on February last. I crossed the Great Slave early in May—"

"And you are . . . Fairfax?" Van Brunt interjected.

The man nodded.

"Let me see . . . John, I think it is, John Fairfax."

"How did you know?" Fairfax queried lazily, half-absorbed in curling smoke-spirals upward in the quiet air.

"The papers were full of it at the time. Prevanche—"

"Prevanche!" Fairfax sat up, suddenly alert. "He was lost in the Smoke Mountains."

"Yes, but he pulled through and came out."

Fairfax settled back again and resumed his smoke-spirals. "I am glad to hear it," he remarked reflectively.

1

The passage is primarily concerned with describing

A) a convivial reunion.
B) the hardships of expeditions.
C) an unexpected encounter.
D) the penury of a village.

2

The passage indicates that once he "penetrated to the white blank spaces on the map" (line 7), Van Brunt

A) was surprised by the bounty he witnessed in uncharted territory.
B) was impressed by the empty and almost lifeless expanses of the Arctic.
C) had achieved his dream of gaining fame by entering unknown land.
D) learned that the maps describing this landscape were old and outdated.

3

The enumerated items in lines 11-13 differ from "timber belts and native villages" (lines 14-15) in that

A) Van Brunt had only suspected the former to exist prior to the expedition.
B) the former were not marked on maps while the latter were already marked.
C) the former occur without the help of humans while the latter require people.
D) only the discovery of the former had the potential to make Van Brunt famous.

4

The passage suggests that Fairfax's current situation could best be characterized as

A) expedient.
B) adverse.
C) unintended.
D) tedious.

5

Which choice provides the best evidence for the answer to the previous question?

A) Lines 63-65 ("Then . . . eyes")
B) Lines 70-73 ("Five years . . . all that")
C) Lines 73-75 ("I came . . . outfit")
D) Lines 91-93 ("Prevanche! . . . out")

6

In line 33, "answered" most nearly means

A) uttered.
B) responded.
C) understood.
D) collaborated.

7

The man's way of scratching the match (lines 58-59) can best be described as one of

A) urgency.
B) fascination.
C) idolatry.
D) caution.

8

The exchange in lines 90-93 indicates that

A) the Smoke Mountains are extremely dangerous.
B) Prevanche had been successfully rescued.
C) Fairfax had made a wrong assumption.
D) Fairfax and Prevanche had been close friends.

9

The passage suggests that the "bearded man" was mainly significant to Van Brunt as

A) a legendary explorer he had thought dead.
B) a presence who denied him a desired exploit.
C) a welcome change to the hostile natives.
D) an acquaintance he had hoped to avoid.

10

Which choice best supports the statement that the bearded man and Van Brunt are probably of the same race?

A) Lines 22-26 ("First . . . him")
B) Lines 33-35 ("But . . . Hello")
C) Lines 35-37 ("He was . . . kind")
D) Lines 55-57 ("The man . . . cunning")

Questions 11-21 are based on the following passage and supplementary material.

In this passage, the author discusses the impact a new technology has had on an experience.

I'm not going to lie to you: I love the Internet. I think it is one of the most revolutionary changes I have experienced in my lifetime. The incredible ease
Line with which we can find and act upon information,
5 the sheer scope of knowledge that I, and more importantly, everyone else, has access to, the rate at which I can now transmit information of many kinds, all of these factors are—for the lack of a better word— breathtaking. I say this not only because it is true, but
10 because I have felt it. Or rather, because I felt it when it first became mainstream in a big way. Nowadays, it's just so easy to take the net for granted.
    That being said, there are some things that I miss because—let's face it—even if a change occasioned an
15 abundance of benefits, it's still a *change*. It means that certain things ceased to be the way they used to be.
    Do you remember vinyl records? Or cassette tapes for that matter? If I were to bring home an archaic vinyl turntable which requires a string of manual
20 actions and corrections to actually play back the song that I want to listen to, my kids would probably call the doctor on me. Why would you want to take a black plastic disc, put it on the platter, pick up the tonearm by the headshell and carefully lower the needle where
25 you deem the right track to be—only to be rewarded by subpar sound fidelity and the need to repeat the whole process when you want to jump to a different track? Why not just listen to that song online using your computer? (It sounds better, too.)
30   I believe the joy I used to feel when listening to a certain song the analog way was an ocean compared to the pond that remains when listening to that same song online. The relative difficulty, the effort of producing the sounds that my ears so craved,
35 was several magnitudes that of just clicking on a browser link. The ownership of the record in itself was satisfying because without it, there was (except for radio which is a medium out of my control) no way to hear this song. These factors made listening a
40 rare experience, and I think I automatically poured more of my heart into listening because it felt like an achievement, however small.
    I used to hang around LP stores browsing dozens of records that were sloppily arranged by genre and
45 artist name. Without an online database to tell me what I was looking at, and without online snippets streaming straight to my phone, I could only rely on available clues such as sleeve art, band name, and song titles to imagine what the music might be like.
50 And without enough money to just go ahead and buy every record I wanted (that sum could have easily bought a car), I simply held the treasures in my hands and I was filled with a deep yearning to experience just once the delectable sounds sealed within. As a
55 result, liking a band and actually knowing most of their songs used to have an aura of initiation and exclusivity to it that in today's world cannot exist.
    Today, when I have music running on my computer, I know I can play it back again anytime. I
60 can find new music within moments and run a search for whatever interests me about it. No effort. So I find myself readily distracted and not a dedicated listener. This gross availability has rendered me, and I dare say many of us, numb to what used to be an inherently
65 intoxicating experience. I can't remember the last time I simply sat down and just *listened*.
    It strikes me as a little bit ironic that we, presented with a medium that brings us endless bounty, find ourselves unable to appreciate each
70 treasure that we receive, that we—if I may twist an old phrase—can't see the trees for the forest.

Chart 1
Music Consumption in Country F

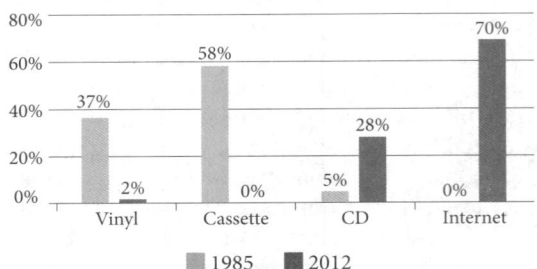

Chart 2
"I listen to music . . ." — 2012 Survey in Country F

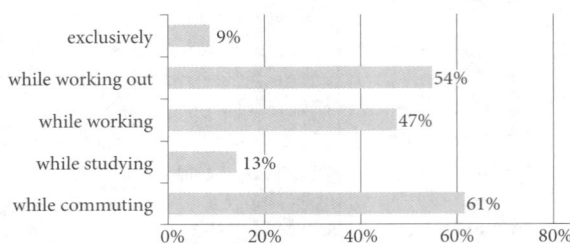

11

The stance the author takes in the passage is best described as that of

A) an evangelist of an innovative technology that deserves more credit.
B) an advocate of abolishing technologies that deprive us of enjoyment.
C) a witness to a development on which he offers a peculiar viewpoint.
D) a defender of older ways of doing things which have fallen out of favor.

12

The main rhetorical effect of the repetition in lines 10-11 ("because I . . . big way") is to

A) concede that his statement could be seen as exaggerated.
B) stress that the Internet has gained in popularity.
C) imply that a certain sensation is no longer felt.
D) qualify a statement by claiming an uncommon point of view.

13

Which of the following best summarizes the point the author makes in lines 13-15 ("That being . . . change")?

A) He believes that even a greatly positive change can result in loss.
B) He thinks change necessarily entails unwanted consequences.
C) He does not believe the gains justify losses incurred due to a change.
D) He prefers the way things are thanks to the changes that occurred.

14

Ultimately, the author regards the "manual actions and corrections" (lines 19-20) as

A) arduous.
B) abnormal.
C) desirable.
D) obsolescent.

15

Which of the following best describes the relationship between paragraph 3 (lines 17-29) and paragraph 4 (lines 30-42)?

A) Paragraph 4 reveals nostalgia that is explained in paragraph 3.
B) Paragraph 4 dramatizes the fallacy of a view presented in paragraph 3.
C) The attitude presented in paragraph 3 is validated in paragraph 4.
D) Paragraph 4 resolves an apparent paradox presented in paragraph 3.

16

The "pond" in line 32 refers to

A) a body of water.
B) a state of being calm.
C) a reduced sensation.
D) the bridge over a gap.

17

As used in line 43, "browsing" most nearly means

A) grazing.
B) leafing through.
C) bookmarking.
D) searching online.

18

The author suggests that the "aura of initiation and exclusivity . . . in today's world cannot exist" (lines 56-57) because

A) listeners nowadays listen to similar kinds of music which prevents exclusivity.
B) LP stores do not exist anymore as they have been supplanted by the Internet.
C) the Internet has removed a restriction that heightened his passion for music.
D) the music he formerly enjoyed is not popular with the current generation.

19

Chart 1 suggests which of the following about music consumption between 1985 and 2012?

A) CDs have enjoyed continuous growth while cassettes have completely disappeared.
B) Cassettes disappeared mostly due to the Internet, and vinyl was directly replaced by CDs.
C) The number of casual listeners has more than doubled over time.
D) The vast majority of music that was consumed has switched media at least once.

20

Taken together, the two charts suggest that people in Country F who listened to music in 2012 most likely

A) downloaded music while they were at school or at work to pass the time.
B) downloaded music and listened to it while doing something else.
C) bought CDs and downloaded music to listen to it while they were not at home.
D) bought CDs only if they were unable to access the Internet.

21

The author would likely attribute the virtual disappearance of certain media in Chart 1 to

A) lower prices that are charged for music bought on the Internet.
B) the disappearance of LP stores that carry such media.
C) the effortless nature that is inherent in current media.
D) the general unwillingness to concentrate solely on music.

CONTINUE →

Questions 22-32 are based on the following passages.

Passage 1 is adapted from Low and Hanley, "A perspective on the importance of within-tree variation in mortality risk for a leaf-mining insect." ©2012. Passage 2 is adapted from Marañón et al., "Mediterranean-climate oak savannas: the interplay between abiotic environment and species interactions." ©2009.

Passage 1

In 2012, Low and Hanley studied a population of the solitary oak leafminer—a leaf-mining moth that feeds on oaks—within an oak grove. It lays eggs singly onto the upper surfaces of leaves, and when larvae
5 hatch, they burrow into the mesophyll layer (the inner tissue) of the leaf. Each larva creates a solitary mine by excavating the leaf mesophyll as it feeds, which creates a visually conspicuous mining scar on the upper surface of the leaf. The aim of the study was to
10 examine survival and performance patterns for insect herbivores against the within-tree variation in abiotic conditions.

They found that mortality occurred most commonly in small and large mines, leaving the
15 intermediate-sized mines as the safest size overall. Mine size might be a reliable cue for natural enemies to detect suitable prey since it corresponds to the size of a larva. In the case of leaf-mining larvae, avian predators may not prefer small leaf-mining larvae
20 because they are difficult to excavate, especially if alternate prey is available.

Given the different levels of danger associated with mine size, they concluded that feeding rates likely play a role in how a leafminer might fare given
25 these risks. Especially for species suffering from restricted mobility, microhabitat conditions are likely to directly affect larval performance and growth. In particular, the result that showed both light intensity and leaf nitrogen content were significant predictors
30 of feeding rate supported the potential importance of both direct and indirect effects on larval performance. Because light alters temperature and humidity, it can affect both larval metabolism and feeding activity. On the other hand, light also influences the
35 photosynthetic efficiency of the leaf, and as a result, larvae are indirectly affected by subsequent changes in the leaf's nutritional quality. Light and nitrogen together can have synergistic effects on larval fitness by affecting their performance and the time of
40 exposure to mortality risks.

Low and Hanley found that greater canopy heights were associated with slower feeding rates and a greater incidence of the unknown category of mortality. Previous research concluded that tree
45 architecture and surrounding landscape can influence microhabitat temperatures and, as a consequence, leafminer growth rate. Since the leaves' nitrogen content did not vary with attachment height, they suggested that there are other factors related to tree
50 architecture and microclimate that limit the growth and development of larvae in the upper canopy. The association between height and unknown mortality causes could reflect the within-tree variability in defense against herbivores such as pathogens
55 that could cause larval death at early stages of development.

Passage 2

Trees attract different kinds of animals, from large herbivores to small invertebrates, which directly or indirectly affect the herbaceous understory[1].
60 Soil may be enriched by feces dropped by wild and domestic herbivores, seeking the oak shade as protection, and hence favoring nutrient-demanding plants underneath the canopies.

Herbaceous fodder under oak trees in Spain's
65 savannas was richer in nutrients than adjacent open grasslands, and similar differences were found for oaks and grasslands in California. Oak trees provide the sub-canopy herbaceous community with mineral elements initially sequestered in the oak litter, which
70 is mineralized and taken up by herbaceous plants, thus becoming available for large herbivores attracted by the oak canopy environment. This tree-induced increase in nutritional value of sub-canopy plants may raise them above the critical threshold for digestion
75 by ruminants grazing in the savanna system.

Birds perch on the trees and disperse seeds underneath, increasing the abundance of bird-dispersed plants in the understory and contributing to the core regeneration of the system. On the contrary,
80 trees may attract small mammals, birds and insects, which will predate seeds and seedlings of the trees and also of the herbaceous plants in the understory. For example, the preferred habitat of the invasive St John's wort plant in shaded areas of California
85 savannas has been interpreted as a consequence of the breeding behavior of the beetle *Chrysolina quadrigemina* (introduced as pest control to fight this invader) that prefers unshaded sites for egg-laying.

At the landscape level, grazing reduces the fuel
90 load of the herbaceous layer, hence diminishing the risk of fire and tree mortality; however, heavy

grazing pressure may suppress tree regeneration. The interaction of grazer—browser—fire strongly influences the tree—grass dynamics.

Tree canopies in savannas are usually kept above the browsing line by large herbivores, which also feed on the herbaceous understory. However, in the Mediterranean landscape there are often closed clumps of tough, horny or spiny shrubs inside of which herbaceous plants may find refuge from large herbivores. In the overgrazed Mediterranean systems, protection from grazing and browsing may be the main cause of facilitation and survival of many palatable plants.

[1] the vegetative layer between the forest canopy and the ground cover

22

The main idea of Passage 2 is that the immediate surroundings of oak trees are affected by

A) their geographical location.
B) harmful and helpful activities of animals.
C) the availability of sufficient nutrients.
D) the level of light intensity in their understory.

23

As used in line 29, "predictors" most nearly means

A) oracles.
B) prophesiers.
C) indicators.
D) hunches.

24

In line 35, "photosynthetic efficiency of the leaf" is primarily mentioned to

A) propose that temperature and humidity are not decisive factors.
B) point out an indirect effect that light intensity has on larvae.
C) provide an explanation for improved larval performance.
D) emphasize that certain kinds of leaves provide more nutrients than others.

25

As used in line 81, "predate" most nearly means

A) poach.
B) forage.
C) stalk.
D) anticipate.

26

In context, the authors of Passage 2 most likely mention "the invasive St John's wort plant" (lines 83-84) in order to

A) describe one of the plants whose seeds might fall prey to insects and other animals.
B) provide an example of a plant that has adapted in response to a human initiative.
C) emphasize that the understory of oak trees provides suitable conditions for a variety of plants.
D) suggest that this plant has adapted in a fashion that runs counter to its preference for shade.

27

Passage 2 mostly suggests which of the following about herbivores that feed in the understories of oak trees?

A) The detrimental effects of their presence outweigh the benefits.
B) Some of them only benefit from a certain subset of a tree's herbaceous understory.
C) If present in sufficient numbers, their grazing prevents tree regeneration.
D) The protective shade of the trees encourages defecation which provides nutrients.

28

Which choice provides the best evidence for the answer to the previous question?

A) Lines 60-63 ("Soil . . . canopies")
B) Lines 64-67 ("Herbaceous . . . California")
C) Lines 72-75 ("This . . . system")
D) Lines 91-94 ("however . . . dynamics")

29

The main purpose of both passages is to

A) discuss the relationship between animals and abiotic conditions in a tree environment.
B) assert that a tree's circumstances are significantly influenced by its denizens.
C) suggest that an animal's success rate depends on the quality of its environment.
D) describe the effects that an organism's circumstances involve.

30

The authors of Passage 2 would most likely add which of the following to Low and Hanley's findings in lines 41-44 ("Low . . . mortality")?

A) Higher mortality at greater canopy heights is likely attributable to birds preying on insects.
B) At greater heights, lack of shade often leads to larvae drying out due to high temperatures.
C) Slower feeding rates result in longer exposure to mortality risks as a larva.
D) The death rate at lower canopy heights might be traced to the presence of large browsers.

31

Which choice provides the best evidence for the answer to the previous question?

A) Lines 67-72 ("Oak . . . environment")
B) Lines 79-82 ("On the . . . understory")
C) Lines 89-91 ("At the . . . mortality")
D) Lines 95-97 ("Tree . . . understory")

32

Passage 1 and Passage 2 respectively describe birds as which of the following?

A) discriminating — two-sided
B) ravenous — useful
C) demanding — beneficial
D) pragmatic — rapacious

Questions 33-42 are based on the following passage.

This passage is from a speech in which Julius Caesar (100 BC–44 BC) responds to calls for an execution without trial of caught conspirators against the state, which would be in violation of their legal rights as Roman citizens.

    I can think of a multitude of examples, senators, in which kings and peoples have, driven by anger or pity, followed ill-advised counsel. Still, I would rather
Line name those in which our forefathers have, resisting
5 the passions in their hearts, acted justly and reasonably.
    In the Macedonian Wars we waged against King Perseus, the glorious and wealthy Rhodian state, which had further grown thanks to the help of the Roman people, was disloyal towards us and hostile.
10 However, when judgment was passed upon the Rhodians after the war had ended, our fathers let them go without punishment so that no one could say the war had been fought for riches rather than righting an injustice.
15   Likewise in the Punic Wars: Even though the Carthaginians committed many abominable atrocities in times of peace as well as during an armistice, our ancestors never committed suchlike even when the opportunity presented itself; they inquired what
20 would befit their dignity rather than what retribution might be permissible by law.
    In the same way, it is up to you, the senators, to ensure the crimes of Publius Lentulus[1] and his accomplices do not outweigh your dignity and to
25 afford less attention to your indignation than to your good reputation. If a punishment commensurate with their crimes can be found, then I approve of this unprecedented measure. However, should the extent of the crime exceed the limits of man's imagination, it
30 is my opinion that we should adhere to such penalties as have been set forth by law.

              * * *

    All bad precedents have originated from good ones. Worse, when government comes into the hands of those who are lesser in competence or good will,
35 this new precedent is likewise transferred from the ones deserving of punishment to those who are not.
    After defeating the Athenians, Sparta installed thirty men to direct the affairs of state. They initially proceeded to execute every wicked and generally
40 hated person without trial which caused much joy among the people: they proclaimed these acts to be justly done. Later, when capriciousness started to reign, the thirty tyrants, down to their whim, killed good men and bad alike and thus terrorized the
45 remainder. The Athenians thus paid a heavy price for their thoughtless exultation: it bought them subjugation and slavery.
    Or consider our own history: when Sulla had Damasippus and others who prospered at the expense
50 of the state strangled, who would not have endorsed this action? All men agreed that these criminal intriguers who had brought on strife through civil unrest had deservedly been executed. This event, however, was the beginning of great bloodshed. For
55 anyone who coveted the next man's house or estate, crockery or clothes, he would go out of his way to have him be counted among those proscribed. Thus the very ones who rejoiced at Damasippus' demise were soon dragged to the scaffold, and the
60 slaughtering did not relent until Sulla had heaped riches unto all of his followers.
    I have no such fears for Marcus Tullius[2], or our own times, but in a great republic, dispositions are numerous and diverse. Is it not possible that in
65 different times, under a different consul, falsehood could be believed instead of the truth? If, following this precedent, that consul should draw the sword heeding the senate's decree, who shall restrain him, and who shall make him see reason?

[1] Publius Cornelius Lentulus Sura was one of the chief conspirators in the Catalinarian conspiracy, a plot to overthrow the Roman Republic.

[2] Marcus Tullius Cicero was a consul in favor of putting the conspirators to death without trial.

33

The primary purpose of the passage is to

A) demand punitive justice whatever the cost.
B) undermine a temperate view on an issue.
C) argue that mercy is always preferable to retribution.
D) present the possible dangers of a course of action.

34

Throughout the passage, Caesar mainly supports his main concern using

A) nostalgic anecdotes.
B) historical instances.
C) impassioned exhortation.
D) poor role models.

35

It can be inferred from the passage that Caesar would disapprove of the "unprecedented measure" (line 28) unless

A) the transgression is beyond man's ability to describe.
B) a fitting way to punish the offender can be conceived.
C) there is no law that addresses the crime in question.
D) the sheer scope of the crime has damaged the senators' reputation.

36

The passage implies that at the outset, the common people perceived the use of violence to right wrongs as

A) dangerous in the long term.
B) gruesome and unnecessary.
C) completely tolerable.
D) somewhat controversial.

37

Which choice provides the best evidence for the answer to the previous question?

A) Lines 15-18 ("Even though . . . suchlike")
B) Lines 38-41 ("They . . . people")
C) Lines 42-45 ("Later . . . remainder")
D) Lines 53-57 ("This . . . proscribed")

38

The question in lines 50-51 mostly functions to

A) imply that a reaction was only natural.
B) accuse Sulla's supporters of shortsightedness.
C) exalt Sulla's actions as honorable.
D) laud the unanimous support Sulla received.

39

The "men" mentioned in line 51 are most similar to

A) "kings and peoples" (line 2)
B) "the Carthaginians" (lines 15-16)
C) "the senators" (line 22)
D) "the people" (line 41)

40

As used in line 57, "counted among" most nearly means

A) regarded as.
B) weighed.
C) hoped for.
D) estimated as.

41

According to the passage, Caesar is mainly concerned that the current proceedings might

A) create grounds for future injustice.
B) give free reign to tyranny and despotism.
C) leave the scope of established Roman law.
D) fail to punish those who justly deserve it.

42

Which choice provides the best evidence for the answer to the previous question?

A) Lines 3-5 ("Still . . . reasonably")
B) Lines 28-31 ("However . . . law")
C) Lines 42-45 ("Later . . . remainder")
D) Lines 66-69 ("If, following . . . reason")

Questions 43-52 are based on the following passage and supplementary material.

This essay was written by a semi-professional swimmer.

I started swimming in elementary school. I do not think I can recall a time I was not on the swim team. I suppose there are those who get sick of it
Line and turn to other sports or hobbies, but personally,
5 I cannot imagine what else I would do with my life. I swim. I flunked Latin, and I am hopeless when it comes to biology, but I do know this sport.
   One of the key moments that informed my swimming experience occurred in middle school.
10 I had just finished a training run, and I was baffled because Coach Brown showed me the time: it was a personal record. I had never made it down the lanes this fast before. What was puzzling, though, was that it did not *feel* like a phenomenal performance. On the
15 contrary, I felt like I could have done better.
   When I mentioned this sentiment to my coach, he asked me whether I liked physics. What does physics have to do with swimming? Even more confused, I answered by asking this question. Coach
20 Brown sat me down after training, and I learned that physics actually has a lot to do with swimming.
   There are Newton's laws of motion, for instance. The first states that an object in motion stays in motion unless acted upon by an outside force, and
25 an object at rest stays at rest unless acted upon by an outside force. For instance, a swimmer who starts moving must first overcome the static friction that resists the motion of water over the swimmer's body. The second law states that acceleration is
30 directly proportional to the net force acting on it and inversely proportional to its mass. When it comes to swimming, this means that a more powerful stroke combined with a reduction in body weight will result in faster acceleration. The final law states that for
35 every action there is an opposite and equal reaction, which also applies to swimming: kick water back, and your body is propelled forward.
   But these laws do not explain what I experienced when I achieved my record time. Why had it felt that
40 way? There is a term in physics, "kinetic energy," that is required to unravel this mystery. Kinetic energy is best understood as mass traveling at a certain speed. This is the energy available to the swimmer. Depending on the swimmer's skills, his actions can
45 either move his body directly toward his goal (positive kinetic energy), or he might direct his energy in another direction (negative kinetic energy), which will take away from his positive kinetic energy.
   For instance, freestyle requires a swimmer to
50 alternate between left and right arms for his strokes. As this happens, the body often twists from side to side with arms and legs pointing in one direction and hips going the other way—kind of like a banana. If this happens, a lot of negative kinetic energy is created
55 because strokes and kicks are not aligned with the end of the lane. Remember, negative energy directly takes away from positive energy. In other words, a lot of energy is wasted and the swimmer loses speed. So when I swam record times, I generated less negative
60 kinetic energy, which meant more positive kinetic energy. By not wasting strength, I was able to achieve more while feeling like I had spent less energy.

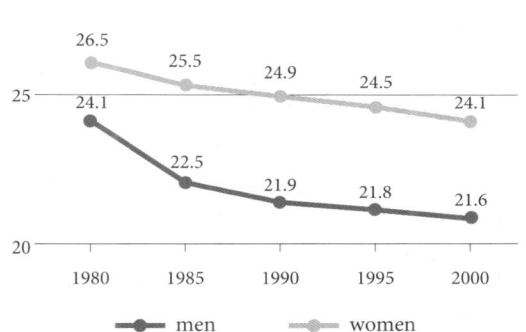

Top Swimming Performance Times (in seconds) for Athletes in Region A

43

In the passage, physics is primarily represented as

A) a basis for understanding various sports.
B) a pretentious way of evaluating swimming.
C) a tool used to analyze an activity.
D) unable to explain a strange occurrence.

44

Over the course of the passage, the main focus shifts from

A) the occurrence of a puzzling phenomenon to a possible explanation.
B) reservations towards an explanation to a sense of reluctant acceptance.
C) the description of a personal preference to an explanation for its existence.
D) viewing a sport through the lens of science to the benefits of doing so.

45

The author indicates which of the following about his training run?

A) It inspired him to consider the sport as a profession.
B) It was the first time he had beaten everyone in his group.
C) He performed better than at his last competition.
D) His results were not in line with his perceived performance.

46

Which choice provides the best evidence for the answer to the previous question?

A) Lines 8-9 ("One of . . . school")
B) Lines 10-12 ("I had . . . record")
C) Lines 13-14 ("What was . . . performance")
D) Lines 16-18 ("When . . . swimming")

47

According to the passage, the coach's question (lines 16-17) initially resulted in

A) annoyance.
B) an admission.
C) comprehension.
D) bewilderment.

48

In line 41, "unravel" most nearly means

A) free.
B) clear up.
C) separate.
D) unfold.

49

According to the description in lines 44-48, which of the following is true about the relationship between positive and negative kinetic energy?

A) Each grows and decreases if the other does the same.
B) If the latter grows, it does so by draining the former.
C) The latter can never be greater than the former.
D) It takes skills for the former to balance the latter.

50

Which of the following, if true, would most undermine the statement in lines 53-56 ("If this ... lane")?

A) Swimming freestyle does not necessarily result in a banana-like form.
B) Even if hips and limbs lose alignment, strokes and kicks do not.
C) Negative kinetic energy does not prevent swimmers from achieving record times.
D) If arms and legs do not align with one's hips, a lot of energy is wasted.

51

Based on the data in the graph, the years 1990-2000 were mostly characterized by

A) higher performance gains than in the previous 10 years for both sexes.
B) decreased rates of improvement for men as compared to the women.
C) a widening of the performance gap towards the middle of the period.
D) fluctuations on the side of the men and steady gains on the side of the women.

52

Which of the following, if converted into action, would be the most relevant in bringing about the results over time as shown in the graph?

A) Lines 26-29 ("For instance ... body")
B) Lines 41-43 ("Kinetic ... swimmer")
C) Lines 51-53 ("As this ... banana")
D) Lines 58-61 ("So ... energy")

STOP

Do not move on to the next section if you finish early.

You may review your answers in this section only.

Answer Keys & Performance Breakdown

1	(C)	Summary	19	(D)	Graph	37	(B)	Evidence
2	(A)	Local	20	(B)	Graph	38	(A)	Context
3	(A)	Local	21	(C)	Graph	39	(D)	Synthesize
4	(C)	Local	22	(B)	Summary	40	(A)	Vocabulary
5	(C)	Evidence	23	(C)	Vocabulary	41	(A)	Local
6	(B)	Vocabulary	24	(B)	Context	42	(D)	Evidence
7	(D)	Local	25	(B)	Vocabulary	43	(C)	Summary
8	(C)	Local	26	(A)	Context	44	(A)	Organization
9	(B)	Local	27	(B)	Local	45	(D)	Local
10	(C)	Evidence	28	(C)	Evidence	46	(C)	Evidence
11	(C)	Stance	29	(D)	Summary	47	(D)	Local
12	(C)	Style	30	(D)	Synthesize	48	(B)	Vocabulary
13	(A)	Local	31	(D)	Evidence	49	(B)	Local
14	(C)	Local	32	(A)	Synthesize	50	(B)	Local
15	(D)	Synthesize	33	(D)	Summary	51	(B)	Graph
16	(C)	Local	34	(B)	Style	52	(D)	Graph
17	(B)	Vocabulary	35	(B)	Local			
18	(C)	Local	36	(C)	Local			

■ Write down the number of correct answers for each question type.

Question Types	Number of Correct Answers
Local	/ 18
Style	/ 2
Vocabulary	/ 6
Evidence	/ 7
Context	/ 3
Organization	/ 1
Summary	/ 5
Stance	/ 1
Synthesize	/ 4
Graph	/ 5
Total	**/ 52**

Answer Explanations

Questions 1-10

1. (C) — Summary

C is the best choice because the passage follows Van Brunt who initially looks forward to being the first white man to set foot in a hitherto unexplored village. He feels chagrin at being greeted by a bearded white man who has been living in that village for five years already, and Van Brunt asks him how he came to be there.

A is incorrect because reunion implies prior acquaintance. Lines 38-40 clearly show they do not know each other. B is incorrect because though "hardships of expeditions" are mentioned, the focus lies on Van Brunt unexpectedly running into Fairfax. D is incorrect because indigence is not brought up or focused on.

2. (A) — Local

A is the best choice because the passage mentions that at this point, he found undreamed-of rich forests and unrecorded tribes which qualify as "bounty." "Uncharted territory" is supported by "white blank spaces on the map" which indicates nothing has been drawn on the map as yet; i.e., it is unexplored.

B is incorrect because the question asks specifically about a certain point in time, after which he finds forests and tribes. C is incorrect because the passage does not mention "achieving" fame. D is incorrect because the maps did not describe this landscape; they were blank.

3. (A) — Local

A is the best choice because the former are mentioned as things he had been intending to do whereas the latter caused him added delight now that he was here. Thus, he had not been aware of the latter's existence.

B is incorrect because he "came to speculate" about the latter, which means they are not a certainty and not on the map. C is incorrect because even though villages are man-made, timer belts do not require people. D is incorrect because no such distinction is made.

4. (C) — Local

C is the best choice because of lines 73-75 (see next question).

A is incorrect because it means "worthwhile" or "advantageous." He has, however, been stuck in this village after his expedition ran into bad luck. B is incorrect because nothing suggests the village is hostile towards him or opposes his presence. D is incorrect because Fairfax never says whether he finds his current life to be tedious.

5. (C) — Evidence

C is the best choice because the lines show the cause of his presence in this village. He mentions mischances, and losing his party and outfit. Therefore, his current situation, living in this village, was not planned.

A, B, and D are incorrect because none of them state how he came to be in this village, or that it was unintended.

6. (B) — Vocabulary

B is the best choice because the two parties are using hand signals to communicate they mean no harm.

A is incorrect because to "utter" indicates verbal communication. C is incorrect because the villagers sent a response instead of simply understanding. D is incorrect because collaboration indicates working together.

7. (D) — Local

D is the best choice because he uses "painstaking care." Also, cherishing the flame as if there were never another expresses the idea that if he loses this flame, he will not be able to summon another. Thus, "caution" is correct.

A is incorrect because "urgency" implies haste. B is incorrect because treasuring something and being careful is different from being amazed or enchanted by it. C is incorrect because it means "worship" or "extreme devotion."

8. (C) — Local

C is the best choice because Fairfax's statement "he was lost . . ." indicates he thought Prevanche had died. The response "but he pulled through and came out" indicates that Prevanche survived his ordeal.

A is incorrect because the Smoke Mountains are not described as extremely dangerous in the specified lines. B is incorrect because the passage does not

Answer Explanations

specify if he received help or got out on his own. D is incorrect because no such information is given in the passage.

9. (B) — Local

B is the best choice because of lines 22-24 (see next question).

A is incorrect because no explorer of legendary status has been mentioned. C is incorrect because though the natives at first seem hostile, they accept his peace sign. In addition, the bearded man was not a welcome sight to Van Brunt. D is incorrect because this choice implies that the two knew each other before.

10. (C) — Evidence

C is the best choice because the sentence states that Van Brunt knew the bearded man to be "his kind."

A, B, and D are incorrect because none of them indicate whether or not Van Brunt and the bearded man are of the same race.

Questions 11-21

11. (C) — Stance

C is the best choice because the author describes how the Internet has changed his experience of listening to music. He contends that he was able to focus more on listening and cherish the music more before the Internet.

A is incorrect because it implies the author recommends the use of the Internet. B is incorrect because the author never recommends that we get rid of the Internet. D is incorrect because "defender" implies a discussion or controversy and upholding one's argument. The passage, however, merely conveys a personal opinion.

12. (C) — Style

C is the best choice because the repetition leaves out the word "have" used in the previous sentence. The change from "I have felt it" to "I felt it" implies he no longer feels something.

A is incorrect because the duration of a feeling would not seem exaggerated. B is incorrect because general opinion is not part of the repeated phrase. D is incorrect because personal opinion is not contrasted against commonly held views.

13. (A) — Local

A is the best choice because "abundance of benefits" (positive change) is contrasted against (still) the emphasized word *change*. The word "still" implies that "change" is seen in contrast to "benefits," and "change" in itself means that the state before and the state after are different; i.e., the state before the change no longer exists (loss).

B is incorrect because "unwanted" implies a lack of intent which is not supported. C is incorrect because it implies a comparison as to which side outweighs the other. D is incorrect because no such preference is suggested.

14. (C) — Local

C is the best choice because after he goes on and describes the manual actions and corrections and what they entail, he states that these inconveniences actually heightened his enjoyment of music (lines 30-42).

A is incorrect because "arduous" means extremely laborious. B is incorrect because this describes how his children would see this matter, not how he himself would feel. D is incorrect because it means outdated and without use.

15. (D) — Synthesize

D is the best choice because paragraph 3 describes how a process is work-intensive and results in lower sound quality whereas paragraph 4 explains that this actually results in higher enjoyment and devotion to listening.

A is incorrect because paragraph 3 does not explain the author's nostalgia. B is incorrect because no view is presented as fallacious in paragraph 3. C is incorrect because paragraph 3 on the surface shows doubt and incomprehension which is then explained and resolved in paragraph 4. Thus, paragraph 4 does not "validate" paragraph 3.

16. (C) — Local

C is the best choice because the pond is compared to an ocean (which is much larger). These bodies of waters are metaphors for the joy experienced when listening to music.

A is incorrect because it is too literal. B is incorrect because placidity is not being discussed. D is incorrect because nothing like bridging a divide is being discussed.

17. (B) — Vocabulary

B is the best choice because in the sentence, the author is "browsing" dozens of records in an LP store. Thus, he is physically looking through records which is similar to "leafing through" (turning pages).

A is incorrect because it means animals eating grass. C is incorrect because "bookmarking" indicates marking a location or spot to return to later. D is incorrect because the author is talking about an LP store (as opposed to using the Internet).

18. (C) — Local

C is the best choice. The sentence in question begins with "as a result" so the previous sentence is of interest. It states that the author did not have enough money to buy and listen to every record, and that this inability filled him with a strong desire to experience the music. Thus, the information available on the Internet has removed this longing. The "aura of initiation and exclusivity" refers to the fact that if you had a record, not everyone else would have it or be able to listen to it.

A is incorrect because converging taste in music genres is not discussed. B is incorrect because LP stores having disappeared is not mentioned. D is incorrect because no comparison is made between the author's and the current generation's taste in music.

19. (D) — Graph

D is the best choice because Vinyl and Cassette, which made up 95% in 1985, made up 2% in 2012. That means almost all of this consumption now happens on a different medium.

A is incorrect because there is not enough data to support "continuous." B is incorrect because the data does not show which medium lost how much to which medium. C is incorrect because casual listening is not part of the data.

20. (B) — Graph

B is the best choice because the question asks what people in 2012 most likely did. Ergo, the highest 2012 percentages are asked for. For Chart 1, this means the Internet (download), and for Chart 2, listening "while doing something else" is easy to support since only 9% listened to music exclusively.

A is incorrect because the person's location while downloading is never specified. C is incorrect because it implies that most people did not want to listen to music at home. Chart 2 does not support this statement. D is incorrect because no such condition is part of the data in Chart 1.

21. (C) — Graph

C is the best choice because Vinyl and Cassette are shown as having mostly disappeared. This fits with the author's idea that older media involved more effort in playing back music as compared to the Internet.

A is incorrect because the passage does not mention this. B is incorrect because "disappearance of LP stores" is not mentioned in the passage. D is incorrect. The passage states that because the Internet makes music so available and listening so facile, people do not focus on music the way they used to. This is not the same as "unwillingness to concentrate."

Questions 22-32

22. (B) — Summary

B is the best choice. (For a short summary, see the explanation for question 28.)

A is incorrect because the passage mainly focuses on the effects of animals, not geographic location. C is incorrect because while this fact was mentioned, it does not encapsulate the main idea. D is incorrect because "light intensity" was not mentioned in Passage 2.

23. (C) — Vocabulary

C is the best choice. The sentence states that light intensity and nitrogen content are significant "predictors" of feeding rate. Thus, knowledge of light intensity and nitrogen content lets one infer the feeding rate. Therefore, "predictors" provide information about something, which makes "indicators" the best choice.

A is incorrect because it means "prophecy" or "divination." B is incorrect because it means "prophets" or "clairvoyants." D is incorrect because it means "inklings" or "feelings."

24. (B) — Context

B is the best choice because the same sentence states that "As a result [of light], larvae are indirectly affected by subsequent changes in the leaf's nutritional quality."

A is incorrect because photosynthetic efficiency is

Answer Explanations

not mentioned to suggest that other factors are not decisive. C is incorrect because nothing in context suggests improved or better performance. D is incorrect because "kinds of leaves" are not mentioned. (Only one kind of leaf is studied.)

25. (B) — Vocabulary

B is the best choice because the sentence mentions animals that "predate" seeds and seedlings. Therefore, "scour" or "forage" is correct.

A is incorrect because it means "trespass" or "smuggle." C is incorrect because it means "ambush" or "creep up on." D is incorrect because it means "predict" or "forestall."

26. (A) — Context

A is the best choice. St John's wort is an example of a plant that small mammals, birds and insects predate seeds and seedlings of (lines 79-82).

B is incorrect because the plant is not mentioned to give an example of its adaptation, but rather as an example of the information in lines 79-82. C is incorrect because "a variety of plants" is not supported. D is incorrect because the passage does not suggest that the plant prefers shade. (The mentioned "beetle" does.)

27. (B) — Local

B is the best choice because of lines 72-75 (see next question).

A is incorrect because the passage does not mention that detrimental effects outweigh benefits with regard to the presence of herbivores. C is incorrect because "prevents" is not supported by the passage. D is incorrect because "encourages" is not supported by the passage.

28. (C) — Evidence

C is the best choice because the lines state that the nutritional value of sub-canopy plants must be above a critical level in order to be digested by ruminants. In other words, ruminants cannot digest just any plant.

A, B, and D are incorrect because none of them show that some herbivores only benefit from a certain subset of a tree's herbaceous understory.

29. (D) — Summary

The main idea of Passage 1 is that different abiotic conditions (leaf size, light, height, etc.) within the same oak tree affect the survival and performance rates of the leafminer (in larval form). The main idea of Passage 2 is that animals affect the understory of oak trees (by dropping feces and providing nutrition, providing and predating seeds, grazing and browsing—the last two activities can be both helpful and harmful).

D is the best choice. Both passages describe organisms (the leafminer and oak trees) that are affected by their circumstances.

A is incorrect because "abiotic conditions" only applies to Passage 1. B is incorrect because it only applies to Passage 2. C is incorrect because it only applies to Passage 1.

30. (D) — Synthesize

D is the best choice because of lines 95-97 (see next question).

A is incorrect because Passage 2 does not mention "birds preying on insects." B is incorrect because Passage 2 does not mention drying out due to lack of shade. C is incorrect because "feeding rates" is not mentioned in Passage 2.

31. (D) — Evidence

D is the best choice because the sentence states that large herbivores keep the tree canopies above a certain line. This suggests that below that line, herbivores eat the tree's leaves (and thus kill any larvae contained within). Therefore, the authors of Passage 2 would likely state that the deaths of larvae at lower canopy heights can be attributed to large browsers (herbivores).

A, B, and C are incorrect because none of them show that the death rate of leafminers at lower canopy heights might be traced to the presence of large browsers.

32. (A) — Synthesize

Passage 1 mentions birds in lines 18-21. Passage 2 mentions birds in lines 76-82.

A is the best choice. Passage 1 indicates that birds will forgo difficult prey if other prey is available (discriminating). Passage 2 states that birds disperse seeds and contribute to the core regeneration of the system, but they also predate seeds (two-sided).

B is incorrect because Passage 1 does not support "ravenous." C is incorrect because Passage 1 does not support "demanding." D is incorrect because Passage 2 does not support "rapacious."

Questions 33-42

33. (D) — Summary

D is the best choice because Caesar opposes the execution of Lentulus without trial. After lauding cases where ancestors exercised restraint instead of acting out of anger, he points out cases where leaders chose violence and the public suffered as a result of these bad precedents. Therefore, Caesar implies that if Lentulus is executed now without trial, the Roman people might suffer as a result of this precedent.

A is incorrect because it is in opposition to Caesar's intentions. B is incorrect because Caesar is advocating a temperate view. C is incorrect because "always" is not supported.

34. (B) — Style

B is the best choice because Caesar uses four examples from history (Macedonian Wars, Punic Wars, Sparta vs. Athens, and Sulla in Rome).

A is incorrect because of "nostalgic." C is incorrect because nothing supports "impassioned." On the contrary, Caesar warns against letting passion take over. D is incorrect because two out of four examples contain positive role models.

35. (B) — Local

B is the best choice because the passage states he would approve of the "unprecedented measure" if a punishment commensurate with the crimes can be found. Therefore, it is also true that Caesar would disapprove if such a punishment cannot be found.

A is incorrect because it is logically the opposite of Caesar's stipulation (that a fitting way to punish is needed). C and D are incorrect because the "law" and the "senators' reputation" are not part of Caesar's stipulation.

36. (C) — Local

C is the best choice because of lines 38-41 (see next question) and because of lines 51-53.

A is incorrect because the passage does not state that

initially, people considered long term consequences. B is incorrect because people initially endorsed the use of violence, which goes against B. D is incorrect because no such controversy was mentioned in the passage.

37. (B) — Evidence

B is the best choice because the lines state that executing every wicked and hated person without trial caused much joy among the people.

A, C, and D are incorrect because they do not deal with initial reactions to the use of violence.

38. (A) — Context

A is the best choice because asking "who would not have endorsed this action?" emphasizes the next sentence which states that "All men agreed . . ." Therefore, it can be said that this endorsement was natural.

B is incorrect because the question itself does not imply shortsightedness. C is incorrect because the question does not imply honor. D is incorrect because it does not praise the fact that there was such support.

39. (D) — Synthesize

D is the best choice because the "men" are those who initially agree to the use of violence and later fall victims to it. This is like "the people" in line 41.

A, B, and C are therefore incorrect.

40. (A) — Vocabulary

A is the best choice because the sentence mentions how one person—out of envy and greed—would try to have another person be "counted among" those proscribed (condemned to death in this context). Thus, "regarded as" is the best choice.

B is incorrect because it means "analyze" or "contemplate," a deliberate study of things. C is obviously incorrect. D is incorrect because it means to "approximate" or to "guess."

41. (A) — Local

A is the best choice because of lines 32-36 which state that bad precedents will result in punishment for those who do not deserve it when those who are unfit govern. Also, there are lines 66-69 (see next question).

B is incorrect because "tyranny" and "despotism"

Answer Explanations

indicate that the current government would collapse. This is not suggested. C is incorrect because even though leaving law behind might set a bad precedent, it is the results of the bad precedent that Caesar is concerned about more than its cause. D is incorrect because Caesar advocates execution after trial in order to avoid setting a bad precedent. This means his main concern is following certain protocols rather than ensuring punishment.

42. (D) — Evidence

D is the best choice because the lines state that a consul might use violence due to "this precedent" which refers to the matter of executing Lentulus. He further implies it would be difficult to restrain that consul and make him "see reason" which indicates that that consul's decision to resort to violence will be unjustified.

A, B, and C are incorrect because none of them state that Caesar was worried about creating grounds for future injustice.

Questions 43-52

43. (C) — Summary

C is the best choice because the passage first mentions that the author was surprised at his personal record because it did not feel like he had been that fast. The coach then explains this phenomenon using physics, and the passage relates several physical laws that apply to swimming.

A is incorrect because only swimming is mentioned. B is incorrect because "pretentious" is not supported. D is incorrect because the passage explains a strange occurrence by resorting to physics.

44. (A) — Organization

A is the best choice because the puzzling phenomenon happens in paragraph 2 (the personal record). The possible explanation happens in the last two paragraphs (kinetic energy).

B is incorrect because even though "reservations" makes sense (lines 17-18), "reluctant acceptance" is not mentioned. C is incorrect because "personal preference" can only refer to the love of swimming. The passage does not explain why that love of swimming came to be. D is incorrect because the passage does not detail benefits of viewing swimming through the lens of physics.

45. (D) — Local

D is the best choice because of lines 13-14 (see next question).

A is incorrect because it is not mentioned. B is incorrect because he only beat his own times. C is incorrect because no previous competitions were mentioned.

46. (C) — Evidence

C is the best choice because the lines state that though he swam a record time, "it did not *feel* like a phenomenal performance" (perceived performance).

A, B, and D are incorrect because none of them state that he actually performed better than he thought he did.

47. (D) — Local

D is the best choice because the first reaction is that he was "more confused."

Therefore, A, B, and C are incorrect.

48. (B) — Vocabulary

B is the best choice because in the sentence, "unravel" is used with "mystery"(or puzzle).

A and C are obviously incorrect. D is incorrect because it means to "spread out" or to "reveal" or "disclose."

49. (B) — Local

B is the best choice because the specified lines state that negative kinetic energy takes away from positive kinetic energy.

A is incorrect because it states that positive and negative kinetic energies increase or decrease at the same time. C is incorrect because no such limit is stated. D is incorrect because skill does not result in balance, according to the passage, but in positive kinetic energy.

50. (B) — Local

B is the best choice. The lines state that negative kinetic energy is created because if hips and limbs are out of alignment, strokes and kicks are not aligned with the end of the lane; i.e., arms and legs do not point directly at or away from the end of the lane.

This is undermined by B because it says that loss of hip-limb alignment does not result in loss of limb-lane alignment.

A, C, and D are incorrect because they do not undermine the given statement.

51. (B)   Graph

B is the best choice because the women improved by 0.4 and 0.4 seconds whereas the men only improved by 0.1 and 0.2 seconds.

A is incorrect because the opposite is true. C is incorrect because the performance gap in 1995 is not wider than the performance gap in 1990. D is incorrect because there are no fluctuations in this graph.

52. (D)   Graph

The results over time, as shown in the graph, represent a steady improvement for both men and women. In other words, swimmers swim faster than they used to.

D is the best choice because the lines mention record times thanks to using energy more efficiently (improved performance).

A, B, and C are incorrect because none of them discuss improved performance.

SAT.Hackers.ac

Hackers New SAT Reading: 10 Practice Tests

TEST 6

Answer Keys & Performance Breakdown
Answer Explanations

Reading Test

65 MINUTES, 52 QUESTIONS

Mark your answers to the questions in Section 1 in the answer sheet provided.

DIRECTIONS

For each of the passages below, there are 10 or 11 questions. Choose the best answer for each of the questions after you have finished reading the passage. The answers to the questions should be based on the information that is stated or implied in the text and any associated graphics.

Questions 1-10 are based on the following passage.

In this passage, the author ponders her childhood days when she had to go to church.

Though I feel obliged to say I never took relish in the thought of having to get up early on Sunday morning to go to church (quite the contrary, to be
Line honest), slouching in one of the wooden pews in the
5 back between my parents and my sister, crowded in between people while at the same time feeling insignificant in that bone-shaded cetacean colossus of a nave held up by those titanic fluted stone ribs week upon week has really branded itself into my
10 memory. It would not be amiss for me to tell you that this recurring hour of dour songs, mindless prayer, kneeling, and stifling incense, the cold church air, the boredom, whispered words with my sister, and stern looks from my mother have come to form a
15 significant part of the cherished memories I now refer to as my childhood. Who would have ever thought I would miss setting foot in the Almighty Father's house? My feet, apparently.

It has been more than 30 years since I was last
20 coerced into getting up in the grey morning hours on Sunday, washing the sleep out of my eyes, and downing some of yesterday's bread for breakfast before being ushered to mass. I distinctly remember the first time I exempted myself (feeling giddy with
25 excitement and quite guilty) and from my bed listened to the sounds of my parents closing the door behind them and walking down the stairs to the car. What freedom! What elation! And yet, nowadays I find myself standing in front of these stone behemoths
30 every once in a while for some unfathomable reason. The rebellious adolescent in me, at least, would have characterized it as unfathomable what with the absence of parental pressure. Sometimes, before I know it, I find myself sitting in one of the hindmost
35 pews of an empty nave, drinking in the quiet, serene air the taste of which affords me such a blessed break from the noisy city that my life has ended up in.

I suspect, however, that it is more than mere escape from my day-to-day that is driving me.
40 It feels like a part of me is calling out, possibly a fragment of the past, some long-lost feeling that has been discarded on the path of growing up and is now making felt its absence. Not knowing what it is I am running after, I indulge in this oblivious
45 somnambulation and sure enough, it is to churches all over town that my lowest extremities lead me. I always enter after the rock whale disgorges its mass of parishioners after mass, and I pore over the vaulted ceilings, the massive organ pipes, and the colored
50 windows depicting saints and suffering, and I wait for something within me to stir, to resonate.

This unseen siren has proved to be elusive. I can almost sense her in the stale incense lingering after big ceremonies; I can almost hear her in the chants
55 and prayers that still echo down the aisles long after everyone has left. She is there, tantalizingly close, but never quite within reach. Somewhere in the vast ocean that lies underneath conscious thought, I feel her beckoning and whispering for sustenance, yet I
60 know neither who she is nor what she requires. Until these questions find an answer, I have no choice but to follow my feet.

1

The primary purpose of the passage is to

A) solve a quaint puzzle.
B) convey a deep-seated urge.
C) criticize mandatory activities.
D) describe a commonplace tendency.

2

The shift between the narration from lines 1-37 and the narration in lines 38-62 is best characterized as a shift from

A) nostalgic recollection to regretful admission.
B) childhood weekends to work life realities.
C) facts and certainty to speculation and uncertainty.
D) hopes of the past to dashed dreams of the future.

3

As used in line 9, "branded" most nearly means

A) labeled.
B) stigmatized.
C) impressed.
D) disgraced.

4

The passage as a whole suggests that the author regards her "feet" (line 18) as

A) a window to a subconscious desire.
B) a symbol representing her guilty conscience.
C) a welcome distraction from inner turmoil.
D) the answer to a nagging question.

5

The description in lines 5-10 ("crowded . . . memory") shows that the author associates a building with

A) intense fright.
B) tedium and monotony.
C) lost family members.
D) a living organism.

6

Which choice provides the best evidence for the answer to the previous question?

A) Lines 19-23 ("It has . . . mass")
B) Lines 33-37 ("Sometimes . . . up in")
C) Lines 46-47 ("I always . . . mass")
D) Lines 57-59 ("Somewhere . . . sustenance")

7

In context, the description in lines 23-28 ("I distinctly . . . elation") primarily serves to

A) imply that an activity is ubiquitous.
B) explain the author's current joy.
C) underscore a lack of understanding.
D) offer a rationale for going to church.

8

In lines 44-45, the phrase "oblivious somnambulation" is used to imply that

A) the author is excited that her feet lead her on their own.
B) going to church leaves the author feeling lethargic.
C) the author does not deliberately choose her destination.
D) the author usually indulges in her walks after dark.

CONTINUE

9

The "siren" mentioned in line 52 most likely refers to

A) the author's sister.
B) an aural signal.
C) a puzzling feeling.
D) an alarming presence.

10

The mood the author probably experiences in lines 52-57 ("This unseen . . . reach") is primarily one of

A) frustration.
B) consummation.
C) contrition.
D) reverence.

Questions 11-20 are based on the following passage.

This passage is adapted from George C. Marshall's speech in 1947. The so-called Marshall Plan Speech proposes an initiative to provide economic support to assist in rebuilding post-World War II Europe.

The truth of the matter is that Europe's requirements for the next three or four years of foreign food and other essential products—
Line principally from America—are so much greater
5 than her present ability to pay that she must have substantial additional help or face economic, social, and political deterioration of a very grave character.
   The remedy lies in breaking the vicious circle and restoring the confidence of the European people
10 in the economic future of their own countries and of Europe as a whole. The manufacturer and the farmer throughout wide areas must be able and willing to exchange their products for currencies the continuing value of which is not open to question.
15   Aside from the demoralizing effect on the world at large and the possibilities of disturbances arising as a result of the desperation of the people concerned, the consequences to the economy of the United States should be apparent to all. It is logical
20 that the United States should do whatever it is able to do to assist in the return of normal economic health in the world, without which there can be no political stability and no assured peace. Our policy is directed not against any country or doctrine but
25 against hunger, poverty, desperation and chaos. Its purpose should be the revival of a working economy in the world so as to permit the emergence of political and social conditions in which free institutions can exist. Such assistance, I am convinced, must not be
30 on a piecemeal basis as various crises develop. Any assistance that this Government may render in the future should provide a cure rather than a mere palliative. Any government that is willing to assist in the task of recovery will find full co-operation I am
35 sure, on the part of the United States Government. Any government which maneuvers to block the recovery of other countries cannot expect help from us. Furthermore, governments, political parties, or groups which seek to perpetuate human misery in
40 order to profit therefrom politically or otherwise will encounter the opposition of the United States.
   It is already evident that, before the United States Government can proceed much further in its efforts to alleviate the situation and help start the
45 European world on its way to recovery, there must

be some agreement among the countries of Europe as to the requirements of the situation and the part those countries themselves will take in order to give proper effect to whatever action might be undertaken
50 by this Government. It would be neither fitting nor efficacious for this Government to undertake to draw up unilaterally a program designed to place Europe on its feet economically. This is the business of the Europeans. The initiative, I think, must come from
55 Europe. The role of this country should consist of friendly aid in the drafting of a European program and of later support of such a program so far as it may be practical for us to do so. The program should be a joint one, agreed to by a number, if not all European
60 nations.

 An essential part of any successful action on the part of the United States is an understanding on the part of the people of America of the character of the problem and the remedies to be applied. Political
65 passion and prejudice should have no part. With foresight, and a willingness on the part of our people to face up to the vast responsibility which history has clearly placed upon our country, the difficulties I have outlined can and will be overcome.

70 I am sorry that on each occasion I have said something publicly in regard to our international situation; I've been forced by the necessities of the case to enter into rather technical discussions. But to my mind, it is of vast importance that our people
75 reach some general understanding of what the complications really are, rather than react from a passion or a prejudice or an emotion of the moment. As I said more formally a moment ago, we are remote from the scene of these troubles. It is virtually
80 impossible at this distance merely by reading, or listening, or even seeing photographs or motion pictures, to grasp at all the real significance of the situation. And yet the whole world of the future hangs on a proper judgment. It hangs, I think, to a large
85 extent on the realization of the American people, of just what are the various dominant factors.

11

The stance Marshall takes in the passage is best described as that of

A) a scholar recounting the effects of a decision.
B) a prophet predicting a dire future.
C) a radical requisitioning extreme measures.
D) a popularizer of a possibly unwelcome idea.

12

The passage suggests that manufacturers and farmers might not want to "exchange their products for currencies" (line 13) if

A) their products are currently undervalued.
B) barter trade is often more lucrative.
C) depreciation of money is a possibility.
D) not selling might drive up product prices.

13

Marshall indicates that "It is logical that the United States should do whatever it is able to do to assist" (lines 19-21) because

A) the U.S. has always acted out of moral obligations.
B) the crisis in Europe affects the U.S. as well.
C) the U.S. stands to profit substantially from a united Europe.
D) the U.S. can afford to lend aid for about four years.

14

The policy in line 23 is best characterized as

A) humanitarian.
B) abiding.
C) altruistic.
D) stable.

15

In line 33, the "palliative" refers to assistance that

A) will provide lasting help to Europe.
B) is granted by governments other than the U.S.
C) falls short of truly solving the crisis in Europe.
D) returns confidence in the strength of European currencies.

16

What does Marshall mainly do in lines 38-41 ("Furthermore . . . States")?

A) He issues a warning.
B) He reiterates a point.
C) He levels an accusation.
D) He offers an interpretation.

17

In paragraph 4 (lines 42-60), Marshall voices concern regarding the efficacy of U.S. assistance unless Europe

A) fails to size up the situation and coordinates the undertaking.
B) determines how its members will cooperate with the U.S.
C) comes up with funding at least equal to that of the U.S.
D) unanimously decides to agree on requirements and takes the initiative.

18

As used in line 68, "placed" most nearly means

A) assigned.
B) located.
C) arranged.
D) recognized.

19

According to the last paragraph, whether people "reach some general understanding" (line 75), or whether they "react from a passion or a prejudice or an emotion" (lines 76-77) hinges on

A) the distance between observer and observed.
B) using different kinds of visual media.
C) the usage of technical explanations.
D) the realization altruism is sometimes required.

20

Which of the following, if true, would most undermine Marshall's statement in lines 79-83 ("It is . . . situation")?

A) Not being able to see a situation with your own eyes renders your judgment of it useless.
B) It is hard to convince people to assist someone else unless these people have something to gain.
C) Mere words, even without pictures, suffice to convey a clear understanding of remote events.
D) Hearing a second-hand account of a situation is always different from being present yourself.

Questions 21-31 are based on the following passages.

These passages discuss a phenomenon related to the pollution of our oceans.

Passage 1

The fact that our planet rotates around its own axis not only results in evenly distributed temperatures across most of its surface—most people simply refer to this as day and night, it has yet another
[5] effect which is less readily apparent to us, earthbound as we are. Termed the Coriolis effect, this centrifugal force can be witnessed when observing objects moving over large distances over time from a high altitude: clouds exhibit clockwise curls and spirals in
[10] the Northern, and counterclockwise patterns in the Southern hemisphere. These wind forces in turn drive oceanic currents, and thanks to the Coriolis effect, colossal rotating systems have taken shape in our seas.

One peculiarity of these rotating currents—ocean
[15] gyres—that has caused quite a stir in the scientific community as well as among environmentalists is that they draw in and trap material in their relatively calm centers. Captain Charles J. Moore inadvertently witnessed this effect in 1997 sailing from Hawaii to
[20] California. He later wrote: "I was confronted, as far as the eye could see, with the sight of plastic. It seemed unbelievable, but I never found a clear spot." He did not know it at the time, but he had stumbled across what would later be referred to as the Great Pacific
[25] Garbage Patch.

The size of the garbage patch can only be roughly estimated since small to miniscule plastic particles constitute the bulk of the waste's mass. Larger items are rare by comparison. This means that sweeping
[30] high-altitude surveys using satellites or airplanes lack efficacy and that localized sea-level water samples have to be used as a basis for extrapolation instead. This introduces a measure of uncertainty that has resulted in vastly diverging conjectures. For instance,
[35] owing to extreme temporal heterogeneity, samples tested for debris collected from the same coordinates only days apart can yield immensely different concentrations of plastic particles.

What adds to this is the virtually impossible task
[40] of pinpointing and quantifying the origins of this plastic flood. Since waste is constantly discharged into the oceans, the size of the patch changes accordingly. We do know the principal culprits are land-based littering and illegal dumping, and we do know that
[45] the relatively smaller contribution is generated on vessels and platforms. Developing an accurate model for these myriad, ever-shifting sources, though, and putting concrete numbers on them remains a formidable undertaking.

Passage 2

[50] Algalita, an organization founded and headed by Charles J. Moore, has been at the forefront of research on marine plastic pollution. Among other studies, it is actively striving to reliably quantify the amount of plastic pollution across our oceans.

[55] In order to get a grip on the sheer mass of plastic that has accumulated in our oceans worldwide, 24 oceanic expeditions have been mounted over the course of several years. Algalita's teams used neuston[1] nets to conduct hundreds of tow sample collections.
[60] Particles greater than 0.33 millimeters were collected in towed nets to be sorted, categorized, analyzed and recorded.

Another method employed were visual survey transects of large plastic debris. This essentially
[65] involved observers who would inspect the waters up to 20 meters off the side of the vessel over a set amount of time. By limiting the distance and the observation time, the teams could later determine the exact area observed. The observers' job was to assign
[70] the noted waste items to one of nine predetermined categories of common debris items. Since the debris could not be collected and weighed, this method at least enabled the researchers to establish estimates as to the mass of larger debris items within a given
[75] parcel of water.

While all of this empirical data is crucial, it does not take factors such as hydrodynamic forces or fragmentation of plastic debris over time into account. The researchers processed the data using
[80] adjustments that took into account ocean currents and wind stress to determine how many particles might be forced downward from the surface and thus escape sample collection. They also applied conservative estimates of fragmentation rates to
[85] determine the actual particle count of ocean waste. These and numerous other adjustments resulted in a model that gives us a pretty precise estimate on how much plastic is polluting our seas—upwards of 268 tons contained within more than 5 trillion particles.

---

[1] Neuston is an umbrella term for organisms or particles that float on the surface of or live right beneath the surface of water.

21

The author of Passage 1 indicates that ocean gyres are ultimately caused by

A) Earth's rotation.
B) calm spots in the sea.
C) cloud patterns.
D) curling wind systems.

22

The author indicates that the "altitude" in line 9 differs from the "altitude" in line 30 in that

A) the former implies much greater height than the latter.
B) the former is a natural effect while the latter is a man-made phenomenon.
C) the former is helpful in an endeavor while the latter is of little consequence.
D) the former represents a prerequisite while the latter presents an obstacle.

23

The author's use of the phrase "stumbled across" (line 23) mainly implies which of the following about Captain Moore?

A) He was not a very capable navigator.
B) His discovery was not intentional.
C) He was dumbfounded by the amount of debris.
D) His vessel had to navigate the garbage patch carefully.

24

As used in line 46 and line 87, "model" most nearly means

A) representation.
B) ideal.
C) miniature.
D) standard.

25

A commenter suggested that Algalita does not sufficiently comprehend the scope of research that quantifying ocean pollution dictates. Which of the following statements from Passage 2 most directly contradicts this claim?

A) Lines 50-52 ("Algalita . . . pollution")
B) Lines 52-54 ("Among . . . oceans")
C) Lines 55-58 ("In order . . . years")
D) Lines 71-75 ("Since . . . water")

26

The author of Passage 2 suggests that a disadvantage of visual survey transects is that

A) an exact count of observed items is impossible.
B) predetermined categories often differ from actual debris.
C) there is a limit to the observable area.
D) this method is inherently imprecise.

27

Passage 2 most strongly implies that the data compiled by way of neuston nets and visual survey transects alone

A) is not truly representative of ocean conditions.
B) yields surprisingly accurate results.
C) defies claims that this kind of effort is futile.
D) is only as good as the observers on the vessels.

28

Which choice provides the best evidence for the answer to the previous question?

A) Lines 64-67 ("This ... time")
B) Lines 76-79 ("While ... account")
C) Lines 79-81 ("The researchers ... stress")
D) Lines 87-89 ("a pretty ... particles")

29

Which statement best describes the relationship between the passages?

A) Passage 2 presents data that calls into question a central claim made in Passage 1.
B) Passage 2 challenges the significance of the phenomenon discussed in Passage 1.
C) Passage 2 offers concrete examples of a solution advocated in Passage 1.
D) Passage 2 places into historical context a development presented in Passage 1.

30

The authors of both passages would most likely agree with which of the following statements about plastic polluting our oceans?

A) Attempting concrete, scientific measurements on it is an impractical proposition.
B) We ought to allocate more resources on quantifying it and finding its various origins.
C) It has been shown that research in this field is viable given enough resources.
D) Attempts to gather reliable data on it involve a variety of challenges.

31

How would the author of Passage 2 most likely respond to the statement in lines 34-38, Passage 1?

A) Repeated measurements will result in reasonable average values.
B) Such phenomena have been successfully taken into account in other research.
C) This problem pales beside the complications caused by plastic fragmentation.
D) This effect is hardly significant compared to the slew of other data available.

Questions 32-42 are based on the following passage and supplementary material.

This passage discusses a scenario developed within game theory that sheds light on human interaction.

The prisoners' dilemma is an interesting paradox developed by the RAND-corporation in 1950. It assumes there are two guilty prisoners
Line being interrogated by the police. Each now has a
5 choice between remaining silent (cooperation) or confessing to their crimes and thereby implicating the other (competition). Regardless of what the other prisoner does, each can improve their own position by confessing: if one sings and the other
10 stays silent, harsher measures will be leveled against the recalcitrant prisoner. If one stays silent, the other will attain better treatment by confessing. According to game theory, therefore, noncooperation is the dominant strategy even though the outcome as a
15 group would be better if both stayed silent.

Of course, the prisoners themselves are not necessarily the item of interest here. The choices and perceived results which lead to a certain pattern of decision-making are significant because they help us
20 get behind certain kinds of behavior that groups of people exhibit in society. As Alistair Peyroux, a noted expert in the field remarked: "This scenario only becomes interesting when its mechanics are applied to other fields like business or social interaction."

25 One such field is competition in business. A simplistic but not unrealistic setup could be two telecommunications companies that, among them, dominate the national market. The best outcome for both might be achieved if both parties cooperated,
30 i.e., kept prices high. However, since the two companies are separate entities and pursue their own objectives, they have to assume the other party will lower prices and thus try to disrupt the first company's sales. After all, in a zero-sum game, my
35 rival's losses directly translate into my gains. In the end, both will likely compete preemptively and try to underbid their rival while still staying profitable.

This kind of me-first attitude also manifests itself on the road. There are countries where driving is an
40 outright frightening affair. I will never forget driving in France where there seems to be little regard for road regulations, and participants will cut in ahead of you without any consideration. Even though it would arguably be much nicer for everyone involved if each
45 participant were to heed rules and common courtesy, the perceived individual gain (arriving marginally faster) obviously outweighs that thought. After all— what good would it do if I were to heed the rules and everyone else would not? Whatever the others might
50 do, I stand to gain more if I do not cooperate.

A question that poses itself at this point is whether or not this egoism is necessarily a negative outcome for society. In the case of the prisoners, it is certainly bad for the prisoners as a group. But
55 to society in general, this self-centeredness ought to be welcome since the worst possible scenario for society would be mutual reticence. As for the telecommunications companies, the tendency to favor non-cooperative strategies also benefits society as a
60 whole because if these companies were to cooperate as a group, everyone else would pay higher prices for their services. When it comes to driving, though, the failure to be considerate is not advantageous to the majority.

65 The reason for these different evaluations lies in the alignment of interests of the group. Criminals and phone companies (this grouping is mere happenstance) have motivations that diverge from that of the public in general, be it eluding punishment
70 or achieving profits at the expense of the public. Drivers, on the other hand, are merely a temporary subset of society. Thus, neither cooperation nor competition is intrinsically preferable. It follows then that the next question should be how to foster
75 cooperation in conditions where such is warranted.

Table
Decision-result Matrix for Two Competing Juice Companies in Region D.

Decisions	Results
Both companies cooperate and do not advertise.	Both companies earn 10 currency units.
Only Juice Company A advertises that it is better than Juice Company B.	Company A earns 15 currency units, Company B earns 0.
Only Juice Company B advertises that it is better than Juice Company A.	Company B earns 15 currency units, Company A earns 0.
Both companies advertise the superiority of their own juice.	Both companies earn 5 currency units.

The companies can either compete (by advertising their product) or cooperate (by refraining from such activities).

Chart
Poll Regarding the Scenario Explained in the table

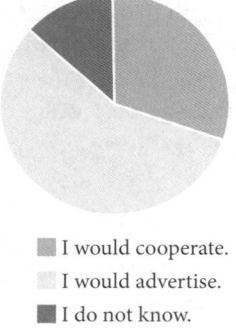

- I would cooperate.
- I would advertise.
- I do not know.

32

The primary purpose of the passage is to

A) analyze the intricacies of a paradoxical theory.
B) consider the consequences of a pervasive tendency.
C) rank human interactions according to their level of egoism.
D) encourage cooperative efforts in various situations.

33

As used in line 10, "leveled" most nearly means

A) surfaced.
B) razed.
C) directed.
D) straightened.

34

The passage mostly suggests which of the following about the prisoners' dilemma?

A) Its application to other fields has made it insignificant.
B) Not all expert opinions are aligned regarding the prisoners' dilemma.
C) The scope of the prisoners' dilemma transcends its origin.
D) It has proven that competition will always be detrimental to society.

35

Which choice provides the best evidence for the answer to the previous question?

A) Lines 12-15 ("According . . . silent")
B) Lines 16-17 ("Of course . . . here")
C) Lines 30-34 ("However . . . sales")
D) Lines 51-53 ("A question . . . society")

CONTINUE

36

According to the passage, the author "will never forget driving in France" (lines 40-41) because

A) traffic laws are hardly observed by drivers.
B) he considers it a phenomenal experience.
C) horrible incidents occurred when he did.
D) the lack of consideration upset the author.

37

What does the author imply about the "nicer" outcome mentioned in lines 43-45?

A) It results in order and courtesy among traffic participants.
B) It is an effective way to ward off egoistical tendencies in drivers.
C) Countries with strictly enforced regulations achieve it more reliably.
D) Desirable though it might be, it is superseded by another factor.

38

By using the word "marginally" in line 46, the author mainly

A) questions the validity of a judgment.
B) raises the exactitude of a statement.
C) emphasizes the impact of a decision.
D) mocks people's failure to cooperate.

39

What ultimately differentiates the examples in paragraph 3 and paragraph 4?

A) The former will likely result in cooperation while the latter will likely end in competition.
B) While the former includes a dilemma, the latter deals with a mundane, choice-free scenario.
C) The former focuses only on the drawbacks of cooperation while the latter details its advantages.
D) Only in the former instance is non-competition undesirable from the viewpoint of the public.

40

The passage indicates that the "prisoners" (line 53) and the "telecommunications companies" (line 58) are similar in that

A) their respective interests do not align with that of people outside the group.
B) both groups have motivations that absolutely preclude cooperation.
C) cooperation among themselves would be advantageous to society in general.
D) both scenarios were developed by RAND-corporation psychologists.

41

Taken together, the table and the chart suggest that the majority of those who participated in the poll

A) prioritize optimal results for the company over optimal results for both companies.
B) would consider the juice company scenario one where the companies' interests run counter to the rest of society.
C) have realized that cooperating benefits the group as a whole more than competition.
D) are risk-friendly since their choice allows for the highest and lowest possible earnings depending on the competition.

42

Is the data in the table an exact match to the author's proposed telecommunications example?

A) Yes, because both feature two companies that dominate their field of business.
B) Yes, because the numbers in Table 1 match the scenario's description of a zero-sum game.
C) No, because the different fields of business change whether cooperation or competition is preferable.
D) No, because the numbers in Table 1 do not match the scenario's description of a zero-sum game.

Questions 43-52 are based on the following passage and supplementary material.

This passage is adapted from Vignoli et al., "Better in the dark: two Mediterranean amphibians synchronize reproduction with moonlit nights." ©2013. The passage describes a study involving two species of anurans[1], H. intermedia and R. dalmatina.

 The interplay of moonlight and animals' nocturnal behavior, especially for prey, is not a zero-one phenomenon (either there is activity
Line or there is none), but a continuum of states that
 5 correspond to different levels of activity, involving a trade-off between activity and safety. When it comes to reproduction, animals often undergo increased predation risk due to increased conspicuousness to predators. As for amphibians, the risk of predation
 10 varies depending on time and space, influencing the various phases of reproduction (site approach, mate search) and actors involved (courting males, other competing males) in a number of ways. Therefore, individual animals are bound to adjust their
 15 reproductive behavior patterns in a way that mitigates predation risk.
 For amphibians, the chance of reproduction and the risk of predation while spawning are two important factors that interact to determine both
 20 spatial and temporal patterns. That is, to maximize reproductive success, amphibians have to balance their decisions on when, where, and how to reproduce against safety considerations. We speculate that an anti-predatory strategy could be among the factors
 25 underlying the seeming correlation between moonless nights and increased activity in anurans. Indeed, *H. intermedia* is intensely hunted by grass snakes, a mainly visually oriented predator, in the observed area during nighttime. The same is not true for *R.*
 30 *dalmatina*, which spawns before the onset of grass snakes' period of foraging activity in late March. However, both species are also targeted by nocturnal birds of prey during the mating period.
 Moreover, moon-related (lunar phobic) activity
 35 patterns similar to those observed in this study have been described for other amphibians as well as for several nocturnal animals. In all these studies, the observed moonlight avoidance by animals has been traced to the increased risk of predation by visually
 40 oriented hunters when exposed in bright moonlight. An experimental study revealed a significant effect of moonlight on the microhabitat use by a visually oriented predator (a snake in this case). This adaptation was likely a reflection of both anti-
 45 predatory strategy on the snake's part and predation avoidance by its prey.
 In general, however, moon luminosity plays less of a role in the activities of nocturnal or cathemeral[2] animals because most of them possess adapted eye
 50 structures enhancing vision in low light. Anurans are usually cathemeral or strictly nocturnal and rely on their tapetum lucidum[3] (most of them display eye-shine) to deal with the darkness. Intraspecific (intersexual) communication and short distance
 55 orientation towards their breeding sites relies mainly on the animals' acoustic and olfactory senses. Hence, apart from the aforementioned anti-predatory strategy, it is possible that visual constraints only marginally regulate frogs' nocturnal reproductive
 60 activities. However, visual stimuli over short distances are important during nighttime for mate selection in *Hyla arborea*, a species which is genetically closely related to *H. intermedia*.
 To our knowledge, the only other study exploring
 65 the effects of the lunar cycle on the reproductive activities of temperate anurans was conducted by Grant et al. in 2009. Although these authors found that various aspects of anuran reproductive phenology were intensified around the full moon
 70 phase, we found in our own two study species indications that quite the contrary is true. We speculate that the observed differences may be due to (i) species-specific effects and/or (ii) a suite of methodological issues, including types of descriptors
 75 used and interpretation of statistical analyses.
 Thus, our study shows discrepancies with an earlier study on species from similar climates and latitudes. This suggests that caution is due when trying to draw general conclusions about the
 80 biological response of amphibian populations to different phases of the moon. Clearly, further studies are still needed to solve this puzzling issue.

[1] Anurans comprise the class of amphibian animals that includes frogs and toads.

[2] an activity pattern which is neither strictly nocturnal nor diurnal, but irregularly active according to prevailing circumstances

[3] an adaptation of the eye which improves the night vision of its bearer

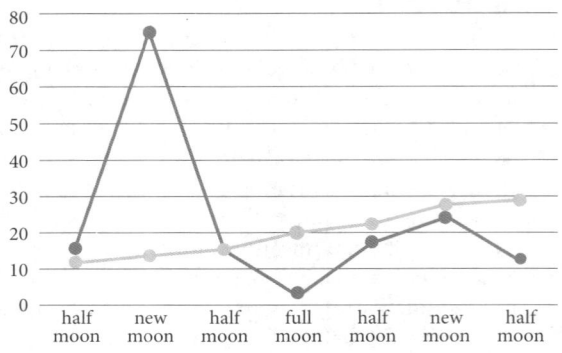

Reproductive Behavior of Frog Species A

— deposited egg clutches
— water temperature

The numbers on the y-axis represent a simple count for egg clutches and degrees Celsius for the water temperature.

43

The main purpose of the passage is to

A) explain the methods scientists use when studying anurans.
B) describe how scientists found the definitive answer to a problem.
C) explain the reasons that might underlie a certain correlation.
D) describe evidence linking reproductive behavior to water temperature.

44

As used in line 40, "oriented" most nearly means

A) located.
B) introduced.
C) familiarized.
D) adjusted.

45

What function does the fourth paragraph (lines 47-63) serve in the passage as a whole?

A) It acknowledges the possibility that the risk of predation might not be the only reason why anurans avoid moonlight.
B) It casts doubt on the studies mentioned in the third paragraph by presenting contrary evidence.
C) It supports the notion that moonlight avoidance might be due to predation since breeding activities do not depend on sight.
D) It gives an overview of the various contradictory results that need to be resolved before an answer can be found.

46

In context, the sentence in lines 60-63 ("However . . . *intermedia*") is best described as

A) a qualification.
B) an illustration.
C) a detailed explanation.
D) a definition.

47

The sentence in lines 71-75 ("We speculate . . . analyses") implies which of the following?

A) The methods the authors used differ from those that Grant used.
B) The results of a study can change depending on procedure and perspective.
C) The traits inherent to the observed species have resulted in differences.
D) Different interpretations necessarily arise when two studies are conducted independently.

48

A scientist claims that the phases of the moon do not play any role in the reproductive activities of anurans. Which choice contradicts that scientist's claim?

A) Lines 13-16 ("Therefore . . . risk")
B) Lines 23-26 ("We speculate . . . anurans")
C) Lines 47-50 ("In general . . . light")
D) Lines 67-71 ("Although . . . true")

49

The passage suggests that the authors' study of anurans

A) has overturned the findings of their predecessors.
B) did not result in generally applicable results.
C) has shed light on how moonlight affects snakes.
D) shows that reproductive urges outweigh safety considerations.

50

Which choice provides the best evidence for the answer to the previous question?

A) Lines 20-23 ("That is . . . considerations")
B) Lines 41-46 ("An . . . prey")
C) Lines 67-71 ("Although . . . true")
D) Lines 78-82 ("This suggests . . . issue")

51

The data in the chart provides most direct support for which idea in the passage?

A) Not every new moon will result in the same levels of increased activity.
B) Less light reduces the risk of predation and allows for reproductive activities.
C) Reproductive activities do not always rely on an animal's visual senses.
D) Along with moonlight, water temperature plays a part in reproductive activities.

52

What statement is best supported by the data in the chart?

A) The lower the water temperature, the more eggs are deposited.
B) Frogs reproduce the least during full moon in order to avoid risks.
C) Frogs prefer a temperature below 20° Celsius for reproduction.
D) Reproduction benefits from dark nights and higher temperatures.

STOP

Do not move on to the next section if you finish early.

You may review your answers in this section only.

Answer Keys & Performance Breakdown

#	Ans	Type	#	Ans	Type	#	Ans	Type
1	(B)	Summary	19	(C)	Local	37	(D)	Local
2	(C)	Organization	20	(C)	Local	38	(A)	Local
3	(C)	Vocabulary	21	(A)	Local	39	(D)	Synthesize
4	(A)	Summary	22	(D)	Synthesize	40	(A)	Synthesize
5	(D)	Local	23	(B)	Style	41	(A)	Graph
6	(C)	Evidence	24	(A)	Vocabulary	42	(D)	Graph
7	(C)	Context	25	(C)	Evidence	43	(C)	Summary
8	(C)	Local	26	(D)	Local	44	(D)	Vocabulary
9	(C)	Local	27	(A)	Local	45	(C)	Context
10	(A)	Local	28	(B)	Evidence	46	(A)	Context
11	(D)	Stance	29	(A)	Synthesize	47	(B)	Local
12	(C)	Local	30	(D)	Synthesize	48	(D)	Evidence
13	(B)	Local	31	(B)	Synthesize	49	(B)	Local
14	(A)	Local	32	(B)	Summary	50	(D)	Evidence
15	(C)	Local	33	(C)	Vocabulary	51	(B)	Graph
16	(A)	Local	34	(C)	Context	52	(C)	Graph
17	(B)	Local	35	(B)	Evidence			
18	(A)	Vocabulary	36	(A)	Local			

■ Write down the number of correct answers for each question type.

Question Types	Number of Correct Answers
Local	/ 20
Style	/ 1
Vocabulary	/ 5
Evidence	/ 6
Context	/ 4
Organization	/ 1
Summary	/ 4
Stance	/ 1
Synthesize	/ 6
Graph	/ 4
Total	**/ 52**

Answer Explanations

Questions 1-10

1. (B) *Summary*

The author mentions that visiting church, though boring, is a significant part of her childhood memories and that unexpectedly, part of her misses going back there (paragraph 1). She remembers the first time she avoided going to church and how happy she was, but that she now, without knowing it, ends up in front of churches from time to time (paragraph 2). She then speculates that something deep within her subconscious is urging her to go even though she cannot quite grasp what that something is (paragraphs 3-4).

B is the best choice.

A is incorrect because the passage does not attempt to solve a puzzle or find an answer. It merely describes a puzzling phenomenon. C is incorrect because criticizing church visits is not the focus. D is incorrect because a personal experience is described. "Commonplace" is not supported.

2. (C) *Organization*

C is the best choice. As can be seen from the explanation for question 1, "facts and certainty" refers to the memories in paragraphs 1-2 while "speculation and uncertainty" refers to the thoughts in paragraphs 3-4. (For a short summary, see explanation for question 1.)

A is incorrect because the last two paragraphs do not focus on or imply regret. B is incorrect because "work life" is not the focus of the latter part. D is incorrect because neither "hopes" (only happiness at staying home) nor "dashed dreams" is mentioned.

3. (C) *Vocabulary*

C is the best choice because in the sentence, a feeling has "branded" itself into memory which means to "impress."

A is incorrect because it means to "describe" or "designate." B is incorrect because it means "set a mark of disgrace upon." D is incorrect because it means "bring shame upon" or "defame."

4. (A) *Summary*

Since the main concern for the author is that she unwittingly goes to churches for some deep-seated reason, and line 18 indicates that it is her feet that lead her there, A is the best choice.

B is incorrect because "guilty conscience" is not mentioned. (She does not surmise that she goes to church because she feels guilty.) C is incorrect because the "feet" stands for that which *leads* the author *to* church. The feet themselves are not characterized as a distraction. D is incorrect because the nagging question is why she goes to church, and the feet provide no answer.

5. (D) *Local*

D is the best choice because church is likened to the insides of a whale (using the phrases "bone-shaded cetacean colossus" and "stone ribs").

A is incorrect because the specified lines do not indicate terror or fear. B is incorrect because the specified lines do not mention boredom. C is incorrect because the specified lines do not mention deceased family members.

6. (C) *Evidence*

C is the best choice because the lines describe the church building as a "rock whale" that "disgorges its mass of parishioners" (living organism).

A, B, and D are incorrect because none of them support that the author associates a building with a living organism.

7. (C) *Context*

The lines describe how joyful the author felt when she did not go to church for the first time. After the specified lines, the author mentions that in contrast, she now finds herself standing in front of church sometimes for some unknown reason.

C is the best choice because the specified lines (joy at not going to church) make the fact that she now goes to church more incomprehensible.

A is incorrect because "ubiquitous" means "pervasive." B is incorrect because no current joy (the author is puzzled) is described. D is incorrect because it is the opposite. It adds confusion instead of offering a reason.

Answer Explanations

8. (C)   Local

"Oblivious" implies that she does not know while "somnambulation" implies sleepwalking, or going somewhere without being conscious of it.

C is the best choice.

A is incorrect because the phrase does not imply excitement. B is incorrect because the phrase does not refer to the effect of walking but to the mode of walking itself. D is incorrect because the phrase does not imply "usually," nor does it specify a time of day.

9. (C)   Local

C is the best choice because this "siren" refers to something that called out to the author (the meaning of siren) in the previous paragraph. (Check lines 40-43.) Thus, the siren is elusive and not well-known which supports "puzzling feeling."

A is incorrect because the siren does not refer to a real person. (Also, no sister is mentioned in context.) B is incorrect because it is too literal. An aural signal is a sound, but the siren is a subconscious feeling. D is incorrect because "alarming" means "causing fear" or "distressing" which is not suggested in context.

10. (A)   Local

A is the best choice because the specified lines state how the author can "almost sense her" and "almost hear her," but she is "never quite within reach."

B is incorrect because it means "achievement" or "fulfillment." C is incorrect because it means "regret" or "remorse." D is incorrect because it means "profound respect."

Questions 11-20

11. (D)   Stance

Marshall first states that Europe cannot pay for basic commodities, and that without help, she will deteriorate. He emphasizes that this will have consequences for the U.S. economy as well, and that assisting Europe is the logical option (paragraphs 1-3). He then stresses that Europeans need to agree on their requirements and the roles they will play before the U.S. can lend further aid (paragraph 4). Finally, he states that it is crucial that the public understands the problem and the remedies if any of this planned aid is to succeed.

D is the best choice since he gives reasons why the U.S. ought to do their best to assist Europe. (Giving financial assistance is the possibly unwelcome part.)

A is incorrect because the speech focuses on a decision that has yet to be made (giving assistance), not the effects of a decision. B is incorrect because Marshall seeks to avoid a dire future. C is incorrect because Marshall does not make demands but seeks consensus.

12. (C)   Local

C is the best choice because the sentence states they must be able and willing to exchange products for currencies, "the continuing value of which is not open to question," or in other words, currencies, "the continuing value of which is guaranteed." This implies they might not want to trade if money might lose in value.

A is incorrect because product value is not mentioned. B is incorrect because "barter trade" is not mentioned. D is incorrect because raising product prices is not suggested.

13. (B)   Local

B is the best choice because lines 17-19 mention that the "desperation of the people concerned" (crisis in Europe) will obviously have "consequences to the economy of the United States."

A is incorrect because "always" is not supported. Also, "logical" refers to practical reasons. C is incorrect because averting drawbacks and profiting are not the same. Also, no "united Europe" is mentioned in context. D is incorrect because this is not mentioned in context or as a reason.

14. (A)   Local

A is the best choice because the policy is directed "against hunger, poverty, desperation and chaos." ("Humanitarian" means relating to measures that improve the happiness or welfare of people.)

B is incorrect because it means "continuing." C is incorrect because it means "free of selfish intentions." D is incorrect because it means "constant" or "fixed."

15. (C)   Local

C is the best choice because a "palliative" refers to something that soothes or relieves without curing. In the sentence, "mere palliative" is contrasted to "cure" while the context discusses aid for Europe.

A is incorrect because it means a real "cure." B is incorrect because no such associations are suggested. D is incorrect because "currencies" are not mentioned in context.

16. (A) Local

A is the best choice because he states that groups with certain motivations "will encounter the opposition of the United States" (lines 40-41).

B is incorrect because he does not repeat himself. C is incorrect because no blame is placed. D is incorrect because no meaning is clarified by way of explanation.

17. (B) Local

B is the best choice because in lines 42-60, Marshall states that without agreement among Europeans as to their requirements and the parts they will play, U.S. efforts to alleviate the situation cannot proceed much further. Also, he states that a unilaterally drawn up plan by the U.S. would be "neither fitting nor efficacious" (lines 50-53).

A is incorrect because it stipulates failure on the part of Europe. (Only if Europe fails at something will U.S. assistance be effective.) C is incorrect because funding contributions are not compared. D is incorrect because unanimous support is not mentioned as a requirement (lines 58-60).

18. (A) Vocabulary

A is the best choice because the sentence mentions that responsibilities are "placed" upon (or assigned to) the U.S.

B is incorrect because it means to "find" or "station." C is incorrect because it means to "put in order" or to "make plans." D is incorrect because it means to "identify" or "understand."

19. (C) Local

C is the best choice because in lines 72-73, Marshall mentions he did not voluntarily enter into "technical discussions." However, he thinks it is important that people reach some general understanding instead of reacting from a passion or prejudice or emotion. Thus, he believes technical explanations are necessary for people to "reach some general understanding."

A, B, and D are incorrect because none of them are mentioned as decisive for this outcome.

20. (C) Local

The specified lines state that it is almost impossible to reach clear understanding of a remote situation through reading, listening, or even looking at photographs or movies.

C is the best choice because it directly undermines the statement.

A, B, and D are incorrect because none of them undermine the given statement.

Questions 21-31

21. (A) Local

A is the best choice because the question asks for the "ultimate" reason. The first cause mentioned in the passage is the rotation of our planet. (This causes curls and spirals in wind systems which in turn influence ocean currents. Thus, circular ocean currents are created.)

B, C, and D are incorrect because none of them identify the ultimate cause.

22. (D) Synthesize

The former "altitude" is mentioned as necessary for observing the Coriolis effect. The latter is mentioned as part of a method that is inefficient. (Since plastic particles are tiny, they cannot be picked out from high altitudes.)

D is the best choice.

A is incorrect because no such comparison is possible based on the information in the passage. B is incorrect because "altitude" itself cannot be said to be a man-made phenomenon. C is incorrect because "little consequence" does not describe "obstacle."

23. (B) Style

The phrase means to "meet with accidentally or unexpectedly."

B is the best choice.

A is incorrect because the phrase does not refer to the way Captain Moore was steering the ship but rather a discovery. C is incorrect because the phrase does not describe the reaction to the debris he found. D is incorrect because the phrase does not suggest careful charting of a course.

Answer Explanations

24. (A) *Vocabulary*

In line 46, the sentence mentions developing an accurate "model" for numerous sources and quantifying them. In lines 86-88, the sentence mentions "estimate" and "adjustments" that resulted in a model that gives us a pretty precise estimate of plastic in our seas.

A is the best choice.

B is incorrect because it means a "goal" or "standard." C is incorrect because it describes a small, physical representation of something. D is incorrect because it means "principle" or "ideal."

25. (C) *Evidence*

C is the best choice because the lines show that Algalita targeted worldwide pollution (large scope) and mounted 24 expeditions over several years (implies a large effort).

A, B, and D are incorrect because none of them support that Algalita understands the massive scope that research on ocean pollution involves.

26. (D) *Local*

D is the best choice because the mass of sighted debris items, since they are not collected, can only be estimated (lines 71-75).

A is incorrect because no such restriction is mentioned for counting. B is incorrect because this is not implied about the categories. C is incorrect. The limited area is not mentioned as the result of an inability to observe more, but rather as a way to calculate the measured area.

27. (A) *Local*

A is the best choice because of lines 76-79 (see next question).

B is incorrect because Passage 2 states that the specified data needs to be adjusted. C is incorrect because no such position is suggested in Passage 2. In addition, this data "alone" is not yet accurate, so the author of Passage 2 would not use it as a basis for defying a claim. D is incorrect because Passage 2 does not portray the observers as the weak link of the process.

28. (B) *Evidence*

B is the best choice because the lines state that this "empirical data" (neuston nets and visual survey transects) does not take certain factors into account.

A and D are incorrect because they do not support that the data mentioned in question 27 is not truly representative of ocean conditions. C is incorrect. Even though it mentions adjusting data to take ocean currents and wind stress into account, it does not (unlike B) directly mention that data does not take certain factors into account.

29. (A) *Synthesize*

Passage 1 explains how ocean gyres come into being before mentioning that these gyres trap large amounts of plastic waste. It states that estimating the size of the garbage patch is a very difficult task. Passage 2 introduces Algalita and mentions the various efforts this company underwent in order to arrive at rather precise measurements of the amount of plastic in the world's oceans.

A is the best choice.

B is incorrect because Passage 2 does not imply that garbage patches are insignificant. C is incorrect because Passage 1 does not advocate a solution. D is incorrect because no historical relationships to other events are mentioned.

30. (D) *Synthesize*

D is the best choice. (For a short summary of the passages, see explanation for question 29.)

A is incorrect because Passage 2 would disagree. B is incorrect because allocation of more resources is advocated in neither passage. C is incorrect because only Passage 2 would agree.

31. (B) *Synthesize*

The specified lines state that water samples from the same location can yield immensely different results. (For a short summary of the passages, see explanation for question 29.)

B is the best choice because paragraph 4, Passage 2 mentions that researchers took hydrodynamic forces into account and arrived at a pretty precise estimate.

A is incorrect because "repeated measurements" is not brought up in Passage 2. C is incorrect because it does not fit the tone for Passage 2, and no such comparison is made in Passage 2. D is incorrect because Passage 2 does not mention glossing over inaccuracies.

Questions 32-42

32. (B) — Summary

The passage discusses the "prisoners' dilemma," a theoretical scenario that looks into cooperation and competition. The passage states that this scenario can be applied to many different fields of human interaction, and it basically shows that even if the best group outcome involves cooperation, individuals choose competition because they prioritize individual gain. Then, the passage explores whether this tendency is good or bad for society.

B is the best choice.

A is incorrect because the intricacies of the theory are not the focus. Rather, its application and consequences are the focus. C is incorrect because no ranking, or putting into order, takes place. D is incorrect because the passage does not encourage, it merely observes.

33. (C) — Vocabulary

C is the best choice because the sentence states that harsh measures (punishment) will be "leveled" against a prisoner.

A is incorrect because it means "come to the top" or "come to the surface." B is incorrect because it means "flatten" or "wipe out." D is incorrect because it means "put in neat order."

34. (C) — Context

Peyroux emphasizes that the prisoners' dilemma is only interesting when applied to other fields like business or social interaction. Before this paragraph, the prisoners' dilemma is explained in terms of prisoners. After this paragraph, other scenarios such as phone companies and driving are discussed.

C is the best choice because of lines 16-17 (see next question).

A is incorrect because the opposite is stated in lines 22-24. B is incorrect because the passage gives no information regarding the alignment of expert opinions (only one expert is cited). D is incorrect because the passage actually states that sometimes, society can benefit from competition.

35. (B) — Evidence

B is the best choice because the lines state that "the prisoners themselves are not necessarily the item of interest," which means that other cases are of interest.

A, C, and D are incorrect because none of them show that the prisoners' dilemma transcends the discussion of prisoners.

36. (A) — Local

A is the best choice because the same sentence states that there is "little regard for road regulations, and participants will cut in ahead of you without any consideration."

B is incorrect because "phenomenal" implies an "astounding" (greatly positive) experience. C is incorrect because "horrible" is too negative. D is incorrect because the passage makes no statement about his emotional state at the time.

37. (D) — Local

D is the best choice because the sentence states "the perceived individual gain obviously outweighs (supersedes) that thought (the nicer outcome)."

A is incorrect because the nicer outcome does not come to pass. B is incorrect because the nicer outcome does not actually come to pass. C is incorrect because the passage does not imply that it is achieved. No other countries are mentioned in context.

38. (A) — Local

A is the best choice because "marginally" implies that the gain (faster) is very small. This implies that not obeying traffic rules and not heeding courtesy are done for a minimal gain.

B is incorrect because "marginally" is not primarily used to add exactitude. Also, "marginally" is not an exact measurement. C is incorrect because "marginally" emphasizes the lack of impact. D is incorrect because "mocks" is not supported.

39. (D) — Synthesize

Paragraph 3 discusses telecommunications companies that undercut each other's prices to compete. Paragraph 4 discusses driving competitively.

D is the best choice because the public profits from lower telecom prices (competition is desirable), but it does not profit from egoistical driving (non-competition is desirable).

A is incorrect because the statement about cooperation is not supported. B is incorrect because driving also involves a choice. C is incorrect because advantages of cooperation are mentioned in the

Answer Explanations

former paragraph (lines 28-30).

40. (A) *Synthesize*

A is the best choice because a good outcome for each group would be negative for society.

B is incorrect because "absolutely preclude" is not supported. C is incorrect because the opposite is correct. D is incorrect because this was only mentioned in connection with prisoners.

41. (A) *Graph*

A is the best choice because the majority of those who participated in the poll chose "I would advertise." This means they competed (prioritized their own company over the group).

B is incorrect. The data in the table and the chart does not indicate how the participants viewed the scenario. C is incorrect because this implies they would choose cooperation, and those who chose cooperation do not constitute the majority. D is incorrect because their choice does not reflect the highest and lowest earnings (15 or 5 depending on the competition).

42. (D) *Graph*

D is the best choice because as described in the passage, zero-sum game means if the opposite gains 1 point, I lose that 1 point. That means the total number of points has to be constant regardless of the choices made. The juice company scenario has 20 points total for total cooperation, 15 points total for partial cooperation, and 10 points total for total competition.

A is incorrect because it is not clear that the two juice companies dominate the field of juice business. B is incorrect since D is correct. (B and D are mutually exclusive.) C is incorrect because both adhere to the prisoners' dilemma. (Competition favors individual gain even if cooperation has a higher group benefit.)

Questions 43-52

43. (C) *Summary*

The passage states that moonlight has an effect on the reproductive behavior of anurans (amphibious animals such as toads and frogs). It is speculated that increased activity on moonless nights is an anti-predation strategy. The passage then explains that visually oriented predators hunt anurans, and that other animals also change their behavior according to moonlight conditions because of predators. Finally, the passage states that for anurans, other activities do not really depend on visibility (which further supports the speculation that anurans are more active on moonless nights due to predators, and not for other reasons).

C is the best choice.

A is incorrect because the passage does not focus on explaining research methods. B is incorrect because no certain results are mentioned, and other studies with very different results are also brought up. D is incorrect because the passage does not mention water temperature.

44. (D) *Vocabulary*

D is the best choice because the sentence mentions higher risk by visually "oriented" hunters in bright moonlight. The hunters in question therefore rely on their visual senses. Thus, "adjusted" as in "adapted" is correct.

A is incorrect because it means "situated" or "placed." B is incorrect because it means "made acquainted" or "familiar with." C is incorrect because it means "made acquainted" or "become knowledgeable about."

45. (C) *Context*

C is the best choice. The previous paragraph mentions studies that trace moonlight avoidance to predator avoidance. The fourth paragraph then states that generally, moon luminosity does not really impact activities, especially reproductive activities. Therefore, the latter paragraph reinforces the notion that moonlight only plays a role because its absence represents greater safety from predators.

A is incorrect because even though an exception is mentioned in lines 60-63, the fourth paragraph states that in general, moonlight has little effect on the activities of animals. B is incorrect because the fourth paragraph does not rebut the third paragraph. D is incorrect because mention of one exception (lines 60-63) does not support "various contradictory results that need to be resolved." (No such stipulation is mentioned.)

46. (A) *Context*

A is the best choice because the species mentioned in the specified lines represents an exception to the general rule mentioned within the paragraph. Therefore, "qualification" is correct.

B is incorrect because the specified lines do not contain an example illustrating their context. C is incorrect because the specified lines do not offer an explanation for their context. D is incorrect because the specified lines do not serve to furnish a definition for a term that was mentioned in context.

47. (B) — Local

B is the best choice because the specified lines state that there were observed differences that might have been due to "methodological issues" (procedure) which could include interpretation of analyses (perspective).

A and C are incorrect because the authors merely speculate here without being certain. D is incorrect because "necessarily" (which implies that this always happens) is not supported.

48. (D) — Evidene

D is the best choice because the lines state that some authors found that "various aspects of anuran reproductive phenology were intensified around the full moon phase." The authors, on the other hand, found "quite the contrary is true." In both cases, the moon plays a role in reproductive activities.

A, B, and C are incorrect because none of them show that the moon plays a role in reproductive activities of anurans.

49. (B) — Local

B is the best choice because of lines 78-82 (see next question).

A is incorrect because the passage only mentions that the authors' study has resulted in different findings compared to other studies. It does not mention that results were overturned. C is incorrect because the authors did not study snakes. D is incorrect because the passage does not state that animals forgo safety in order to reproduce.

50. (D) — Evidence

D is the best choice because the lines state that "caution is due when trying to draw general conclusions about the biological response of amphibian populations to different phases of the moon."

A, B, and C are incorrect because none of them show that the authors' study of anurans did not result in generally applicable results.

51. (B) — Graph

B is the best choice because reproductive behavior (as indicated by the number of deposited egg clutches) increases with decreasing light and vice versa.

A is incorrect because this idea did not appear in the passage. C is incorrect because the chart has no data on visual senses. D is incorrect because water temperature was not mentioned in the passage.

52. (C) — Graph

C is the best choice. The chart includes two "half moon—new moon—half moon" intervals. The interval on the left (water temperature below 20°) has a much higher peak egg count than the interval on the right (water temperature above 20°).

A is incorrect because the statement disregards the phases of the moon. For example, the egg decreases after the second "new moon" even though the water temperature increases. B is incorrect because no such motivation is represented in the chart. D is incorrect because the chart shows fewer eggs for higher water temperatures during similar moon phases.

SAT.Hackers.ac

Hackers New SAT Reading: 10 Practice Tests

TEST 7

Answer Keys & Performance Breakdown
Answer Explanations

Reading Test

65 MINUTES, 52 QUESTIONS

Mark your answers to the questions in Section 1 in the answer sheet provided.

DIRECTIONS

For each of the passages below, there are 10 or 11 questions. Choose the best answer for each of the questions after you have finished reading the passage. The answers to the questions should be based on the information that is stated or implied in the text and any associated graphics.

Questions 1-10 are based on the following passage.

This passage is adapted from a novel. The narrator, Raul, is visiting his hometown, the fictional city of Santiago.

"So it's been what—20 years since last time?" Alex's forehead creased up like it always did when he was trying to think.

Line
5   "Something like that. Gotta tell you though, I don't recognize a thing."

Alex proudly pointed out the broad, uniformly tiled pedestrian walkways, the steel-and-glass office buildings and the brand-new shopping center.

"Yeah, it's a real city now. Remember the dirt
10 roads? And all them . . . souvenir shops and folk art shops?" He looked around again. "It's all been cleaned up," he said with a smile.

"Yeah," I said. But I remembered.

I remembered the smell of the old Santiago. Those
15 *dirt roads used to be lined with food stands, bursting with the fragrances of roasting corn and tortillas which would mix with that of brightly hued fruit stands. The smell of ripe and sweet pineapples and mango mingled with the sounds of playing children, begging children*
20 *and stray dogs.*

And woven into that heartbeat, the ever-present tourists picking through multicolored blankets and cheap shoes.

I remembered cooling off amid the bustle with Celia
25 *at—what was the name of that café again? I remembered the off-white plastic tables on that colorful, tiled courtyard. Wasn't that around the time of her birthday?*

Alex must have said something because he was looking at me.

30   "Huh?"

He laughed. "Anyway, you don't look too excited. Yeah . . . I know it's not like LA."

I shook my head. "No, that's not it. Not at all. I gotta say, it's much cleaner than the part of town
35 I live in. I just kinda miss the dirt. I don't know . . . I sorta miss all the kitsch and . . . the dogs. And . . . you know? The way it used to be."

"You're crazy, Raul. Why would you ever wanna go back to that?"

40   "Because . . . how can I say it? Because the noise and dirt . . . all the clutter . . . it just felt right. Like home, really."

I looked around the modern buildings, neat walkways and the shiny shop signs.

45   *I looked around the small backstreets. Celia's birthday was coming up, and I didn't have anything for her yet, so I had wandered off into the backstreets, away from the hubbub. I looked into a tiny store full of carved and painted art representing animals and saints.*
50 *As I stepped closer to inspect the jewelry laid out amid random baubles and trinkets, I espied another shop entrance that somehow spoke to me.*

The shop was dark, and once my eyes had adjusted, I made out shelves lined with dusty bottles and flacons[1],
55 *gleaming under their coat of neglect. Old wax and furniture floated in the air, spices and flowers, and perfumes sprayed into the air by testers lingered heavily. This store was filled with old European perfumes, some of which had been discontinued.*

60   *Excitement welled up inside of me, and I approached the kid who was minding the place.*

"You know that perfume I got Celia?"
"You mean, before she ran away?" Alex grinned

at me.

"Yeah yeah. Before she ran away. Do you remember though?"

"Maybe. Why?"

"You know . . . that store's gone. And . . . they don't even make that perfume anymore."

"We have much better stores now. It's because you haven't seen them yet. Come on, I'll show you." He started walking.

"I suppose," I gave in and followed him inside.

[1] vials or bottles

1

The passage primarily contrasts

A) a city's metropolitan appeal to another city's earlier dinginess.
B) Raul's vivid recollections to his impotence at expressing them.
C) Alex's boastful eloquence to Raul's impassive apathy.
D) Raul's naïve hopes in the past to his present, hard-boiled realism.

2

What does Alex mostly want to convey to Raul?

A) Raul has hardly changed at all since they last met.
B) Unlike Raul, he misses the way Santiago used to be.
C) Raul should move back from LA to Santiago.
D) He is proud of the way Santiago has changed.

3

Which choice provides the best evidence for the answer to the previous question?

A) Lines 1-3 ("So it's . . . think")
B) Lines 9-12 ("Yeah . . . up")
C) Lines 24-27 ("I remembered . . . birthday")
D) Lines 31-33 ("He laughed . . . at all")

4

As used in line 52, "spoke to" most nearly means

A) uttered.
B) enticed.
C) seemed familiar.
D) unhinged.

5

The shop's interior, as presented in lines 53-57, can most aptly be described as

A) dark and desolate.
B) fragrant and dilapidated.
C) dim and rich.
D) rapt and alluring.

6

In context, it can be inferred that Raul felt excitement welling up inside of him (line 60) because

A) all of the perfumes in the store were rare.
B) the shopkeeper was not present.
C) the scents in the air made him feel lightheaded.
D) he had found what he was looking for.

7

By asking "Do you remember though?" (lines 65-66), Raul mainly

A) reprimands Alex for touching on a painful chapter of his past.
B) guides the conversation back towards the point he originally wanted to make.
C) acknowledges an embarrassing episode of his past that Alex brought up.
D) questions Alex's ability to correctly remember what happened long ago.

CONTINUE

8

The passage suggests that Raul gives in (line 73) because

A) he cannot make himself understood to Alex.
B) he realizes Alex's point of view is correct.
C) he wants to look for a better gift for Celia.
D) the new store reminds him of old Santiago.

9

The passage indicates that Raul's memories of the old Santiago are colored by

A) the unpleasant reminder of being left by his former girlfriend.
B) the distortions inherent in remembering events in the distant past.
C) wistfulness born of the awareness that he cannot return to those times.
D) a certain event that steers his recollections in a specific direction.

10

Which choice provides the best evidence for the answer to the previous question?

A) Lines 24-27 ("*I remembered . . . birthday*")
B) Lines 50-52 ("*As I . . . me*")
C) Lines 60-61 ("*Excitement . . . place*")
D) Lines 62-66 ("*You know . . . though*")

Questions 11-21 are based on the following passage and supplementary material.

This passage is adapted from Haile Selassie I's address to the United Nations General Assembly in 1963.

It is the sacred duty of this Organization to ensure that the dream of equality is finally realized for all men to whom it is still denied, to guarantee that exploitation is not reincarnated in other forms in
5 places whence it has already been banished.
   As a free Africa has emerged during the past decade, a fresh attack has been launched against exploitation, wherever it still exists. And in that interaction so common to history, this in turn, has
10 stimulated and encouraged the remaining dependent peoples to renewed efforts to throw off the yoke which has oppressed them and its claim as their birthright the twin ideals of liberty and equality. This very struggle is a struggle to establish peace,
15 and until victory is assured, that brotherhood and understanding which nourish and give life to peace can be but partial and incomplete.
   In the United States of America, the administration of President Kennedy is leading a
20 vigorous attack to eradicate the remaining vestige of racial discrimination from this country. We know that this conflict will be won and that right will triumph. In this time of trial, these efforts should be encouraged and assisted, and we should lend our sympathy and
25 support to the American Government today.
   Last May, in Addis Ababa, I convened a meeting of Heads of African States and Governments. In three days, the thirty-two nations represented at that Conference demonstrated to the world that when the
30 will and the determination exist, nations and peoples of diverse backgrounds can and will work together in unity, to the achievement of common goals and the assurance of that equality and brotherhood which we desire.
35 On the question of racial discrimination, the Addis Ababa Conference taught, to those who will learn, this further lesson: That until the philosophy which holds one race superior and another inferior is finally and permanently discredited and abandoned;
40 that until there are no longer first class and second class citizens of any nation; that until the color of a man's skin is of no more significance than the color of his eyes; that until the basic human rights are equally guaranteed to all without regard to race; that
45 until that day, the dream of lasting peace and world citizenship and the rule of international morality will

remain but a fleeting illusion, to be pursued but never attained. And until the ignoble and unhappy regimes that hold our brothers in Angola, in Mozambique
50 and in South Africa in subhuman bondage have been toppled and destroyed; until bigotry and prejudice and malicious and inhuman self-interest have been replaced by understanding and tolerance and good-will; until all Africans stand and speak as free beings,
55 equal in the eyes of all men, as they are in the eyes of Heaven; until that day, the African continent will not know peace. We Africans will fight, if necessary, and we know that we shall win, as we are confident in the victory of good over evil.
60 The United Nations has done much, both directly and indirectly to speed the disappearance of discrimination and oppression from the earth. Without the opportunity to focus world opinion on Africa and Asia which this Organization provides, the
65 goal, for many, might still lie ahead, and the struggle would have taken far longer. For this, we are truly grateful.

But more can be done. The basis of racial discrimination and colonialism has been economic,
70 and it is with economic weapons that these evils have been and can be overcome. In pursuance of resolutions adopted at the Addis Ababa Summit Conference, African States have undertaken certain measures in the economic field which, if adopted
75 by all member states of the United Nations, would soon reduce intransigence to reason. I ask, today, for adherence to these measures by every nation represented here which is truly devoted to the principles enunciated in the Charter.

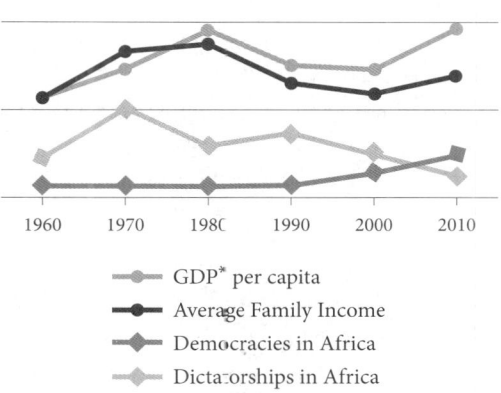

Average Prosperity Indices vs. Forms of Government in Africa

- GDP* per capita
- Average Family Income
- Democracies in Africa
- Dictatorships in Africa

*gross domestic product (the monetary value of all goods and services produced over a certain amount of time)

11

The primary purpose of the passage is to

A) detail the damages discrimination has wrought.
B) compile a list of stipulations necessary for peace.
C) assign blame for an intolerable situation.
D) request cooperation towards achieving a goal.

12

In paragraph 1, the Organization is primarily characterized as

A) bound.
B) revered.
C) liberated.
D) altruistic.

13

Which of the following best describes the function of paragraph 3?

A) It shows that the conflict for equality in Africa is not an isolated event.
B) It calls for crucial moral support for the Civil Rights Movement in America.
C) It justifies the measures that Africa will have to take by referring to a related struggle.
D) It implies that America has won its conflict and the UN should now focus on Africa.

14

The phrase "remaining vestige" in line 20 suggests that

A) racial discrimination was once rampant.
B) the fight against racism has progressed very far.
C) only a single location remains in which racism is an issue.
D) complete victory in the struggle against inequality is imminent.

15

The main rhetorical effect of the series of conditions in lines 37-57 ("That until . . . peace") is to

A) propose a concise plan for overcoming inequality.
B) imply that discrimination is almost impossible to overcome.
C) show that peace is a precondition for attaining equality.
D) assert the resolute decision not to compromise.

16

Within the context of the passage as a whole, lines 60-67 mainly serve to

A) summarize the current state of affairs.
B) shift the focus away from Africa to Asia.
C) recommend a certain approach to a problem.
D) concede that progress has been made.

17

As used in line 76, "reason" most nearly means

A) rationale.
B) justification.
C) sensibleness.
D) intention.

18

The passage most strongly suggests that which of the following is an effective way to combat inequality?

A) Passing new legislative measures
B) Managing a broad adoption of economic measures
C) Emulating the American fight against discrimination
D) Finding a purely Africa-based solution

19

Which choice provides the best evidence for the answer to the previous question?

A) Lines 18-22 ("In the United . . . triumph")
B) Lines 30-34 ("nations . . . desire")
C) Lines 35-37 ("On the question . . . lesson")
D) Lines 73-76 ("African States . . . reason")

20

In the graph, which statistic sees the highest resulting increase between the years 1970 and 2000?

A) GDP per capita
B) Average Family Income
C) Democracies in Africa
D) Dictatorships in Africa

21

Does the graph provide support for the author's claim that racial discrimination and colonialism can be overcome with economic weapons?

A) Yes, because the number of democracies consistently rises along with income levels.
B) Yes, because autocracies only disappear in years where the GDP rises.
C) No, because the number of democracies moves independently from average income levels.
D) No, because the data does not address changes in racial discrimination in Africa.

Questions 22-31 are based on the following passage.

This passage is adapted from Gene Stratton-Porter, "Moths of the Limberlost, with water color and photographic illustrations from life." Originally published in 1912.

In that same country garden where my first Cecropia was found, Deilephila Lineata was one of my earliest recollections. This moth flew among the flowers of especial sweetness all day long, just as did
[5] the hummingbirds; and I was taught that it was a bird also—the Lady Bird. The little tan and gray thing hovering in air before the flowers was almost as large as the hummingbirds, sipping honey as they did, swift in flight as they; and both my parents thought it a
[10] bird.

They did not know the hummingbirds were feasting on small insects attracted by the sweets, quite as often as on honey, for they never had examined closely. They had been taught, as I was, that this
[15] other constant visitor to the flowers was a bird. When a child, a hummingbird nested in a honeysuckle climbing over my mother's bedroom window. My father lifted me, with his handkerchief bound across my nose, on the supposition that the bird was so
[20] delicate it would desert its nest and eggs if they were breathed upon, to see the tiny cup of lichens, with a brown finish so fine it resembled the lining of a chestnut burr, and two tiny eggs. I well remember he told me that I now had seen the nest and eggs of the
[25] smallest feathered creature except the Lady Bird, and he never had found its cradle himself.

Every summer I discovered nests by the dozen, and for several years a systematic search was made for the home of a Lady Bird. One of the unfailing
[30] methods of finding locations was to climb a large Bartlett pear tree that stood beside the garden fence, and from an overhanging bough watch where birds flew with bugs and worms they collected. Lady Birds were spied upon, but when they left our garden they
[35] arose high in air, and went straight from sight toward every direction. So locating their nests as those of other birds were found, seemed impossible.

Then I tried going close the sweetest flowers, those oftenest visited, the petunias, yellow day lilies,
[40] and trumpet creepers, and sitting so immovably I was not noticeable while I made a study of the Lady Birds. My first discovery was that they had no tail. One poised near enough to make sure of that, and I hurried to my father with the startling news. He
[45] said it was nothing remarkable; birds frequently lost their tails. He explained how a bird in close quarters has power to relax its muscles, and let its tail go in order to save its body, when under the paw of a cat, or caught in a trap.

[50] That was satisfactory, but I thought it must have been a spry cat to get even a paw on the Lady Bird, for frequently hummingbirds could be seen perching, but never one of these. I watched the tail question sharply, and soon learned the cats had been after every Lady
[55] Bird that visited our garden, or any of our neighbours, for not one of them had a tail. When this information was carried to my father, he became serious, but finally he said perhaps the tail was very short; those of hummingbirds or wrens were, and apparently some
[60] water birds had no tail, or at least a very short one.

That seemed plausible, but still I watched this small and most interesting bird of all; this bird that no one ever had seen taking a bath, or perching, and whose nest never had been found by a person so
[65] familiar with all outdoors as my father. Then came a second discovery: it could curl its beak in a little coil when leaving a flower. A few days later I saw distinctly that it had four wings but I could discover no feet. I became a rank doubter, and when these
[70] convincing proofs were carried to my father, he also grew dubious.

22

The primary purpose of the passage is to

A) relate the origins of the author's favorite pastime.
B) evaluate different methods of scientific observation.
C) relate a transformative event in the author's life.
D) describe events that resulted in a re-evaluation.

23

The passage indicates that the author's father would most likely describe hummingbirds as

A) a kind of insect.
B) difficult to observe.
C) sensitive creatures.
D) adept at surviving.

24

Which choice provides the best evidence for the answer to the previous question?

A) Lines 3-6 ("This moth . . . Lady Bird")
B) Lines 17-21 ("My father . . . upon")
C) Lines 23-26 ("I . . . himself")
D) Lines 33-37 ("Lady Birds . . . impossible")

25

The search mentioned in paragraph 3 (lines 27-37) can best be characterized as

A) deliberate but futile.
B) thorough but elusive.
C) well-planned and rewarding.
D) strenuous and vain.

26

The passage indicates that the author's father initially considered the author's discoveries about Lady Birds to be

A) vain speculations of an ignorant child.
B) an observation resulting from mundane facts.
C) sufficiently consequential to reassess his opinion.
D) an feat he himself was not capable of.

27

The passage implies that the author believes which of the following about the theory that Lady Birds lose their tails to cats?

A) It is highly unlikely since Lady Birds, unlike hummingbirds, do not stop flying and are harder to catch.
B) It is very likely since birds can shed their tails when they find themselves in a precarious situation.
C) It must be correct because not a single Lady Bird has a tail which means every one of them has been attacked by a cat.
D) It is doubtful since her father came up with the theory in spite of his inability to find a single nest.

28

Which choice provides the best evidence for the answer to the previous question?

A) Lines 46-49 ("He explained . . . trap")
B) Lines 50-53 ("That . . . these")
C) Lines 53-56 ("I watched . . . tail")
D) Lines 61-65 ("That . . . father")

29

As used in line 51, "spry" most nearly means

A) robust.
B) sprightly.
C) agile.
D) spirited.

30

What does the author's father mainly do in lines 56-60 ("When . . . one")?

A) He earnestly considers the author's opinion for a moment, but in the end discards it in favor of his own.
B) He shows his dislike of the author's findings and explains what she saw using well-established facts.
C) He points out the author's logical flaws but encourages her to continue her investigation.
D) He takes his time to interpret the author's observation based on his own speculation.

31

In context, the author most likely includes the activities in lines 63-64 ("taking . . . found") in order to

A) emphasize that her father has spent long years studying the wild.
B) suggest that a certain kind of bird is really not a bird at all.
C) list discoveries that no one before her had been able to make.
D) explain why she believes her father's position to be plausible.

Questions 32-41 are based on the following passages.

In both passages, adoption of the metric system (centimeters, meters, and kilograms as opposed to the inches, feet, and pounds of the old, imperial system) in the United States is discussed. This adoption is also referred to as metrication. Both passages were written in 2014.

Passage 1

In 2012, a petition bearing the weight of close to 50,000 signatures brought attention to a long-standing issue: the need to can the imperial system
Line of measurement. Why are we still relying on decrepit
5 and sometimes obscure units such as ounces, feet, fathoms, and furlongs? Besides being convoluted and requiring more mental math for conversion, there is the fact that the U.S. is one of the only nations left on this planet that even uses the old system.
10   In his response to this petition, the Under Secretary of Commerce for Standards and Technology essentially waves our champions of progress away with what I imagine to be a patronizing smile. To summarize, he claims that we are already using the
15 metric system since our units of measurement have been defined in terms of metric units since 1890. He also states that the fact that we are using both the metric and the imperial system in trade and commerce makes us a truly bilingual nation, as if this
20 were a fact to applaud. He goes on to say that using metric terms of measurement is a voluntary act, and that if personally you wish to do so, you may. In short, nothing is going to change.
  The half-hearted spirit of inaction evident in
25 the government's answer comes as no surprise. This was not the first time people have attempted in vain to bring logic and clarity to our numbers. In 1968, the U.S. Metric Study was conducted as a way of determining the feasibility of metrication. Given
30 the importance of trade and the growing impact of technology in the U.S., the greater part of participants believed that conversion to the metric standard was the right decision.
  Thus, in 1975, the Metric Conversion Act "to
35 coordinate and plan the increasing use of the metric system in the United States" was passed by Congress. However, it lacked the punch necessary to root out that moldy heritage passed down from the British Empire and to guarantee a fresh start: the act initiated
40 a voluntary conversion, and the United States Metric Board—given life to coordinate the effort—was not invested with sufficient power to bring about the envisioned changes before it was disbanded in 1982

due to spending cuts.

Passage 2

It is undeniable that when the United States does officially leave behind the U.S. Customary System in favor of the metric system, it will be one of the last nations to make this step. It seems baffling that this has not yet come to pass. And while there are certainly
50 those who see the U.S. government's lethargic approach concerning the matter as the main culprit, I believe there is more than one reason for this state of affairs.

In 1790, Thomas Jefferson envisioned units based on a decimal system, but this vision required
55 verification of the exact metric unit of length in France, a costly trip. What with wary relations turning sour during those years, the financial aspect was not the only roadblock that kept the metric system out of American reach. Franco-American relations turned
60 outright hostile in 1795, which meant the U.S. was not to partake in an international presentation of the metric system in Paris in 1798.

Admittedly, when the U.S. government "went metric" in 1975 with the Metric Conversion Act, it
65 was a letdown. By failing to decree a deadline and by declaring the conversion voluntary, it robbed the move of much of its steam. Globalization brought on another push, as increased exports of U.S. goods and outsourced production facilities in countries abroad
70 called for usage of metric units, be it on product labels or heavy machinery. However, amendments to the Metric Conversion Act in 1988, stating that the metric system is the "preferred system of weights and measures for United States trade and commerce"
75 were, again, voluntary, which is like putting up signs in a restaurant that say "no smoking (if you want to cooperate)."

There are signs that the wind is shifting, though. In 2013, Hawaii has seen the introduction of a
80 non-voluntary bill. Should it be passed into law, Hawaii will be the first state to effectively replace the old imperial system with the "new," more effective metric units.

Another factor that still warrants attention is
85 the sheer cost of the undertaking. It will involve a stupendous amount of time and effort to change every label, drawing, machine, display, sign, and whatnot to the metric system. Nevertheless, it is about time we made that investment.

32

Both passages support which statement about the metric system?

A) It represents a desirable advance as a system of measurement.
B) The headway it has recently made presents grounds for hope.
C) The United States government is mainly to blame for its absence.
D) The advantages of its adoption will be worth its heavy price.

33

Which best describes the author's tone in Passage 1, lines 4-9 ("Why . . . system")?

A) Amazement
B) Exasperation
C) Wrath
D) Curiosity

34

What does the author mainly do in lines 10-13 ("the Under . . . smile")?

A) He adds his own interpretation of an action.
B) He analyzes the underlying reasons for a decision.
C) He qualifies an assertion made previously.
D) He questions the logic leading to a response.

35

In context, the "Study" (line 28) and its results are mentioned mainly to

A) scrutinize the reasons for advocating the abolition of the metric system.
B) illustrate the half-hearted spirit of inaction displayed by the government.
C) point out the rationale behind making the Metric Conversion Act a law.
D) spell out the factors that initially prevented metrication from being adopted.

CONTINUE

36

The author of Passage 1 would most likely characterize the voluntary nature that has been part of an implementation as

A) no longer critical.
B) morally questionable.
C) a restricting obstacle.
D) a galvanizing oversight.

37

Which choice provides the best evidence for the answer to the previous question?

A) Lines 20-22 ("He goes . . . you may")
B) Lines 25-27 ("This was . . . numbers")
C) Lines 29-33 ("Given . . . decision")
D) Lines 39-43 ("the act . . . changes")

38

The simile in lines 75-77 primarily serves to

A) convey the author's preference for the metric system.
B) characterize a step as paradoxical and void.
C) advocate the enforcement of certain rules.
D) imply that people will not smoke in spite of this sign.

39

The author of Passage 1 would most likely respond to lines 85-89, Passage 2 ("It will . . . investment"), with

A) cautious acceptance.
B) reserved skepticism.
C) open indifference.
D) general agreement.

40

Which statement summarizes an important difference between the two passages?

A) While Passage 1 focuses on shortcomings of the U.S. government, Passage 2 seeks to exonerate its decisions.
B) While Passage 1 blames a single entity for a situation, Passage 2 attempts to incorporate a broader perspective.
C) Passage 1 maintains a hopeful outlook concerning the adoption of the metric system which Passage 2 categorically rejects.
D) Passage 1 draws heavily upon recent events and decisions whereas Passage 2 is exclusively based on early history.

41

Which choice provides the best evidence for the answer pertaining to Passage 2 within the previous question?

A) Lines 51-52 ("I believe . . . affairs")
B) Lines 53-56 ("In 1790 . . . trip")
C) Lines 63-67 ("Admittedly . . . steam")
D) Lines 78-80 ("There are . . . bill")

Questions 42-52 are based on the following passage and supplementary material.

This passage has been adapted from Marti et al., "Evolution of Ossoue Glacier (French Pyrenees) since the end of the Little Ice Age." ©2015.

The Pyrenees[1] host the southernmost glaciers in Europe, all below 43° N latitude. Their small sizes (less than 1 km²), relatively low elevations, and
[Line 5] southern locations make them particularly vulnerable to climate warming. Pyrenean glaciers are strongly out of balance with regional climate and are quickly retreating. While Pyrenean glaciers are in jeopardy, little is known about their evolution since the end of the Little Ice Age (LIA). Comparisons with other
[10] mountain range glaciers are rare, and hampered by fragmented data sets.

Due to the paucity of meteorological measurements, especially at high altitude, Pyrenean climate proxy records are useful to complete past
[15] climate fluctuations at secular scales. A part of this is that glaciers are considered robust climate proxies; their reconstruction may provide further independent evidence that the climate is changing. More generally, however, retreat of Pyrenean glaciers could affect
[20] local ecosystems by diminishing the diversity of species in Pyrenean streams. Furthermore, the natural heritage and visual perception of the high mountain landscape could also be irrevocably affected.

The last favourable period to glacier development
[25] in the Pyrenees was the Little Ice Age, which occurred between the 14th and 19th centuries. LIA climate cooling in the Pyrenees led to the formation and advancement of glaciers in 15 massifs[2]. In the middle of the 19th century, after the respective advance and
[30] recession phases, the Pyrenean glacier fronts reached positions close to their maximum LIA extent. At that time, the area of Pyrenean glaciers is estimated to have been slightly over 20 km². Since then, their area covered 8 km² in 1984, 6 km² in 2004, and
[35] approximately 3 km² in 2013.

Due to their remote locations and small sizes, Pyrenean glaciers have not benefited from long-term glaciological studies. That said, early topographic measurements were made by "Pyreneists," alpinists
[40] who became enthusiasts in the exploration and observation of the Pyrenees. However, it was not until the *Commission internationale des glaciers* (CIG) was created in 1894 in Zürich that the situation slightly improved. Its first president, the Swiss scientist
[45] François-Alphonse Forel, promoted the organized monitoring of glaciers in the Pyrenees for comparison to the evolution of the glaciers in the Alps.

Prince Roland Bonaparte established and communicated to the Commission the first regular
[50] observations of glacier frontal variations between 1874 and 1895. Next, Gaurier monitored the glaciers over the period 1904–1927, which was interrupted by World War I. On the French side of the Pyrenees, *Eaux et Forêts*, the French national agency in charge
[55] of forest and water management, took over the measurements in 1932 and after World War II, during the 1945–1956 period.

At the end of the 1970s, under the initiative of François Valla from the *Centre Technique du Génie*
[60] *Rural et des Eaux et Forêts* and with the support of the *Parc National des Pyrénées*, the first, to our knowledge, mass balance measurements in the Pyrenees were performed at Ossoue and Taillon glaciers between 1978 and 1984 (with only qualitative data taken in
[65] 1983 and 1984). This initiative led to the creation of the *Groupe d'Etudes des Glaciers des Pyrénées* (GEGP), a collaborative group comprising the *Institut National de l'Information Géographique et Forestière* and researchers at Pau University. Two topographic
[70] maps, dated 1948 and 1983, were produced by the GEGP. However, this group lasted only a few years, so that, for the period between 1957 and 2001, only raw terrestrial and aerial images are available for reconstructing glacier front and area variations.
[75] Since 2001, a group of volunteer glaciologists called the *Association Moraine* have performed regular glaciological field measurements.

On the Spanish side, the institutional program *Evaluación de los Recursos Hídricos Procedentes*
[80] *de la Innivación* (ERHIN) has monitored Spanish glaciers since the 1990s. Since 1991, this program has collected an uninterrupted glaciological mass balance time series of the Maladeta Glacier.

In spite of all these efforts, observations of the
[85] Pyrenean glaciers remain scarce and irregular. Hence, there are few available reconstructions of glacier evolution since the Little Ice Age, and quantitative studies are even rarer.

[1] a European mountain range

[2] a large mountain mass or a group of mountains within a mountain range

Chart
Length of the Ossoue Glacier in the Pyrenees
(from 1840 to a Projected 2020)

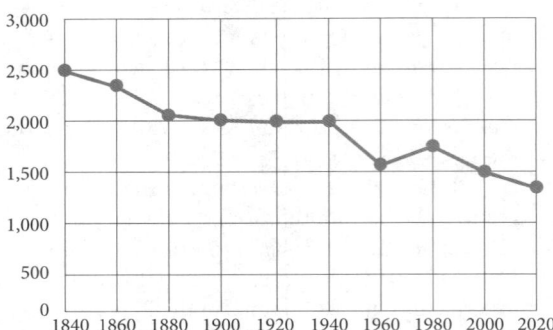

Ossoue Glacier length (meters)

Table
Temperature and Precipitation Data
for the Ossoue Glacier

Time-frame	Mean Temperature (°C)	Summer Temperature (°C)	Precipitation (mm)
1858-1890	-1.3	5.8	no data
1890-1894	-1.4	4.6	1,071
1905-1913	-1.8	4.1	1,165
1928-1949	-1.2	5.1	993
1950-1982	-1.4	4.8	1,068
1983-2013	-0.4	6.1	1,042

42

As used in line 15, "secular" most nearly means

A) nonreligious.
B) temporal.
C) profane.
D) worldly.

43

It can be reasonably inferred from paragraph 2 (lines 12-23) that the Pyrenean glaciers are of interest because

A) their ecosystems contain an exceptional diversity of aquatic species.
B) they contain historical data that would otherwise be hard to obtain.
C) not a lot of scientific work has been successfully conducted there.
D) the loss of their natural heritage further corroborates climate change.

44

The passage indicates that studies of the Pyrenean glaciers initially gained traction due to

A) enthusiastic alpinists who chose to explore and observe.
B) the first mass balance measurements at Ossoue and Taillon.
C) worries that climate change strongly affects the glaciers.
D) interest in the history of another geographic landmark.

45

Which choice provides the best evidence for the answer to the previous question?

A) Lines 2-7 ("Their . . . retreating")
B) Lines 38-41 ("That said . . . Pyrenees")
C) Lines 44-47 ("Its first . . . Alps")
D) Lines 65-69 ("This initiative . . . University")

46

The author suggests that which of the following is an obstacle to research of the Pyrenean glaciers?

A) Armed conflict
B) Insufficient funding
C) Reliance on volunteers
D) Their vast size

47

Which choice provides the best evidence for the answer to the previous question?

A) Lines 31-35 ("At that . . . 2013")
B) Lines 36-38 ("Due to . . . studies")
C) Lines 54-57 ("*Eaux* . . . period")
D) Lines 75-77 ("Since . . . measurements")

48

The author would ultimately characterize the efforts undertaken by the GEGP as

A) groundbreaking.
B) fleeting.
C) rewarding.
D) inspiring.

49

What function does the final paragraph (lines 84-88) mainly serve?

A) It laments the current state of affairs.
B) It calls for additional research efforts.
C) It puts the mentioned studies into perspective.
D) It denigrates the studies that have been conducted.

50

Taken together, the chart and the table suggest that the length of Ossoue Glacier

A) decreases due to increases in temperature and precipitation.
B) held steady when the mean temperature stayed below -1 °C.
C) increases if the mean temperature is below -1.3 °C and the summer temperature below 5 °C.
D) decreased when precipitation levels tended to be relatively low.

51

Based on data in the chart, which of the following intervals displays the highest decrease in glacier length?

A) 1860-1880
B) 1940-1960
C) 1960-1980
D) 2000-2020

52

The author of the passage would most likely consider the information in the table to be

A) proof for his claim that the study of Pyrenean glaciers suffers from fragmented data sets.
B) plain evidence corroborating his belief that the area covered by Pyrenean glaciers is shrinking.
C) an excellent example of data that climate change deniers try to gloss over.
D) a laudable attempt which is unfortunately useless without mass balance data.

STOP

Do not move on to the next section if you finish early.

You may review your answers in this section only.

Answer Keys & Performance Breakdown

1	(B)	Summary	19	(D)	Evidence	37	(D)	Evidence
2	(D)	Summary	20	(C)	Graph	38	(B)	Local
3	(B)	Evidence	21	(D)	Graph	39	(D)	Synthesize
4	(B)	Vocabulary	22	(D)	Summary	40	(B)	Synthesize
5	(C)	Local	23	(C)	Local	41	(A)	Evidence
6	(D)	Context	24	(B)	Evidence	42	(B)	Vocabulary
7	(B)	Local	25	(A)	Local	43	(B)	Local
8	(A)	Local	26	(B)	Local	44	(D)	Local
9	(D)	Summary	27	(A)	Local	45	(C)	Evidence
10	(A)	Evidence	28	(B)	Evidence	46	(A)	Local
11	(D)	Summary	29	(C)	Vocabulary	47	(C)	Evidence
12	(A)	Local	30	(D)	Local	48	(B)	Local
13	(A)	Context	31	(B)	Context	49	(C)	Context
14	(B)	Local	32	(A)	Synthesize	50	(D)	Graph
15	(D)	Style	33	(B)	Local	51	(B)	Graph
16	(D)	Context	34	(A)	Local	52	(A)	Graph
17	(C)	Vocabulary	35	(C)	Context			
18	(B)	Local	36	(C)	Local			

■ Write down the number of correct answers for each question type.

Question Types	Number of Correct Answers
Local	/ 19
Style	/ 1
Vocabulary	/ 4
Evidence	/ 9
Context	/ 6
Organization	0 / 0
Summary	/ 5
Stance	0 / 0
Synthesize	/ 3
Graph	/ 5
Total	/ 52

Answer Explanations

Questions 1-10

1. (B) *Summary*

In the passage, Raul returns to his hometown and finds it significantly changed. His friend Alex proudly points out the modern face of the city, but Raul finds himself nostalgically remembering the way the city used to be.

B is the best choice because although Raul's memories are described in detail, he is unable to convey these impressions in his conversation with his friend.

A is incorrect because no other city's earlier appearance is brought up. C is incorrect because Raul is not impassive or disinterested; he tries to convey his feelings to his friend. D is incorrect because "present, hard-boiled realism" is not supported by the passage. Also, the passage does not indicate that Raul used to be "naïve."

2. (D) *Summary*

Alex repeatedly brings up how much better the city is now compared to how it used to be.

D is the best choice.

A is incorrect because it is not mentioned. B is incorrect because it is Raul who feels this way, not Alex. C is incorrect because it is not mentioned.

3. (B) *Evidence*

B is the best choice because the lines state that now, Santiago is a "real" city. (It did not use to be a real city.) Also, the things of the past have been "cleaned up" which also indicates satisfaction with the way things are now.

A, C, and D are incorrect because none of them show that Alex is proud of the way the city has changed.

4. (B) *Vocabulary*

B is the best choice because the sentence states that after he approached a shop to inspect its wares, another shop entrance "spoke to" him. Thus, the other shop entrance told him to step closer, or "enticed" him.

A is incorrect because it is too literal which does not fit the context of the word. C is incorrect because it implies that he feels he has been there before. D is incorrect because it means to "mentally unbalance" or literally "take off its hinges."

5. (C) *Local*

C is the best choice because the shop was dark (dim) and the air smelled of wax, furniture, spices, flowers, and a lot of perfume (rich as in "intense sensation").

A is incorrect because "desolate" is not supported. B is incorrect because "dilapidated" means "in ruins or disrepair" which is too strong to describe dusty perfume bottles. D is incorrect because "rapt" means "enthralled" or "completely fascinated" or "mesmerized" which is not supported by the specified lines.

6. (D) *Context*

Raul feels excitement at the sight of rare perfumes. Rarity aside, the only other hint in context that explains his excitement is in lines 45-47 that state he is looking for a birthday present.

D is the best choice.

A is incorrect because "all" is not supported. B is incorrect because the fact that the shopkeeper is absent is mentioned after, and not as a reason for his excitement. C is incorrect because the context does not suggest he feels intoxicated by the scents.

7. (B) *Local*

B is the best choice because he basically reiterates the question he asked before in line 62 ("You know . . . Celia?") after which Alex changed the topic to Celia running away.

A is incorrect because "reprimand" means "rebuke" which is not supported. Also, "painful" is not supported. C is incorrect because "embarrassing" is not supported. Also, Raul does not answer Alex's question here, but rather returns to his original point. D is incorrect because Raul does not indicate that Alex remembers things incorrectly.

8. (A) *Local*

A is the best choice because in line 68, Raul's words imply that he somewhat misses the perfume store. He mentions things that are now irretrievable which hints at a sense of loss. Alex, however, counters that today's stores are "much better" and implies he will think differently once he has seen them. This shows that Alex does not understand Raul's nostalgic point of view.

Answer Explanations

B is incorrect because it is not implied that Raul agrees with Alex now. C is incorrect because getting a better gift is not suggested. D is incorrect because no similarity or familiarity is suggested.

9. (D) *Summary*

Raul's memories come up twice. In the first part, general impressions of Santiago's streets are described, followed by a memory of sitting in a coffee shop with Celia prior to her birthday. The second part shows Raul browsing stores looking for a birthday gift for Celia.

D is the best choice because the memory of sitting with Celia prior to her birthday is followed by more, related memories.

A is incorrect because nothing in the memories implies that she left him. B is incorrect because the passage does not indicate his memories are skewed. C is incorrect because nothing in the memories themselves indicates nostalgia or longing.

10. (A) *Evidence*

A is the best choice because the lines mention the event that influences the rest of his memories in the passage.

B, C, and D are incorrect because none of them mention an event that colors Raul's memories.

Questions 11-21

11. (D) *Summary*

The speaker states that it is the duty of the UN to ensure equality and to combat exploitation (paragraph 1). He then states that this fight is still ongoing in Africa, and that in a convention, African leaders successfully worked toward common goals (lines 6-34). He further grants that Africa owes much in this fight to the UN's help (lines 60-67), but says that the UN can do more to help Africa in the form of economic support (lines 68-79).

D is the best choice.

A, B, and C are incorrect because the speaker primarily asks for economic support for Africa.

12. (A) *Local*

A is the best choice because the Organization has a "sacred duty." It is "obliged" to do something.

B is incorrect because the respect it receives is not mentioned. C is incorrect because the Organization is not described as "freed" from something. D is incorrect because selfishness or lack thereof is not mentioned.

13. (A) *Context*

Paragraph 3 lauds and encourages the fight against discrimination in America. The remainder of the passage discusses the fight against discrimination in Africa.

A is the best choice.

B is incorrect because "crucial" is not supported. C is incorrect because no measures in Africa are excused in this paragraph. D is incorrect because according to the paragraph, the fight is still ongoing (lines 19-21).

14. (B) *Local*

B is the best choice because "vestige" means "trace," so the phrase suggests that only a very small amount of discrimination is left. Therefore, the fight against racism is mostly over.

A is incorrect because one cannot infer from this phrase that something used to be "rampant." C is incorrect because the phrase signifies a degree or an amount, not exact locations. D is incorrect because a degree or amount of something does not reliably inform the remaining duration of a process.

15. (D) *Style*

"Until" is repeated numerous times which leads up to lines 56-57 which state that "the African continent will not know peace." In essence, Haile Selassie makes numerous stipulations that all have to be fulfilled before Africa will stop fighting.

D is the best choice.

A is incorrect because goals are listed, not steps in achieving them. B is incorrect because Selassie is not pessimistic. Rather, he is defiant (lines 57-59). C is incorrect because cause and effect are switched.

16. (D) *Context*

The paragraph shows that the UN's help has shortened the fight against oppression. (The fight has progressed further thanks to the UN.) Before and after this paragraph, Selassie emphasizes that the fight is not over and asks the UN for further help in the fight.

D is the best choice.

A is incorrect because though the paragraph itself does show a state of affairs, the purpose in context is to acknowledge that help has been given before asking for more help. B is incorrect because even though Asia is mentioned, the focus stays on Africa. C is incorrect because no recommendations are made.

17. (C) *Vocabulary*

C is the best choice because "reason" stands in opposition to "discrimination," "colonialism," and "evil." Therefore, the best choice is "sensibleness" as in "sound judgment."

A and B are incorrect because they mean "reason" as in "cause for something." D is incorrect because "intent" or "motivation" does not make sense in context.

18. (B) *Local*

B is the best choice because of lines 73-76 (see next question).

A is incorrect because laws are not mentioned. C is incorrect because the passage merely calls for support for the fight in America; it does not recommend emulating it. D is incorrect because the passage does not state a purely African solution would be best. Also, Haile Selassie asks for help from the UN (which is not a purely Africa-based solution).

19. (D) *Evidence*

D is the best choice because it states that economic measures, if adopted by all member states of the UN (broad adoption), would "reduce intransigence to reason." ("Intransigence" refers to racial discrimination and colonialism in lines 68-69, so it means "inequality.")

A, B, and C are incorrect because none of them mention economic measures to fight inequality.

20. (C) *Graph*

C is the best choice because just comparing the values for 1970 and 2000, "Democracies in Africa" gains the most. "Average Family Income" and "Dictatorships in Africa" decrease while "GDP per capita" only sees a miniscule gain, smaller than that of "Democracies in Africa."

Therefore, A, B, and D are incorrect.

21. (D) *Graph*

D is the best choice because the graph only shows the development of relative affluence over time, and the relative development of government types over time. None of these give information on the level of racial discrimination.

A is incorrect because democracies do not actually rise with income levels according to the graph. B is incorrect because autocracies also disappear in years where the GDP drops (2000). A and B are also incorrect since the Graph has no data on racial discrimination. C is incorrect because the lack of correlation between democracies and income levels does not make a statement about racial discrimination.

Questions 22-31

22. (D) *Summary*

The passage first states that a moth called Lady Bird was thought to be a bird, not an insect. The author as well as her parents had been taught so. Finding their nests, in contrast to those of other birds, however, proved to be futile. The passage then mentions three field observations that make the author, and ultimately the author's father, doubt whether Lady Birds are really birds.

D is the best choice.

A is incorrect because the passage does not focus on why the author enjoys a certain hobby. B is incorrect because different ways of observing and evaluating them are is not the focus of the passage. C is incorrect because the passage does not focus on a single event. Also, none of these events are stated to be life-altering.

23. (C) *Local*

C is the best choice because of lines 17-21 (see next question).

A is incorrect because the passage only mentions Lady Birds as insects, not hummingbirds. B is incorrect because the father showed his daughter a nest. Also, the passage does not suggest that the father thinks hummingbirds are difficult to observe. D is incorrect because the passage does not mention whether the father thinks this way.

Answer Explanations

24. (B) *Evidence*

B is the best choice because the lines state that the father blocked the author's nose with a handkerchief because he supposed that "the bird was so delicate" it might fly away if breathed upon.

A, C, and D are incorrect because none of them show that the father would characterize hummingbirds as sensitive creatures.

25. (A) *Local*

A is the best choice because she used an unfailing method (deliberate), but locating nests as those of other birds seemed impossible (futile).

B is incorrect because it is not the search that is elusive but the quarry that is elusive. C is incorrect because the search is not rewarding. D is incorrect because "strenuous" is not supported in context.

26. (B) *Local*

B is the best choice. The first discovery the author makes happens in paragraph 4 (lines 38-49). Here, the father says that the author's finding is "nothing remarkable" and that birds frequently exhibit this behavior.

A is incorrect because neither "vain" nor "ignorant" is supported by the father's reaction. C is incorrect because the father does not change his opinion. D is incorrect because the passage does not indicate that the author's father was unable to do what the author did.

27. (A) *Local*

A is the best choice because of lines 50-53 (see next question).

B and C are incorrect. First of all, it would take a very nimble cat to catch these never-perching Lady Birds. Secondly, in spite of this difficulty, cats caught every single Lady Bird's tail without exception. This implies that the author finds the theory unlikely. D is incorrect because the passage does not state that she doubts her father's opinion on account of his inability to find a nest.

28. (B) *Evidence*

B is the best choice because the lines state that it would take a very nimble cat to catch these never-perching Lady Birds which is a fact that run against the father's theory, which implies that the author feels the theory is unlikely.

A, C, and D are incorrect because none of them show that the author finds the theory to be highly unlikely since Lady Birds do not stop flying and are harder to catch.

29. (C) *Vocabulary*

C is the best choice because the sentence describes cats that can successfully attack a Lady Bird which never perches. Thus, "spry" means "nimble" or "agile."

A is incorrect because it means "healthy" or "strong." B is incorrect because it means "vivacious" or "lively." D is incorrect because it means "showing mettle" or "lively."

30. (D) *Local*

D is the best choice because the father "became serious, but finally he said" (he takes his time) that perhaps (speculation) the tail was very short. He says this because those of hummingbirds or wrens are also short.

A is incorrect because he does not discard the author's opinion (which is that Lady Birds have no tail). B is incorrect because the specified lines do not support "dislike of the author's findings." C is incorrect because neither "logical flaws" nor encouragement is supported by the specified lines.

31. (B) *Context*

B is the best choice because the context discusses a bird that does not behave like a bird (the specified lines describe normal bird behavior) and that has four wings and no feet; a fact which instills doubt in the author and her father.

A is incorrect because the specified activities do not provide support for her father's experience. C is incorrect because the passage does not indicate that she is the first to discover these activities. D is incorrect because the context does not mention that the author believes her father's position to be plausible.

Questions 32-41

32. (A) *Synthesize*

A is the best choice because Passage 1 mainly complains about the lethargy of the U.S. government which has so far prevented the adoption of the metric system over the imperial system, and Passage 2 mainly states that there are reasons besides the one stated in Passage 1 for this state of affairs, but there is hope. Both see the metric system as a desirable advance as compared to the current system.

B is incorrect because only Passage 2 would support this choice. C is incorrect because only Passage 1 would support this choice. D is incorrect because though Passage 1 would in essence agree, no "heavy price" was mentioned.

33. (B) — Local

B is the best choice because the author asks for justification for using a convoluted and complicated system that most nations do not use anymore.

A is incorrect because it is too positive. C is incorrect because "wrath" or "anger" is too extreme. D is incorrect because rather than trying to investigate, the author is pointing out an undesirable state of affairs.

34. (A) — Local

A is the best choice because the author imagines that the Under Secretary of Commerce for Standards and Technology put on a "patronizing smile" when responding to a petition. Whether or not this is true is unknown, so it's the author's own interpretation.

B is incorrect because the author does not analyze anything—he just imagines a smile. C is incorrect because the sentence in lines 10-13 does not limit or qualify the contents of the previous paragraph. D is incorrect because a "patronizing smile" implies condescension, but it makes no statement about "logic."

35. (C) — Context

C is the best choice because in the next sentence, the result of the study calls for metrication and therefore (line 34), the Metric Conversion Act was passed by Congress. So "rationale" is correct. (The study was the reason, the Metric Conversion Act the result.)

A is incorrect because the "abolition of the metric system" is not mentioned in context. Also, abolition without prior adoption does not make sense. B is incorrect because the "half-hearted spirit" (line 24) refers to the voluntary nature of metrication measures. The study was a preliminary tool to gauge whether conversion was necessary. Execution, and thus the question of voluntary versus mandatory came later. D is incorrect because the study was actually designed to possibly facilitate metrication.

36. (C) — Local

C is the best choice because of lines 39-43 (see next question).

A is incorrect because it only says that now, as ever, metrication is a voluntary measure (lines 20-25). But it never says that the question of voluntariness has lost its importance. B is incorrect because moral issues are not mentioned. D is incorrect because "galvanizing" implies shocking someone into action, whereas according to the passage, the voluntary nature of legislation has resulted in lethargy.

37. (D) — Evidence

D is the best choice because the lines imply that the Metric Board, dealing with a voluntary conversion, lacked in power and thus failed to effect changes. Thus, the "voluntary nature" was a restricting obstacle.

A, B, and C are incorrect because none of the lines show that the voluntary nature of conversion became a restricting obstacle.

38. (B) — Local

B is the best choice because the clause within the parentheses makes a restriction dependent on someone's willingness to cooperate. Therefore, if someone does not want to cooperate, they do not have to follow the restriction. This makes the restriction meaningless, and putting up a restriction like that is paradoxical.

A is incorrect because the simile disparages the voluntary nature of a policy. C is incorrect because the simile itself does not advocate enforcing anything. D is incorrect because the simile serves to make a point about metrication policies, not about smoking.

39. (D) — Synthesize

D is the best choice because the author of Passage 1 complains about the failure to convert to the metric system. Thus he would agree with lines 88-89. Before lines 88-89, it says that metrication will take a lot of time and effort which does not contradict Passage 1 even though Passage 1 does not discuss these points either. Thus, "general" agreement is correct.

A is incorrect because "cautious" implies reservations or worries. There is nothing in lines 85-89 that would make the author of Passage 1 hesitate. B is incorrect because "skepticism" is the opposite of what the author of Passage 1 would feel. C is incorrect because the inclusion of lines 83-89 means that the author of

Answer Explanations

Passage 1 would agree rather than directly state that they do not care.

40. (B) — Synthesize

B is the best choice because Passage 1 blames the lethargy of the U.S. government for the failure to adopt the metric system and Passage 2 states that there were additional factors besides the one mentioned in Passage 1.

A is incorrect because Passage 2 does not try to exonerate the U.S. government. C is incorrect because Passage 1 is resigned rather than hopeful while Passage 2 is actually hopeful. D is incorrect because Passage 2 does not exclusively talk about early history (line 79).

41. (A) — Evidence

A is the best choice because the lines state that there is more than one reason for this state of affairs. Therefore, "broader perspective" is supported.

B, C, and D are incorrect because none of them support the idea that Passage 2 takes on a "broader perspective" than Passage 1.

Questions 42-52

42. (B) — Vocabulary

B is the best choice because the sentence mentions past climate fluctuations at "secular" scales. Thus, "secular" becomes a time-related word.

A is incorrect because it means "not religious." C is incorrect because it means "immoral" or "irreverent." D is incorrect because it means "material" or "mundane."

43. (B) — Local

B is the best choice because according to paragraph 2, Pyrenean records are useful since there is a "paucity of meteorological measurements, especially at high altitude," making the Pyrenean data that's otherwise hard to obtain. Since Pyrenean records are useful to "complete past climate fluctuations at secular scales," "historical data" is supported.

A is incorrect because "exceptional" is not supported. C is incorrect because "paucity" (line 12) does not refer to the Pyrenees. D is incorrect because the loss of natural heritage is not stated to be evidence for climate change.

44. (D) — Local

D is the best choice because of lines 44-47 (see next question).

A is incorrect because the "enthusiasts" are mentioned before studies gained traction (CIG in 1894). B is incorrect because these measurements happen much later and thus cannot be the cause. C is incorrect because results of climate change are not mentioned in this context.

45. (C) — Evidence

C is the best choice because the lines state that the first president of the CIG promoted the monitoring of Pyrenean glaciers for comparison to the evolution of the glaciers in the Alps (another geographic landmark).

A, B, and D are incorrect because none of them show that studies gained traction due to interest in another geographic landmark.

46. (A) — Local

A is the best choice because of lines 54-57 (see next question).

B is incorrect because "funding" is not mentioned. C is incorrect because the passage does not suggest that volunteers are an obstacle to research. D is incorrect because the opposite is true. Their small size was the reason Pyrenean glaciers did not benefit from more studies.

47. (C) — Evidence

C is the best choice because the lines state that studies took place before and after, but not during World War II.

A, B, and D are incorrect because none of them show that armed conflict presented an obstacle to research.

48. (B) — Local

B is the best choice because the passage states that the group "lasted only a few years" (line 71).

A is incorrect because the inception of the GEGP was the result of an innovation (the first mass balance measurements in the Pyrenees), not its cause. C is incorrect because even though maps were produced, the question mentions "ultimately" which points at the short duration of the group. D is incorrect because there was no mention of anyone who was influenced by the work of this group.

49. (C) Context

C is the best choice because it relates the studies mentioned in the passage to a broad overview. (Research remains scarce and irregular.)

A is incorrect because "laments" is not supported. B is incorrect because nothing is called for or demanded. D is incorrect because "denigrates" is not supported.

50. (D) Graph

D is the best choice because the lowest two values of precipitation (1928-1949 and 1983-2013) correspond to significant drop-offs in glacier lengths.

A is incorrect because the highest precipitation values actually correspond to periods with little loss in glacier length compared to periods with relatively low precipitation. B is incorrect because between 1840 and 1880, the glacier lost a lot of length though the temperature was below -1 °C. C is incorrect because the glacier decreased in length between 1890 and 1894 even though the mean temperature was below -1.3 °C and the summer temperature below 5 °C.

51. (B) Graph

B is the best choice because in the given period, the length starts out pretty much at 2,000 m and at the end of the period, it drops to around 1,600 m. No other period displays that much of a decrease.

A, C, and D are therefore incorrect.

52. (A) Graph

A is the best choice because the data in the table is incomplete. It misses precipitation data, and the records do not seamlessly connect before 1928. In lines 9-11 of the passage, the author states that comparisons of the Pyrenees with other mountain ranges are "hampered by fragmented data sets."

B is incorrect because the table itself has no data on the area covered by Pyrenean glaciers. Thus, "plain evidence" is not supported. C is incorrect because the passage does not mention "climate change deniers." D is incorrect because the author does not mention that certain data is useless unless mass balance data is included.

SAT.Hackers.ac

TEST 8

Hackers New SAT Reading: 10 Practice Tests

Answer Keys & Performance Breakdown

Answer Explanations

1

Reading Test
65 MINUTES, 52 QUESTIONS

Mark your answers to the questions in Section 1 in the answer sheet provided.

DIRECTIONS

For each of the passages below, there are 10 or 11 questions. Choose the best answer for each of the questions after you have finished reading the passage. The answers to the questions should be based on the information that is stated or implied in the text and any associated graphics.

Questions 1-10 are based on the following passage.

This passage is adapted from a memoir. In this excerpt, the child of an immigrant family moves from the city to a more rural area.

  I was born and raised here, in one of the big cities. Melting pot, people call it, and for good reason. You grow up around all kinds there. Black, brown,
Line yellow, white, and all those kids you just cannot place.
  5 I remember this one kid down the street, Kyle, who was this weird mix of—I have no idea, actually. Not important. Nor was it a bad thing. Nor did I care. That's just the way it was: no one really cared what you looked like, and no one asked where you were
 10 from. It was obvious, see? You were from here.
  There came a day Dad told us we were moving. I didn't really know what that meant. I guess I was too young for the right synapses in my brain to go 'fire!', and paint a picture of a new life somewhere else. I
 15 think it was something about his job—with him, it was always something about his job. Anyhow, one day these big, burly strangers showed up at home and started loading our belongings into a big truck. When I asked mom what was going on, she just laughed and
 20 called me an idiot—she always did—before telling me we were moving. That's when it struck me. Moving, as in moving to another place. Taking everything you have and unloading at some unknown destination.
  I don't remember much about the actual drive.
 25 Except I probably asked a hundred times where we were moving *to*. Dad being Dad, and I suspect this might also be an Asian thing, he just said "You will like it there." That's the thing about him. Patience like a stone. You just can't wear him down, so that was all I
 30 could coax out of him.
  Things were different around our new home.

Of course, he had been wrong: I didn't like it. Not a bit. I think I was the only non-white kid in our neighborhood. Back then, China was the only Asian
 35 country widely known in the United States. So the first—and only semi-intelligent—question I was asked would always be "Are you Chinese?" Worse inevitably followed. Eventually, though, I made some good friends. There's that.
 40 Nowadays, I am in college, and I'm still here. It's nice and safe here, according to Dad. He says it's important to keep the family together. He claims he heard this college I'm attending is prestigious. Don't ask me what for—it is something he heard but can't
 45 explain. I strongly suspect he really just likes the tuition fees being prestigiously low. Be that as it may. I have my friends around here, and I'm not really that worried about my future, so I'm pretty happy with things as they are.
 50 This part of the States being predominantly white and all, most of my friends are white. Not that that matters, really. The attitude, though, does. I figure there are three ways the majority deals with ethnic minorities—people like me. One is to dislike them
 55 just because they look different. I respect that. It's honest, and I respect honesty. Then there is the overly politically correct type that shows this contrived interest in "what it's like to be Asian." I hate those guys—they make me feel like a zoo exhibit. I wish
 60 they would just ignore me instead of showing off how accepting and tolerant they are. Dime a dozen, guys like that. And then finally, every once in a while, you meet someone who genuinely couldn't care less about your background. All they care about is whether
 65 you're fun. Whether you watch the right shows on TV. Whether you go to the ball games or not. Suchlike. I guess I am lucky I have found a couple of friends like that.

Of course, that doesn't mean I don't have to deal
70 with any stereotypes whatsoever. See, my friend Carl
once went to get himself a tattoo. And somehow he
got it into his thick head to get a Chinese character
inked onto his forearm. I thought it would look
extraordinarily stupid, but he didn't take me along
75 for my opinion. Turns out, he took me along because
he somehow presumed I knew how to read Chinese
characters. So when he asked me for a character that
not only looked awesome, but also meant something
cool, I just looked at him. You know, I gave him the
80 *look*. It took him a minute, but the penny eventually
dropped.
"So you don't know any Chinese?"
"Much as you do. I was born here, you know?
And my parents aren't even Chinese."
85 "Yeah, I know. It's just that . . . you know. You
look like you might know."
I had to laugh in spite of myself.
"I guess I do at that."

1

The passage is primarily concerned with

A) the gradual decline of racism over time.
B) the influence of ethnicity on perception.
C) the importance of friends and family.
D) the ignorance of immigrant children regarding their origins.

2

The passage indicates that the narrator is fond of his birthplace due to the

A) abundance of young children.
B) auspicious lack of discrimination.
C) unique diversity of inhabitants.
D) mishmash of different languages.

3

Which choice provides the best evidence for the answer to the previous question?

A) Lines 1-3 ("I was born . . . there")
B) Lines 3-7 ("Black . . . thing")
C) Lines 8-10 ("That's . . . here")
D) Lines 31-34 ("Things . . . neighborhood")

4

As used in line 30, "coax" most nearly means

A) tease.
B) allure.
C) con.
D) soothe.

5

The passage as a whole suggests that the narrator "didn't like" (line 32) his new home primarily because

A) he had to start over and make new friends.
B) his ethnicity became more of an issue than before.
C) he did not really know anything about the place.
D) he was teased for being the only Asian in the neighborhood.

6

The narrator uses the phrase "Worse inevitably followed" (lines 37-38) in order to imply that

A) he always had to put up with uninformed questions.
B) he invariably got into fights over being Asian.
C) he met decent friends in spite of prevailing discrimination.
D) he disliked talking about his country of origin the most.

7

As described in the passage, the narrator's attitude towards college and his future is mostly

A) vacuous.
B) precipitous.
C) nonchalant.
D) averse.

8

The passage indicates that the narrator likes people the best who

A) share his hobbies and other interests.
B) demonstrate their tolerance of other ethnicities.
C) are not interested in his origin.
D) avoid asking him obtuse questions about his background.

9

Which choice provides the best evidence for the answer to the previous question?

A) Lines 35-39 ("So the . . . friends")
B) Lines 56-58 ("Then there . . . Asian")
C) Lines 62-64 ("And then . . . background")
D) Lines 66-68 ("I guess . . . like that")

10

In context, it can be inferred that the narrator "just looked at" Carl in line 79 because

A) Carl had not asked the narrator for his opinion on the tattoo.
B) the narrator was disappointed by Carl's racist remark.
C) the narrator did not want to admit that he did not know Chinese.
D) Carl made a wrong presumption based on appearance.

Questions 11-20 are based on the following passage and supplementary material.

This passage is from John F. Kennedy's address to the American People on Civil Rights in 1963.

The Negro baby born in America today, regardless of the section of the Nation in which he is born, has about one-half as much chance of
Line completing a high school as a white baby born in
5 the same place on the same day, one-third as much chance of completing college, one-third as much chance of becoming a professional man, twice as much chance of becoming unemployed, about one-seventh as much chance of earning $10,000 a year,
10 a life expectancy which is 7 years shorter, and the prospects of earning only half as much.
    This is not a sectional issue. Difficulties over segregation and discrimination exist in every city, in every State of the Union, producing in many
15 cities a rising tide of discontent that threatens the public safety. Nor is this a partisan issue. In a time of domestic crisis men of good will and generosity should be able to unite regardless of party or politics. This is not even a legal or legislative issue alone. It
20 is better to settle these matters in the courts than on the streets, and new laws are needed at every level, but law alone cannot make men see right. We are confronted primarily with a moral issue. It is as old as the scriptures and is as clear as the American
25 Constitution.
    The heart of the question is whether all Americans are to be afforded equal rights and equal opportunities, whether we are going to treat our fellow Americans as we want to be treated. If an
30 American, because his skin is dark, cannot eat lunch in a restaurant open to the public, if he cannot send his children to the best public school available, if he cannot vote for the public officials who will represent him, if, in short, he cannot enjoy the full and free
35 life which all of us want, then who among us would be content to have the color of his skin changed and stand in his place? Who among us would then be content with the counsels of patience and delay?
    One hundred years of delay have passed since
40 President Lincoln freed the slaves, yet their heirs, their grandsons, are not fully free. They are not yet freed from the bonds of injustice. They are not yet freed from social and economic oppression. And this Nation, for all its hopes and all its boasts, will not be
45 fully free until all its citizens are free.
    We preach freedom around the world, and we

mean it, and we cherish our freedom here at home, but are we to say to the world, and much more importantly, to each other that this is the land of the
[50] free except for the Negroes; that we have no second-class citizens except Negroes; that we have no class or caste system, no ghettoes, no master race except with respect to Negroes?

Now the time has come for this Nation to fulfill
[55] its promise. The events in Birmingham and elsewhere have so increased the cries for equality that no city or State or legislative body can prudently choose to ignore them. The fires of frustration and discord are burning in every city, North and South, where
[60] legal remedies are not at hand. Redress is sought in the streets, in demonstrations, parades, and protests which create tensions and threaten violence and threaten lives.

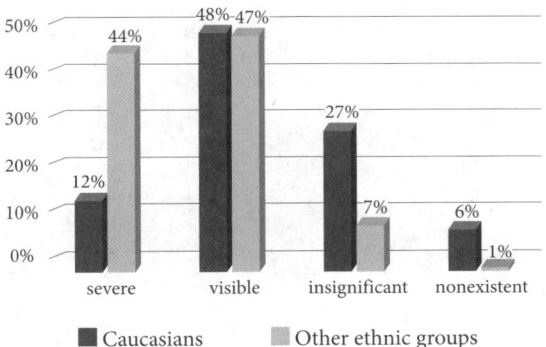

How Discrimination Was Perceived in 2012 (Independent Poll)

11

The stance Kennedy takes in the passage is best described as that of

A) a moralist deriding a nation's past efforts.
B) an idealist questioning his own aspirations.
C) a custodian of forgotten American ideals.
D) an advocate striving for a needed change.

12

The main rhetorical effect of the repeated use of numbers in paragraph 1 is to

A) drive home the disparity between two different groups.
B) exaggerate the injustice that young African Americans face.
C) tally up the progress that has been achieved over time.
D) imply that certain problems are unlikely to be solved.

13

The statement in line 12 ("This is . . . issue") mainly serves to emphasize that

A) every country has to deal with the problem of discrimination.
B) a problem should not be seen as a localized occurrence.
C) a holistic approach including all demographics is needed.
D) racism has become the most pressing problem in every U.S. state.

14

As used in line 20, "settle" most nearly means

A) straighten out.
B) lull.
C) dwell.
D) land.

CONTINUE

15

In paragraph 3 (lines 26-38), Kennedy likens equal rights and equal opportunities to

A) a slow process that will require time and patience.
B) Americans being able to do anything they want.
C) the willingness to trade places with any American.
D) a way to morally educate the American people.

16

Lines 43-45 ("And this . . . free") primarily serve to

A) establish a condition for reaching a goal.
B) reprimand a shortcoming of the past.
C) offer up prospects of a better future.
D) question the possibility of attaining true freedom.

17

The question in lines 46-53 implies that Americans preach a concept that

A) can never be achieved due to America's bigotry.
B) is only possible to achieve in America.
C) is celebrated but not completely realized.
D) has successfully done away with class distinctions.

18

The passage suggests that the "events in Birmingham and elsewhere" (line 55) are significant in terms of

A) their role as an example for equality.
B) their power to rally people to a cause.
C) the scope of change they have brought about.
D) the unprecedented violence witnessed there.

19

The data in the figure best supports the view that, taken as a whole, Caucasians regard discrimination with more

A) nonchalance.
B) urgency.
C) deliberation.
D) enmity.

20

Which of the following statements is supported by the passage and by the information in the figure?

A) The racial divide in America has grown worse in the last 50 years.
B) The problem addressed in the passage has not yet been fully resolved.
C) The quest for equal rights and opportunities has been discarded.
D) Different ethnic groups cannot arrive at the same conclusions.

Questions 21-30 are based on the following passage.

This passage is adapted from Pugnaire et al., "Evolutionary changes in correlations among functional traits in *Ceanothus* in response to Mediterranean conditions." ©2006.

Plant species characteristic of infertile environments reveal consistent correlations among traits such as low growth rate, high root-to-shoot
Line ratio, high concentrations of secondary metabolites,
5 and low nutrient absorption rate, which are a response to low availability of resources. This combination of attributes represents a strategy to cope with high levels of stress and enables plants to successfully colonize infertile environments.
10 The set of trait attributes is sufficiently consistent among different low-resource environments that it constitutes what could be termed a stress resistance syndrome (SRS). Environmental pressures have presumably selected for this specific profile of
15 attributes in response to stressful environments.
The presence of a similar suite of trait attributes in different species irrespective of evolutionary lineage supports the idea that the SRS evolved in a synchronous manner rather than by parallel selection
20 for each individual trait. In other words, evolutionary changes leading to stress tolerance in plants might occur through only a few mutations in genes with large pleiotropic[1] effects rather than by accumulation of many small mutational events. However, this
25 hypothesis has not been rigorously tested by statistical analysis of the relationships among traits in plant groups whose evolutionary relationships are known.
Also, different species might have such evolutionary changes in common either because they
30 are linked by a network of shared ancestry or because the traits are adaptations to common environments. Therefore, when analyzing species traits to look for selective pressures or ecological trends, it is important to determine the phylogenetic[2] relationships among
35 species and the extent to which changes in one set of characters is associated with evolutionary changes in another set.
Ceanothus is a highly diversified genus that is widespread in California. It has two well
40 differentiated sections, the subgenera *Ceanothus* and *Cerastes*, both of which have species present in a wide range of environments, from coastal scrub to dry chaparral habitats to sub alpine elevations in Sierra Nevada. Species differ widely in size, allocation
45 patterns and reproductive strategies, which are conditioned by disturbance regime[3]. Adult individuals of the *Cerastes* species are killed by fire but produce a number of large seeds whose germination is triggered by fire. In contrast, most species in the subgenus
50 *Ceanothus* resprout from the root crown when the aerial part is removed by fire or grazing and produce fewer, smaller seeds.
Most species of the genus *Ceanothus* now present in California appeared after an Eocene climatic
55 change when a drier, more seasonal climate favored the recurrence of fires. Phylogenetic analyses using chloroplast DNA suggest that the two subgenera diverged 18-39 million years ago, whereas species within each subgenus diverged more recently.
60 Subgenus *Ceanothus* species share a large number of traits with other *Rhamnaceae* species, particularly regarding leaf traits and rooting depth, and can be considered ancestral, while *Cerastes* species with smaller, thicker leaves and shallow root systems
65 different from other *Rhamnaceae*, are considered to have evolved later and are better suited to thrive under a Mediterranean climate....
... [I]n response to new, drier conditions, evolution might enhance traits related to stress
70 tolerance such as small leaves while the higher frequency of fires in Mediterranean-type climate could affect recruitment traits, enhancing the seeder habit.

[1] referring to the production of two or more effects by a single gene

[2] referring to the evolutionary history of a group of organisms

[3] ways that an environment's flora is replaced on a large scale (such as fire, wind, or flood)

21

Over the course of the passage, the focus shifts from

A) the apparent connection among a group of adaptations to a detailed analysis of each.
B) various strategies to cope with infertile environments to examples of successful plants.
C) a commonality among plants adapted to harsh environments to probing its possible origins.
D) casting doubt on an unproven theory to the examination of concrete examples to find answers.

22

As used in line 17, "irrespective" most nearly means

A) heedless.
B) inattentive.
C) regardless.
D) disrespectful.

23

Which of the following can be inferred about the "evolutionary changes" mentioned in lines 20-21?

A) They can only be thought of as pleiotropic if no evolutionary relationships exist.
B) They occur in a synchronous manner since they are a response to environmental stresses.
C) They cannot be attributed to one certain evolutionary process without additional research.
D) They result in a similar group of attributes due to mutations in pleiotropic genes.

24

According to the passage, "it is important to determine the phylogenetic relationships among species" (lines 33-35) in order to

A) distinguish between inherited traits and traits that evolved due to an environment.
B) determine how one species is related to another species.
C) rule out certain traits that are result of environmental pressures.
D) prove the existence of pleiotropic mutations as opposed to single mutations.

25

As used in line 35, "set" most nearly means

A) scene.
B) position.
C) sect.
D) series.

26

The author implies that the genus *Ceanothus* found in California

A) owes most of its attributes to a Mediterranean climate.
B) has adapted to deal with a variety of habitats.
C) is well capable of resisting climate change.
D) displays only qualities that reflect its evolutionary lineage.

27

Which choice provides the best evidence for the answer to the previous question?

A) Lines 28-31 ("Also . . . environments")
B) Lines 39-44 ("It has . . . Nevada")
C) Lines 53-56 ("Most . . . fires")
D) Lines 60-63 ("Subgenus . . . ancestral")

28

Which choice does the author explicitly cite as a reproductive strategy used by plants?

A) Resprouting from small seeds
B) Root-to-shoot ratio
C) Seeds that need fire
D) Small and thick leaves

29

Which choice provides the best evidence for the answer to the previous question?

A) Lines 46-49 ("Adult . . . fire")
B) Lines 49-52 ("In contrast . . . seeds")
C) Lines 63-67 ("while . . . climate")
D) Lines 68-73 ("[I]n response . . . habit")

30

The author most likely mentions "other *Rhamnaceae* species" (line 61) in order to

A) illustrate specific stress resistance syndrome characteristics.
B) show how environmental adaptations can overrule ancestral similarities.
C) aid the contrast between environmental and inherited attributes.
D) emphasize that leaf adaptations are the most prominent among the SRS traits.

Questions 31-41 are based on the following passages.

These passages discuss ecotourism.

Passage 1

I keep stumbling across this word "ecotourism" everywhere, in all kinds of contexts, advertisements, and discussions. Mostly, it appears to be a catchword
Line for luring in conscientious tourists. It seems to be the
5 new thing. But what is it really? While there is a lot of doubt concerning the viability of ecotourism as a concept, I believe it is really up to the individual's decision to honor the "eco": keeping in mind the environment and respecting the local culture.

10   On a recent trip I took to Southeast Asia, I traveled across Vietnam using the same transportation the locals use. The nature I witnessed was breathtakingly beautiful, and I stood *inside* of it. It was utterly unlike the sanitized versions created for
15 tourists with little shops lining the exits. I stayed in villages and paid for rooms in local homes instead of hotels. What a profoundly rewarding experience: the love and generosity extended to me was heartwarming, and glad does not come close to describing how I felt
20 about paying locals instead of some huge multinational hotel chain. In addition, I am quite confident the carbon footprint of my travel was insignificant.

   If you do it right, ecotourism means visiting and thus supporting the local, especially the rural
25 scene which is often ignored by big operators. If you do it right, ecotourism means spending money at these locations rather than some big resort and thus supporting the local community. If you do it right, ecotourism means walking or using transportation
30 instead of driving everywhere in your own car. By leaving the trodden track, you will have opportunities to meaningfully connect with people. By visiting national parks and reserves and paying their entrance fees, you will contribute to protecting endangered
35 habitats and species. And by deciding to practice ecotourism, you will reward yourself with an uplifting experience.

   Of course, there are businesses that have nothing to do with ecotourism beyond their self-advertisement.
40 A good rule of thumb is that bigger, more convenient, and more modern usually means less eco-friendly. If more and more travelers decide to forgo these "green-washed" operators, these businesses will eventually be forced to change their myopic and
45 egotistical practices.

Passage 2

The idea of ecotourism arose from the criticism leveled against traditional mass tourism. Mass tourism, according to critics, results in observable adverse effects on the local ecology and culture.
50 Thus a working definition of sustainable tourism was developed, referred to as alternative tourism, which in essence states that tourism needs to be conducted in a manner and adhere to a scale which will remain viable indefinitely and will not degrade
55 the environment or change it. Ecotourism is another term for this concept.

   There are certainly benefits to this kind of tourism. For instance, the income generated thanks to this industry can become grounds for preservation
60 of natural assets. National parks have seen significant expansion thanks to ecotourism. In certain countries, the income generated by this kind of tourism can have a momentous impact on the national economy. In addition, on a local level, a rise in the standard of living
65 can often be at least partially attributed to this industry.

   On the other side of the equation are, needless to say, the problems that come with ecotourism. Fundamentally, the lack of laws and regulations that mandate certain procedures and standards is an
70 issue that needs to be addressed. Due to the absence of legislation, companies with little experience or little intent to adhere to the principles of ecotourism can set up shop without fear of punitive measures. Another result of lack of regulation is that the money
75 generated through this "ecotourism" which ought to end up in the local community is instead often rerouted to some national tour operator, or even to an international entity.

   Another problem is the matter of over-visitation.
80 An attractive site for tourists might eventually cause its own demise by drawing too much attention. One must remember that natural habitats are fragile systems, and the arrival of great numbers of humans will cause a strain through their very presence by
85 disrupting the habitat, littering, and causing pollution. Similarly, local communities that were previously quite isolated now have to cope with and adapt to the presence of numerous tourists which goes against the standards of preservation prescribed by alternative
90 tourism.

   While doubtlessly an admirable concept in theory, ecotourism has yet to be implemented in a way that truly honors its spirit.

31

Which of the following does the author of Passage 1 imply about businesses?

A) Certain operators resort to misleading strategies to draw tourists.
B) Small businesses cannot compete against bigger operators.
C) If left unchecked, some will represent an active threat to ecotourism.
D) Their success solely depends on their amenities.

32

Which choice provides the best evidence for the answer to the previous question?

A) Lines 1-4 ("I keep . . . tourists")
B) Lines 14-17 ("It was . . . hotels")
C) Lines 32-35 ("By visiting . . . species")
D) Lines 40-41 ("A good . . . eco-friendly")

33

In line 14, "sanitized" most nearly means

A) dissimilar.
B) artificial.
C) decontaminated.
D) glamorous.

34

In response to the assertions in Passage 1, lines 23-28 ("If you . . . community"), the author of Passage 2 would most likely respond by

A) agreeing that ecotourism by itself has the power to lift local communities out of poverty.
B) arguing that this interaction can be problematic because it might alter local ways of life.
C) adding that experiencing unadulterated nature can be an inspiring reward.
D) contending that most tourists prefer convenient hotel resorts to this style of travel.

35

The function of the second paragraph in passage 2 (lines 57-65) is to

A) advocate a practice.
B) make a concession.
C) dispel expectations.
D) honor an achievement.

36

In line 78, "entity" most nearly means

A) body.
B) organism.
C) visitor.
D) business.

37

Which of the following describes a situation most similar to that of the "attractive site" in line 80?

A) A cave, popular for its beauty, has deteriorated significantly due to wind and weather.
B) A famous garden needs to be maintained carefully in order to receive guests in spring.
C) A car show has to contend with wear and tear on its cars due to intense visitor traffic.
D) A gorgeous canyon becomes so crowded with visitors that it is hard to enjoy the view.

38

The author of Passage 1 would most likely view the final sentence in Passage 2 with

A) relief due to the grueling conditions ecotourism prescribes.
B) alarm due to the spread of pessimism regarding ecotourism.
C) doubt thanks to the decline of "green-washed" tour operators.
D) skepticism since travelers can choose to adhere to ecotourism.

39

Which choice provides the best evidence for the answer to the previous question?

A) Lines 7-9 ("I believe . . . culture")
B) Lines 32-35 ("By visiting . . . species")
C) Lines 38-39 ("Of course . . . self-advertisement")
D) Lines 42-45 ("If more . . . practices")

40

Unlike the author of Passage 1, the author of Passage 2 implies that ecotourism

A) means forgoing luxury for authenticity.
B) has always failed to live up to its mandate.
C) involves protecting the local population.
D) scrutinizes travelers' carbon footprints.

41

Which statement best summarizes an important difference between the two passages?

A) Passage 1 stresses individual agency, whereas Passage 2 looks at broader factors.
B) Passage 1 lists the pros and cons of a practice, whereas Passage 2 only considers the benefits.
C) Passage 1 offers a solution to a problem, whereas Passage 2 argues for a different solution.
D) Passage 1 takes an ambivalent stance towards an issue, whereas Passage 2 is more optimistic.

Questions 42-52 are based on the following passage and supplementary material.

This passage is adapted from an essay about information science.

We are becoming data. More and more of our lives is being recorded, stored, and evaluated on interconnected devices, and the resulting,
Line unprecedented confluence of information is changing
5 the way we interact with data.

In the 1960s and 1970s, early computer-driven database systems were conceived to capture data in structures that allowed for improved data modeling and access. This period saw the development and rise
10 of relational database systems that granted users easy, customizable and flexible access to data. While these represented a landmark achievement over simple text file data storage, data at that time existed only in dark, tiny hamlets, separated like islands, entered manually
15 by specialists and technicians.

Data as a part of everyday life did not begin until the 1990s when the World Wide Web (the Internet) started seeing widespread adoption. Millions of households used personal computers and modems[1] to
20 dial into the World Wide Web. Certain services such as e-mail, weblogs, or chat rooms require personal information, and this user information along with the usage history (a log of actions undertaken by each user) was recorded in database systems. The
25 hamlets had grown into small, brightly lit towns interconnected by tenuous pathways.

Twenty years later, mobile devices connected to the Internet have completely transformed this picture. In 2014, more than 1.5 billion smartphones
30 were in use worldwide. These devices, always at hand, ceaselessly take pictures, record sound, send digital messages, upload status updates to our social networking sites, and allow us to handle payments for shopping and banking. The list only grows each day.
35 While twenty years ago, we had to sit down in front of a computer and use a keyboard to enter data that might be captured online, it has now become quite a challenge to avoid leaving quite a holistic picture of our activities online.

40 Not only do mobile devices lead users to capture more of their data, but online corporations are actively working towards painting a more complete picture of them. The most successful online entities that serve hundreds of millions of users provide an
45 array of products and services that enable them to not only learn about a user's demographical data, but to combine that knowledge with search activity, consumption habits, leisure time preferences, and so forth. Every "free" service is really paid for with a bit
50 of information. The little towns have now given way to sprawling, radiant megacities connected by pulsing traffic arteries blazing with data. With each day, the glare grows more blinding.

We are becoming data. Collected data on
55 innumerable users, incessantly updated and added to, presents a great challenge to those who would make use of this transformation. In light of the colossal commercial benefits latent in such big data, interest in data mining (also referred to as Knowledge Discovery
60 from Data) has understandably surged.

In essence, data mining describes a process that entails the preparation of information, searching it for meaningful patterns, and their presentation to the user.

Since data mining is often applied to immense
65 amounts of data collected from countless users using different devices, the data needs to be preprocessed. Faulty or inconsistent data is removed, and information from different sources and databases is consolidated into a single database to be searched.

70 The "mining" part consists of the search for meaningful patterns. The prepared data is analyzed by the data mining system to either *describe* the data—to classify the information that resides in the database according to user requirements—or to *predict* outcomes
75 —to use the data as a basis for assumptions about the future. For instance, an online shopping mall may want to use data mining to describe its users in ways such as "Which gender spends more money here?" or "What age group has made repeated purchases?"
80 The same shopping mall may try to mine predictive data in the vein of "What product is a client likely to purchase if he has just purchased a certain book?"

After the patterns have been extracted, they need to be rendered in a humanly readable fashion
85 so that the miner may take appropriate action. Notwithstanding this simplistic introduction, data mining is actually a challenging subset of information science that is as complex as it is lucrative.

[1] a device used to connect a personal computer to the Internet

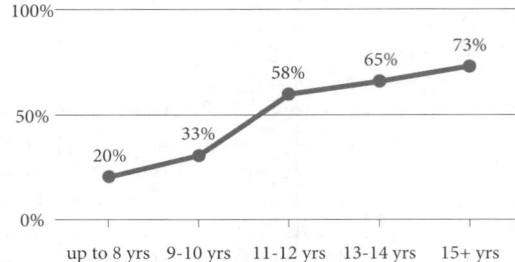

Figure 1
Age Groups Posting Personal Information
(Region A, 2012)

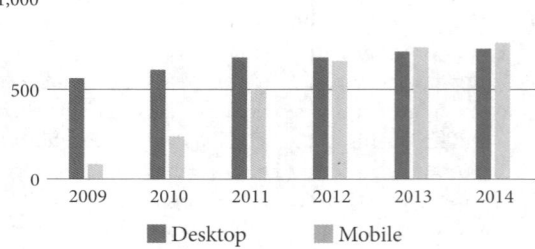

Figure 2
Internet Usage Measured
in Consumption Units (CI)

42

Over the course of the passage, the focus shifts from

A) the fact that more consumer data is being stored online to concerns about the resulting lack of consumer privacy.
B) the observation of a global trend to an attempt to predict the outcome of this trend should it be allowed to continue.
C) the inception and proliferation of a technology to a way this technology is employed in a commercial context.
D) the discovery of a technology in a remote area to its worldwide application and successful commercialization.

43

Which choice provides the best evidence for the answer to the previous question?

A) Lines 16-18 ("Data . . . adoption")
B) Lines 50-53 ("The little . . . blinding")
C) Lines 57-60 ("In light . . . surged")
D) Lines 86-88 ("Notwithstanding . . . lucrative")

44

The passage implies that which of the following is most directly responsible for the fact that we commonly leave traces of our everyday lives in online databases?

A) The birth of the World Wide Web
B) The adoption of mobile devices
C) Successful online entities
D) Interest in data mining

45

Which choice provides the best evidence for the answer to the previous question?

A) Lines 16-18 ("Data . . . adoption")
B) Lines 37-39 ("it has . . . online")
C) Lines 40-43 ("Not only . . . them")
D) Lines 54-57 ("Collected data . . . transformation")

46

The author mentions successful online entities that offer various services in order to suggest that

A) small online ventures are not viable in today's economy.
B) trying to glean more data from users is the only way these businesses can make profits.
C) holistic user information is an inherently valuable commodity.
D) certain companies actively exploit credulous users by exposing their private data.

47

In lines 70-76 ("The . . . future"), the author mainly

A) explicates the way a process is utilized towards certain goals.
B) illustrates a concept using different examples.
C) differentiates between use cases in terms of how meaningful they are.
D) explains two stages in data mining in order of execution.

48

Which choice best supports the claim that data mining benefits those who wish to commercially exploit big data?

A) Lines 1-5 ("More and . . . data")
B) Lines 54-57 ("We are . . . transformation")
C) Lines 67-69 ("Faulty . . . searched")
D) Lines 80-82 ("The same . . . book")

49

As used in line 84, "rendered" most nearly means

A) presented.
B) ceded.
C) carried out.
D) translated.

50

The author of the passage would probably consider the information in figure 1 to be

A) an indication that among children, mobile device ownership grows with age.
B) evidence that personal information counts the least among pre-teens.
C) representative of the adage that caution decreases with age.
D) compelling confirmation that more private data is divulged every year.

51

Based on the data in figure 2, mobile usage overtook desktop usage for the first time in

A) 2009.
B) 2012.
C) 2013.
D) 2014.

52

According to the data in figure 2, the latter half of the time period depicted was characterized by

A) faster growth in mobile usage than in the first half.
B) a decline in mobile usage as compared to desktop usage.
C) constantly larger mobile consumption than desktop consumption.
D) a decline in growth rate of mobile consumption units.

STOP

Do not move on to the next section if you finish early.

You may review your answers in this section only.

Answer Keys & Performance Breakdown

1	(B)	Summary	19	(A)	Graph	37	(C)	Local
2	(B)	Local	20	(B)	Graph	38	(D)	Synthesize
3	(C)	Evidence	21	(C)	Organization	39	(A)	Evidence
4	(A)	Vocabulary	22	(C)	Vocabulary	40	(B)	Synthesize
5	(B)	Summary	23	(C)	Local	41	(A)	Synthesize
6	(A)	Local	24	(A)	Local	42	(C)	Organization
7	(C)	Local	25	(D)	Vocabulary	43	(C)	Evidence
8	(C)	Local	26	(B)	Local	44	(B)	Local
9	(D)	Evidence	27	(B)	Evidence	45	(B)	Evidence
10	(D)	Context	28	(C)	Local	46	(C)	Local
11	(D)	Stance	29	(A)	Evidence	47	(A)	Local
12	(A)	Style	30	(C)	Context	48	(D)	Evidence
13	(B)	Context	31	(A)	Local	49	(A)	Vocabulary
14	(A)	Vocabulary	32	(A)	Evidence	50	(A)	Graph
15	(C)	Local	33	(B)	Vocabulary	51	(C)	Graph
16	(A)	Local	34	(B)	Synthesize	52	(D)	Graph
17	(C)	Local	35	(B)	Context			
18	(B)	Local	36	(D)	Vocabulary			

■ Write down the number of correct answers for each question type.

Question Types	Number of Correct Answers
Local	/ 17
Style	/ 1
Vocabulary	/ 7
Evidence	/ 9
Context	/ 4
Organization	/ 2
Summary	/ 2
Stance	/ 1
Synthesize	/ 4
Graph	/ 5
Total	**/ 52**

Answer Explanations

Questions 1-10

1. (B) — Summary

The passage compares the narrator's first city (no one cares what he looks like) to a place he moves to later. (He is the only Asian and has to contend with what he thinks are uninformed questions about his ethnicity.) The narrator states he likes people who do not care about ethnicity at all, and he finally recounts an episode where his friend mistakenly thinks that he knows Chinese due to his background.

Therefore, B is the best choice.

A is incorrect because "decline" is not supported and "racism" is partially too strong. C is incorrect because the importance of friends and family is not the focus. D is incorrect because the focus is on how other people see the narrator, not on what immigrant children like the narrator know about their origins.

2. (B) — Local

B is the best choice because of lines 8-10 (see next question).

A is incorrect because "abundance" is not supported. C is incorrect because "unique" is not supported. D is incorrect because "different languages" is not suggested.

3. (C) — Evidence

C is the best choice because the lines state that no one cared what you looked like or asked where you were from. This implies that no one cared about ethnicity, which means there was a lack of discrimination.

A, B, and D are incorrect because none of them indicate that the narrator's birthplace was characterized by a lack of discrimination.

4. (A) — Vocabulary

The sentence itself does not give decisive hints, but the context does. Lines 25-28 state that the narrator repeatedly asked his father about the destination, but all he would get by way of response would be "You will like it there." That was all the narrator could "coax" out of him.

A is the best choice as it means "provoke" or "pester" through some persistent action.

B is incorrect because it means "seduce." C is incorrect because it means "deceive" or "trick." D is incorrect because it means "allay" or "assuage."

5. (B) — Summary

The passage states that he did not like the new neighborhood because he was the only non-white kid and he was asked questions about his background which he did not like. This did not happen in the city he used to live in (paragraph 1).

B is the best choice.

A and C are incorrect because neither of them are mentioned as a reason for dislike. D is incorrect because the passage does not state he was teased for this specific reason.

6. (A) — Local

"Worse" refers to the semi-intelligent question "Are you Chinese?" Therefore, "worse" here signifies less intelligent questions that inevitably (always) followed.

A is the best choice.

B is incorrect because "fights" is not supported. C is incorrect because it is a positive development. D is incorrect because the context does not support "the most."

7. (C) — Local

C is the best choice because the narrator dismisses the fact that his school is not very prestigious by saying "Be that as it may." Also, he indicates he is not really worried about the future, so he is pretty happy which in essence means he does not care too deeply about college.

A is incorrect because it means "airheaded" or "unintelligent." B is incorrect because it means "steep" or "abrupt." D is incorrect because it means "hostile" or "opposing."

8. (C) — Local

C is the best choice because of lines 66-68 (see next question).

A is incorrect because shared hobbies are not mentioned as the narrator's reason for liking someone. B is incorrect because it is the opposite of what the passage states. D is incorrect because avoiding

Answer Explanations

something he dislikes does not equal him liking someone the best.

9. (D) — Evidence

D is the best choice because it shows he considers himself lucky to have friends like that (which refers to people who do not care about his background).

A, B, and C are incorrect because none of them support the fact that he likes people the best who are not interested in his origin.

10. (D) — Context

In context, it is clear that it is a meaningful look. In lines 80-82, Carl finally understands that the author does not know Chinese (which was implied by the look). And he goes on to explain that he assumed the narrator would know Chinese because of the way he looks (lines 85-86).

D is the best choice.

A is incorrect because Carl actually asks him for his opinion. B is incorrect because "racist" is not supported. C is incorrect because the passage does not support the idea that the author is reluctant to admit to this fact.

Questions 11-20

11. (D) — Stance

Kennedy first emphasizes that African Americans do not have the same chances as whites which he calls a moral issue. He emphasizes that 100 years after Lincoln freed the slaves, African Americans still suffer inequality and that this contradicts American rhetoric of freedom. He concludes that now is the time to remedy this shortcoming.

D is the best choice.

A is incorrect because the nation's past efforts are not *belittled*. They are characterized as insufficient, which is different. B is incorrect because he does not question his own aims. C is incorrect because "forgotten" is not supported.

12. (A) — Style

Each number shows that African Americans are much worse off than white people.

A is the best choice.

B is incorrect because there is no indication that the numbers have been altered for dramatic effect. C is incorrect because the numbers show shortcomings, not progress. D is incorrect because no such conclusions about the future are drawn.

13. (B) — Context

"Not a sectional issue" in context means that it is a prevalent issue that affects every city in every state.

B is the best choice.

A is incorrect because "country" means nation. Only the U.S. is discussed. C is incorrect because "demographics" is not mentioned in context. D is incorrect because the statement does not imply a degree of urgency.

14. (A) — Vocabulary

A is the best choice because the sentence says it is better to "settle" these matters (problems) in the courts. "Settle" therefore means to "resolve" which is like "straighten out."

B is incorrect because it means to "soothe." C is incorrect because it means to "inhabit a certain location." D is incorrect because it means to "come ashore" or to "alight on a surface."

15. (C) — Local

C is the best choice because of lines 34-37.

A is incorrect because "patience and delay" refers to the consolation that African Americans have to make do with since they are not treated equally. This does mean that equal rights are a process that is necessarily slow. B is incorrect because "do anything they want" is extreme and not supported. D is incorrect because no method of moral education is discussed.

16. (A) — Local

A is the best choice because the sentence makes full freedom dependent on (not until) the freedom of all citizens.

B is incorrect because the past is not criticized in these lines. C is incorrect because a better future is not simply presented, it is made dependent on a condition. D is incorrect because pointing out a condition for something and doubting it are not the same.

17. (C) Local

C is the best choice because in line 47, it says we "cherish" freedom (celebrated), but lines 48-53 indicate that we are only free and equal except for African Americans (not completely realized).

A is incorrect because "never" is extreme and unsupported. B is incorrect because no such distinction is made. D is incorrect because "successfully done away" implies that no more class distinctions exist.

18. (B) Local

The specified events refer to a catalyst for "the cries for equality that no city or State or legislative body can . . . ignore." Furthermore, the fires of frustration (cries for equality) are burning in every city. In essence, the specified events caused nationwide, passionate protests against inequality.

B is the best choice.

A is incorrect because the events caused anger and frustration. C is incorrect because the events have triggered protests, not change. D is incorrect because "unprecedented" is not supported.

19. (A) Graph

The data shows that Caucasians perceive discrimination as less severe and more insignificant.

A is the best choice because "nonchalance" means "lack of concern" or "casualness."

B is incorrect because this is true for the other ethnic groups. C is incorrect because it means "careful consideration" before a decision. D is incorrect because it means "hostility."

20. (B) Graph

The data in the graph shows that other ethnic groups (non-white) view discrimination as more of an issue than Caucasians. This unequal perspective implies that the other ethnic groups do not feel they are treated equally. The main point of the passage is that the U.S. needs to make equality a reality instead of a preached concept.

B is the best choice.

A is incorrect because the numbers in the passage are not directly comparable against the data in the graph. C is incorrect because the graph does not support the notion that equal rights have been given up on. D is incorrect because the passage does not support it, and the graph has no data to support or deny it.

Questions 21-30

21. (C) Organization

The passage first mentions a set of attributes common to plants that grow in infertile environments. This might be caused by many simple mutations or a few pleiotropic mutations. Also, these attributes could either be due to inheritance in the case of genetically related plants or due to environmental pressures. The passage then gives a detailed example of an adapted plant.

C is the best choice.

A is incorrect because the passage does not analyze each adaptation in detail. B is incorrect because rather than various strategies, the passage focuses on one common set of attributes which makes up one strategy. D is incorrect because "casting doubt on" is not supported by the passage.

22. (C) Vocabulary

C is the best choice because within the sentence, there are similarities in different species "irrespective" of evolutionary lineage. Evolutionary lineage is therefore discounted. Thus, "regardless" is correct.

A is incorrect because it means "careless" or "reckless." B is incorrect because it means "negligent" or "distracted." D is incorrect because it means "insulting" or "impolite."

23. (C) Local

C is the best choice because lines 21-24 state that these changes could be due to pleiotropic effects instead of many small mutations. The next sentence states that this hypothesis has not been sufficiently tested.

A is incorrect because the absence of evolutionary relationships is not mentioned as a condition. B is incorrect because there is no certainty yet as to whether the changes occurred in a synchronous manner or not. D is incorrect because there is no certainty yet as to whether the changes are due to changes in pleiotropic genes or not.

24. (A) Local

A is the best choice. The specified sentence starts with "therefore," so the previous sentence should be focused on. It states that species might have traits in common either because of shared

Answer Explanations

ancestry (inheritance) or because of adaptations to environments.

B is incorrect because the interspecies relationships are not stated as a reason. C is incorrect because rather than ruling out environmental pressures, it is important to determine whether environmental pressures are a cause. D is incorrect because proving pleiotropic mutations is not stated as a reason.

25. (D) — Vocabulary

D is the best choice because the sentence describes how changes in "one set of characters" are connected to changes in "another set," characters being genetic traits in context. Thus, "set" means "group" or "collection," which makes "series" correct.

A is incorrect because it means "setting" or "incident" or "culture." B is incorrect because it means "physical place" or "stance" or "belief." C is incorrect because it means "creed" or "cult."

26. (B) — Local

B is the best choice because of lines 39-44 (see next question).

A is incorrect because only one of the two subgenera (subspecies) mentioned in the passage has adapted to a Mediterranean climate. This does not imply that all of genus *Ceanothus* owes the majority of its attributes to this climate. C is incorrect because the passage only mentions that *Ceanothus* appeared after a climatic change which does not support the general statement found in C. D is incorrect because one subspecies of *Ceanothus* displays environmental rather than inherited adaptations.

27. (B) — Evidence

B is the best choice because the lines state that the subgenera of *Ceanothus* can be found in a wide range of environments.

A, C, and D are incorrect because none of them show that *Ceanothus* has adapted to deal with a variety of habitats.

28. (C) — Local

C is the best choice because of lines 46-49 (see next question).

A is incorrect because the passage only mentions resprouting from the root crown, not from seeds. B and D are incorrect because the passage does not indicate that these are reproductive strategies.

29. (A) — Evidence

A is the best choice because the lines state that adult plants that die of fire produce seeds whose germination is triggered by (i.e., that need) fire.

B, C, and D are incorrect because none of them show that seeds that need fire are a reproductive strategy used by plants.

30. (C) — Context

C is the best choice because *Rhamnaceae*, being similar to one subgenus, is stated to be ancestrally related to that subgenus. The other subgenus, being different from *Rhamnaceae*, is stated to be different having evolved to deal with its climate. Thus, one subgenus has a number of inherited traits (*Rhamnaceae*) while the other got its traits from a Mediterranean climate.

A is incorrect because *Rhamnaceae* is not mentioned to point out traits but rather *similarities* or *differences* in traits. B is incorrect because overruling ancestral traits is not mentioned in context. D is incorrect because "most prominent" is not supported in context.

Questions 31-41

31. (A) — Local

A is the best choice because of lines 1-4 (see next question).

B is incorrect because Passage 1 does not mention this. C is incorrect because the author does not mention businesses potentially posing an "active threat" to ecotourism. Passage 1 also states that ecotourism is up to the individual, not the business. D is incorrect because no such dependence is mentioned (check lines 39-41).

32. (A) — Evidence

A is the best choice because it says "ecotourism" is used as a catchword for luring in tourists. "Luring" implies businesses use the word "ecotourism" to mislead customers.

B, C, and D are incorrect because none of them mention that businesses resort to misleading strategies.

33. (B) — Vocabulary

B is the best choice because in the sentence, "sanitized" refers to something created for tourists. This is contrasted to standing inside of nature like the locals do (ergo not created for tourists).

A is incorrect because "sanitized" as in "cleaned up" is contrasted to a natural state. "Dissimilar" does not express that. C is too literal and thus does not fit the context of the word. D is incorrect because "glamorous" means "lovely" or "alluring."

34. (B) — Synthesize

Lines 23-28 state that correct ecotourism means visiting the local scene and spending money there supporting the locals instead of consuming at big resorts. Passage 2 discusses the aspect of locals in lines 74-78 and lines 86-90.

B is the best choice because of lines 86-90.

A is incorrect because Passage 2 does not mention this. It also goes against the main opinion of Passage 2. C is incorrect because Passage 2 does not mention this kind of reward. D is incorrect because no such statement is made in Passage 2.

35. (B) — Context

The second paragraph admits that there are benefits to ecotourism. In the following paragraph, the author focuses on the problems with ecotourism which is followed by another problem in paragraph 4.

B is the best choice.

A is incorrect because the author does not recommend this kind of tourism. C is incorrect because dispelling expectations means to talk about the negative sides of something. D is incorrect because though positive aspects are listed, the author does not want to give praise but merely concede several points. (Check line 57 where it says "certainly.")

36. (D) — Vocabulary

D is the best choice because in the sentence, "entity" is another word for "tour operator" which is a business.

Therefore, A, B, and C are incorrect.

37. (C) — Local

The "attractive site" suffers from over-visitation. It causes its own demise (details on this demise can be found in lines 83-85) by attracting too many tourists.

C is the best choice because too many people (intense visitor traffic) cause damage (wear and tear on cars).

A, B, and D are incorrect because they do not mention damage due to too many people.

38. (D) — Synthesize

The final sentence of Passage 2 states that ecotourism only exists as a concept, and that it has not yet been implemented according to its principles (viable indefinitely and does not degrade or change the environment). Passage 1's main point is that ecotourism is a personal choice and that if one so chooses, one can adhere to its principles (lines 7-9).

D is the best choice.

A is incorrect because "grueling conditions" does not fit the author's outlook. B is incorrect because "spread of pessimism" is not supported by the final sentence of Passage 2. Also, Passage 1 does not focus on this aspect. C is incorrect because the "green-washed" tour operators are not seen as an obstacle to ecotourism.

39. (A) — Evidence

A is the best choice (see previous question).

B, C, and D are incorrect because none of them state that ecotourism really depends on the individual.

40. (B) — Synthesize

B is the best choice (last sentence of Passage 2, see explanation for question 38).

A is incorrect. Passage 1 would support this. C is incorrect because both passages would agree. D is incorrect because both passages would agree.

41. (A) — Synthesize

Passage 1 emphasizes that ecotourism depends on the individual traveler's decisions. Passage 2 is skeptical of ecotourism because there is a lack of legislation and regulation. Also, over-visitation might degrade ecosystems and alter the way of life of the locals.

A is the best choice.

B is incorrect because Passage 2 also has cons. C is incorrect because Passage 2 does not argue for a solution. D is incorrect because Passage 1 is optimistic whereas Passage 2 is skeptical.

Answer Explanations

Questions 42-52

42. (C) — Organization

C is the best choice because lines 6-53 show how database technology has grown until nowadays, and how it is inextricably linked with our daily lives. From line 54, the passage shows how data mining uses this data to reap commercial benefits.

A is incorrect because privacy concerns are not mentioned. B is incorrect because no predictions as to the outcome of a trend are attempted. D is incorrect because the passage does not mention that database technology was discovered in a remote area.

43. (C) — Evidence

C is the best choice because the lines show the transition from databases (such big data) to their employment (data mining) in a commercial context (colossal commercial benefits).

A, B, and D are incorrect because they either talk about databases or data mining, but not both.

44. (B) — Local

B is the best choice because of lines 37-39 (see next question).

A is incorrect because the "World Wide Web" is mentioned in a much earlier context. C is incorrect because "successful online entities" is mentioned in a later context. D is incorrect because "interest in data mining" is a result, not a cause of leaving traces of our everyday lives in databases.

45. (B) — Evidence

B is the best choice because the lines show that it has now (twenty years later, due to mobile devices) become a challenge to avoid leaving quite a holistic picture of our activities online.

A, C, and D are incorrect because they do not show that mobile devices are the reason we leave traces of our lives in online databases.

46. (C) — Local

In lines 43-50, it essentially says that services enable online entities to combine a user's demographical data with search activity, consumption habits, leisure time preferences, etc. The next sentence indicates these are free services, and that what the company gains is therefore not money but information.

C is the best choice.

A is incorrect because it is not mentioned. B is incorrect because the passage does not state there is no other way. D is incorrect because exposing data is not mentioned.

47. (A) — Local

A is the best choice because the lines in essence state that mining means searching for meaningful patterns which are used to either describe or predict.

B is incorrect because the specified lines do not contain examples. C is incorrect because the lines do not state whether one use is more meaningful than the other. D is incorrect because the lines do not suggest that two stages are carried out in a certain order.

48. (D) — Evidence

D is the best choice because the lines show how data mining can give predictive information about purchasing decisions of customers.

A, B, and C are incorrect because they do not show commercial benefits of data mining.

49. (A) — Vocabulary

A is the best choice because the sentence describes data patterns that, after extraction, need to be "rendered" in a humanly readable fashion. Therefore, "rendered" means "showed" or "presented."

B is incorrect because it means "surrendered" or "relinquished." C is incorrect because it means "executed." D is incorrect because it means "converted" or "interpreted."

50. (A) — Graph

The information in figure 1 shows that the older children become, the more personal information is posted. The author of the passage says the main reason for personal information ending up in online databases is mobile devices.

A is the best choice.

B is incorrect because the passage does not make any statements as to which age groups value personal information. C is incorrect because no such adage is mentioned in the passage. D is incorrect because the passage does not discuss the disclosure of data.

51. (C) Graph

C is the best choice because the column that represents mobile is larger than the desktop column only in 2013 and 2014. Since the question asks for the first time, 2013 is correct.

A, B, and D are therefore incorrect.

52. (D) Graph

The question asks about the latter half of the time period depicted, ergo 2012-2014.

D is the best choice because the column representing mobile usage grows at much lower rates than in 2009-2011.

A is incorrect because the opposite is true. B is incorrect because the opposite is true. (Desktop usage falls behind mobile usage.) C is incorrect because in 2012, desktop consumption still ranks above mobile consumption.

SAT.Hackers.ac

Hackers New SAT Reading: 10 Practice Tests

TEST 9

Answer Keys & Performance Breakdown
Answer Explanations

1

Reading Test
65 MINUTES, 52 QUESTIONS

Mark your answers to the questions in Section 1 in the answer sheet provided.

DIRECTIONS

For each of the passages below, there are 10 or 11 questions. Choose the best answer for each of the questions after you have finished reading the passage. The answers to the questions should be based on the information that is stated or implied in the text and any associated graphics.

Questions 1-10 are based on the following passage.

This passage is adapted from a novel. The protagonist, Anna, is in high school.

Anna strode briskly across the quad towards the back fence. School was just depressing after classes were out, being completely deserted. Stupid detention
Line again. Looking at the dead, empty windows made
5 her feel like she was missing out on something, somewhere else. Of course, she didn't really have anywhere to be. Tuesday afternoon. Only Tuesday. With a heavy sigh, she adjusted her headphones and approached the fence.
10 You weren't supposed to climb the fence to access the parking lot. She expertly handled the fence and jumped down the other side. Carla had once said only losers went the long way. Dusting off her hands, she stopped and thought. Her friends would be hanging
15 out at the spot. Should she go? She always did, though of late, something seemed different. Somehow Carla . . . she didn't know. She could always go home and hope mom wasn't in.
"Anna!" The addressee almost wet herself.
20 "Finally—I seriously thought they were, umm, gonna pen you up all day. Did you see Mr. Morgan's face?" Megan laughed. "Actually, umm, you should take a look in the mirror—close your mouth for Chrissakes—did I startle you? Sorry!" She smiled
25 and took Anna's arm as she always did, and started walking towards the spot.
Court was in full session. Gorgeous Carla was passing judgment on the class' newcomers *in absentia*. Anna was pretty sure this was how it was
30 used. Talking about people who weren't there. Carla acknowledged her with a fiendishly attractive grin that sent her pulse racing and then went on to Scan the Surroundings, as she called it. "Gotta know what's going on around you," she would say. Shielding her
35 eyes against the non-existing sun-glare, she squinted off into the distance to her left and right. Anna and everyone else had gotten used to it. It's not like anyone would say anything. That was just unthinkable. Only thing was, Anna was thinking it now.
40 "Hey," Anna said to the others while trying not to blush. Her MP3 player was blasting *Two Hearts*— a song she secretly enjoyed. God forbid the others found out. Definitely not cool. She could only hope Carla would continue her barrage against somegirl
45 Smith's name.
The bubble of hope burst instantly.
"Look who's late! Our very own bad girl Anna. Going for a makeover? Only, they say . . . you know . . . listening to love songs and *playing* tough doesn't
50 really go together that well. I'd definitely have to agree with that."
'She spells definitely *definately*,' Anna thought. 'And who are *they* anyway?' Anna felt her face growing hot. She glared at the others daring them
55 to laugh. Strained expressions all around except for Megan who rolled her eyes in sympathy as much as she dared while Carla droned on.
"So anyhow, this new girl Ebsidy? I was like . . . I was thinking. That's definitely not a real name.
60 I mean . . . I have never heard this name before. So . . ."
Excitedly, she started rummaging in her bag and produced . . . Mr. Ingram's attendance list for the class! She held it up triumphantly.
"Carla! Sheesh—did you steal that offa Mr. Ingram's
65 desk?" Michelle looked around in panic.
"Oh, shut up, Michelle. Y'all take a look at this."
Her finger stabbed at a name on the list. The girls huddled around and looked. It said "Abcde Smith." *Ebsidy*! Anna couldn't help it. She was kind of sore at

Carla, but this was so absurd, she couldn't help but
burst out laughing. So did everyone else.
    Megan literally *squealed* clutching her stomach.
"That's *sooo* messed up," she managed under tears.
    When the laughter subsided, Carla looked at
Anna. Newborn angel's eyes.
    "Not mad, are you, Anna?" Her voice a soothing
cool.
    "Umm . . . no." At that moment she just couldn't
hate her. She was an idiot.

1

In the passage, Anna is primarily concerned with

A) reflecting on a pivotal event in her school life.
B) finding ways to fit in with her group of friends.
C) her jumbled feelings towards one of her peers.
D) her self-disdain owing to her inability to express her feelings.

2

The description of school in paragraph 1 primarily conveys Anna's

A) exuberance at the prospect of leaving.
B) anxiety to be with her friends.
C) forlorn and frustrated feelings.
D) amusement at life's vicissitudes.

3

Lines 10-12 ("You weren't . . . side") and lines 20-22 ("Finally . . . laughed") are similar in that both imply that Anna

A) has repeatedly engaged in an activity.
B) feels resentment towards her teachers.
C) is not an exemplary student.
D) is easily influenced by others.

4

The passage indicates that Carla's behavior in lines 34-36 is perceived by the girls as

A) a persistent idiosyncrasy that is best not brought up.
B) a sign of uneasiness regarding their surroundings.
C) an embarrassing habit that did not warrant a reaction.
D) an intimidating gesture that allowed Carla to wield influence.

5

Which choice most strongly supports the idea that Anna has crossed a boundary?

A) Lines 14-17 ("Her friends . . . know")
B) Lines 37-39 ("It's not . . . now")
C) Lines 52-55 ("She spells . . . laugh")
D) Lines 76-79 ("Not mad . . . idiot")

6

It can be inferred from the passage that Anna is "trying not to blush" (lines 40-41) because

A) she remembers the shame of being mocked previously.
B) the other girls know she was listening to *Two Hearts*.
C) she is anxious that a fact about her may come to light.
D) she believes she is going to be ostracized if found out.

7

As presented in the passage, Megan is best described as

A) mischievous but also outright silly.
B) loyal and sympathetic but slightly cowed.
C) academically weak but warm and generous.
D) outwardly friendly but really underhanded.

8

Which choice provides the best evidence for the answer to the previous question?

A) Lines 21-24 ("Did you . . . Sorry!")
B) Lines 24-26 ("She . . . spot")
C) Lines 55-57 ("Strained . . . on")
D) Lines 72-73 ("Megan . . . tears")

9

According to the passage, the laughter of the girls was caused by

A) Megan's exaggerated way of expressing amusement.
B) a printing error on the class attendance list.
C) the revelation of a surprising idiosyncrasy.
D) Carla's inclination to misspell certain words.

10

In context, which of the following best characterizes Carla's behavior toward Anna in lines 74-77 ("When . . . cool")?

A) Innocuous and artless
B) Frank and confrontational
C) Ingratiating and flattering
D) Affable and manipulative

Questions 11-21 are based on the following passage and supplementary material.

This passage is adapted from an essay about psychology.

Let the setting be an office. Let us imagine a certain Mr. Doe is sitting here, waiting for an interview with President Smith of Dowell Company.
Presently, a door opens and two persons walk in:
a Caucasian man in a suit followed by an African American woman carrying a coffee tray. Without hesitation, Mr. Doe springs up from his seat and grasps the man's hand, exclaiming "It is such an honor to meet you, President Smith!" The greeted man's eyes widen in shock, he shakes his head and nods at the woman who entered the office with him. It takes a minute or two, but after the ensuing embarrassment and laughter, things are sorted out.

It may take you, the reader, a moment or two to figure out why things needed to be "sorted out." Others might take even longer, or they might even need to be told what happened. What went wrong? Mr. Doe assumed that the company's president is the man while it is, in fact, the title held by the woman who entered the office after him.

Regardless of the time required to divine what occurred here, this little scenario shows us something about the workings of the human mind: so-called tacit assumptions permeate our thinking and shape much of the mental construct that we use in order to understand the world around us. When presented with certain problems or situations, our minds automatically resort to the most plausible or the most "natural"-feeling possibilities in order to fill in unknown variables.

Tacit assumptions should be thought of as an evolutionary leg up. We could not function as efficiently as we do if we were to question and analyze every single situation that we encounter in our daily lives. Assuming that the probable will turn out to be true has contributed to our success as a species since this tendency frees our minds to focus on problems that warrant dealing with. We do not wonder whether the store is really going to exchange goods for money. Instead, we consider what we need to buy or if the price is adequate. Or, when leaving our apartment, we do not ponder whether the air outside will be breathable today. We might think about what to wear instead.

However, this automation does not always confer an advantage. In the case of Mr. Doe (and many others), the man's gender, Caucasian descent, and not carrying beverages elicited a stronger association with the conception of a company's president than did his companion's attributes. A conclusion was drawn without conscious effort. Thus his mind was freed up for other tasks such as deciding what to say. The problem that arose from this, though, is obvious: had Mr. Doe consciously pondered the question of who among the two persons could actually be the president, his initial reaction would have been more circumspect.

Tacit assumptions and their acceptance tell us a lot about our mindsets as individuals and even as a society. After all, was it not "natural" for Mr. Doe to react the way he did? Even if you do not agree, are you not able to understand why he immediately assumed the man was the president? It is certainly not outlandish to react as he did even though it would be desirable if it were.

I am relieved to think that nowadays, this particular tacit assumption will encounter more resistance, and immediate resistance at that, than it would have 40 years ago. That being said, a host of these assumptions still roam our minds, governing us without even triggering our awareness.

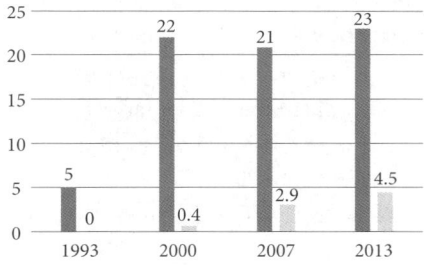

Statistics Regarding Female Bosses in Country A

■ % prefer a female boss
■ % female CEOs in Fortune 500 Companies

11

Within the passage as a whole, the second paragraph (lines 14-20) mainly serves to

A) lead from an example to the psychological concept behind it.
B) suggest that different readers possess different cognitive capacities.
C) introduce a situation that might result in a misunderstanding.
D) criticize Mr. Doe for his biased presumptions based on race and gender.

12

Lines 21-26 ("Regardless . . . us") suggest which of the following about tacit assumptions?

A) They enable us to interpret our environment once we acquire them.
B) The model that underlies our perception would differ without them.
C) They are an evolutionary advantage that is common to our species.
D) There exist various terms to describe this concept.

13

As used in line 38, "warrant" most nearly means

A) certify.
B) ensure.
C) call for.
D) permit.

14

Which of the following best summarizes the author's main point in lines 31-57?

A) An alternative to tacit assumptions is to replace automation with conscious efforts to judge which situations need attention.
B) Tacit assumptions allow us to prioritize problems that need our attention instead of pondering obvious outcomes.
C) The drawbacks of tacit assumptions are that some automatic conclusions are incorrect and should be avoided.
D) There are drawbacks in addition to advantages to our ability to relegate certain decisions to mental automation.

15

In the passage, the author indicates which of the following as the reason for the "embarrassment and laughter" mentioned in lines 12-13?

A) Mr. Doe's racist background and bias
B) Our society's evolving notions of propriety
C) A process Mr. Doe was not aware of
D) President Smith's unseemly behavior

16

Which choice provides the best evidence for the answer to the previous question?

A) Lines 4-6 ("Presently . . . tray")
B) Lines 23-26 ("so-called . . . us")
C) Lines 47-51 ("Caucasian . . . effort")
D) Lines 66-69 ("I am . . . ago")

17

As used in line 60, "natural" most nearly means

A) unrefined.
B) artless.
C) essential.
D) common.

18

The passage suggests most strongly that the author of the passage considers our current society's mindset to be

A) colored to an objectionable degree by tacit assumptions.
B) unable to overcome the handicap that tacit assumptions impart.
C) dangerously tolerant of old-fashioned preconceptions.
D) free from the burden of parochial tacit assumptions.

19

Which choice provides the best evidence for the answer to the previous question?

A) Lines 31-35 ("Tacit . . . lives")
B) Lines 40-44 ("Instead . . . instead")
C) Lines 61-65 ("Even if . . . were")
D) Lines 69-71 ("That . . . awareness")

20

The data in the graph about female bosses most strongly supports which of the following statements?

A) Female CEOs in Fortune 500 Companies directly contributed to the popularity of female bosses.
B) The increase in preference for female bosses grew steadily until 2013.
C) The number of people preferring a female boss dropped sometime after 2000.
D) The issue of female CEOs had never been discussed prior to the 1990s.

21

The data in the graph provides the most direct support for which of the following ideas in the passage?

A) Tacit assumptions are fundamental to the way we understand our environment.
B) We have been able to overcome sexism thanks to research into tacit assumptions.
C) Tacit assumptions about gender roles have decreased over the years.
D) The undeniable success of female CEOs has overturned a lot of tacit assumptions.

Questions 22-31 are based on the following passage and supplementary material.

This passage is adapted from Wamelink et al., "Can Plants Grow on Mars and the Moon: A Growth Experiment on Mars and Moon Soil Simulants." ©2014.

Lunar and Martian explorations have provided information about the mineral composition of their respective soils. In addition to rocks, they contain
Line large amounts of sand-like soils or regoliths. All the
5 essential minerals for the growth of plants appear to be present in sufficient quantities in both soils with the likely exception of reactive nitrogen. The latter's absence may be overcome by using nitrogen-fixing plant species. In symbioses with bacteria, these
10 nitrogen fixers are able to bind nitrogen from the air and transform it into nitrates, a process which requires nitrogen in the atmosphere. However, there is no atmosphere on the moon; the one on Mars can only be called minimal and contains mere traces of
15 nitrogen.

During the earlier Apollo project, no experiments concerning plant growth on the moon were conducted. However, experiments on Earth have been carried out using retrieved moon material. Plants
20 were exposed to moon stones through direct contact and small amounts were even added to the growth medium. These results indicated that there were no toxic effects of moon soil on short term plant growth.

Our goal was to investigate whether or not plants
25 would germinate and live long enough to go through the first stages of plant development on artificial Mars and moon regoliths. If so, it would be conceivable that plant growth is possible within an artificial surrounding on the surfaces of Mars and our moon
30 even though our experiment was to be conducted on Earth with its deviating gravity. Moreover, we assumed that such plant cultivation would be carried out within sealed surroundings under Earth-like light and atmospheric conditions.

35 For the study, Mars and moon regolith simulants manufactured by NASA were purchased. Since these regoliths are (at least in mineral composition) comparable to Earth soils, they can be mimicked by using volcanic Earth soils, as has been done by NASA.
40 As a control, we used coarse river Rhine soil extracted from a stratum 10 m below the surface which is nutrient poor and free from organic matter and seeds. Analysis revealed that the moon regolith simulant is truly nutrient poor though it contains a small amount
45 of nitrates and ammonium. The Mars regolith simulant also contains traces of nitrates, ammonium and also a significant amount of carbon.

Plant species were selected from three groups: four different crops, four nitrogen fixers, and six wild
50 plants. Only species with relatively small seeds were chosen so that the nutrient stock in the seeds would be quickly depleted and the plant becomes totally dependent on what is available in the soils for its growth.

55 Small pots were filled with 100 g moon soil simulant, 100 g Earth soil or 50 g Mars soil simulant, and 25 g demineralized water was added to each pot. The mass of the simulants added differed since we wanted to fill the pots up to approximately similar
60 volumes to attain the same column height.

On average, plant species in Martian soil simulant performed significantly better than plants in our Earth's control soil with respect to biomass increment. Even though the coarse and very nutrient-poor soil is far
65 from the best choice to grow crops on, we expected it to perform at least as well as the extraterrestrial alternatives. However, during warmer periods, it was difficult to maintain the water level in the pots even though water was administered twice a day. The Mars
70 soil simulant resembles loess-like[1] soils from Europe and retains water better than the other two soils. Moon soil simulant dried out the fastest. It is therefore recommended that further research be conducted on the physical characteristics of extraterrestrial soils in
75 order to explore potential irrigation techniques.

[1] a silt which forms fertile topsoil

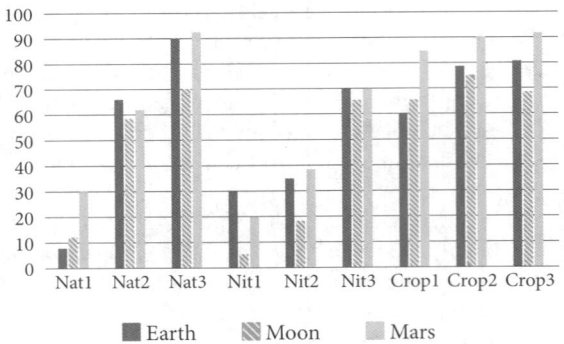

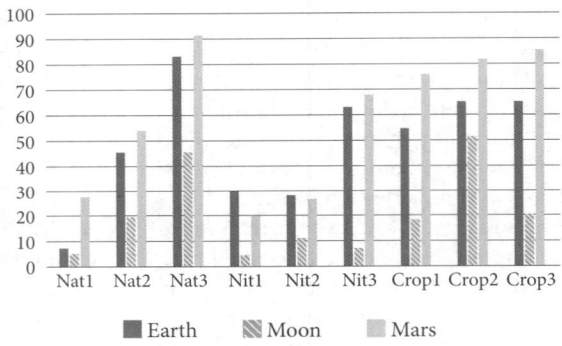

Charts 1 and 2 show partial results of the study described in the passage. Nat1-Nat3 refers to naturally occurring plants, Nit1-Nit3 refers to nitrogen fixers, and Crop1-Crop3 refers to crops.

22

As used in line 22, "medium" most nearly means

A) surroundings.
B) mechanism.
C) mode.
D) climate.

23

The passage implies that the authors believe which of the following about lunar and Martian regoliths?

A) It is possible to create interchangeable substitutes for them using resources from Earth.
B) Plants might suffer from detrimental effects if exposed to them over long periods of time.
C) The absence of an atmosphere means they lack most of the nutrients plants require.
D) They are actually inferior to Earth's soils when it comes to growing plants.

24

Which choice provides the best evidence for the answer to the previous question?

A) Lines 9-15 ("In symbioses . . . nitrogen")
B) Lines 19-23 ("Plants . . . growth")
C) Lines 35-39 ("For the . . . NASA")
D) Lines 63-67 ("Even . . . alternatives")

25

As used in line 40, "control" most nearly means

A) authority.
B) standard.
C) supervision.
D) limitation.

26

The authors imply that which of the following is a factor that favors the accuracy of the study's results?

A) Selection of plants
B) Size of seeds
C) Planetary gravity
D) Water quality

27

Which choice provides the best evidence for the answer to the previous question?

A) Lines 27-31 ("If so . . . gravity")
B) Lines 48-50 ("Plant . . . plants")
C) Lines 50-54 ("Only . . . growth")
D) Lines 55-57 ("Small . . . pot")

28

The authors mention "column height" in line 60 most likely to

A) point out the exactitude which is required in order to attain reliable results.
B) underscore an essential requirement that had to be satisfied.
C) explain the process according to which the experiment was conducted.
D) offer the rationale behind a decision that was made regarding the study.

29

Which of the following statements is best supported by the passage and by the information in Chart 1?

A) Crops perform better than nitrogen fixers on moon soil since crops suffer less from lack of hydration.
B) Naturally occurring plants performed surprisingly well on Martian soil compared to that of Earth.
C) The poor water retention rate of moon soil only becomes a significant factor after 50 days.
D) Simulated regolith is made of Earth soil which explains why the plants grew best on Mars simulant.

30

Taken together, the two charts suggest that naturally occurring plants

A) mostly last 50 days after sprouting unless planted into moon soil.
B) will most likely die if they are planted into moon regolith.
C) thrive for the most part if they are planted into Mars regolith.
D) die the least after germination if planted into Earth soil.

31

What statement is best supported by the data in Chart 2?

A) For each soil, crops are categorically stronger survivors than nitrogen fixers.
B) None of the survival rates on moon soil surpasses any of the other shown survival rates.
C) The survival rate on Earth for any given plant always trails that of Mars.
D) The values for naturally occurring plants define the boundaries for Earth soil.

Questions 32-41 are based on the following passage.

This passage is adapted from President Woodrow Wilson's first inaugural address in 1913. In this part of his speech, Woodrow Wilson addresses the price of progress.

    We have built up, moreover, a great system of government, which has stood through a long age as in many respects a model for those who seek to set liberty
Line upon foundations that will endure against fortuitous
5 change, against storm and accident. Our life contains every great thing, and contains it in rich abundance.
    But the evil has come with the good, and much fine gold has been corroded. With riches has come inexcusable waste. We have squandered a great part
10 of what we might have used, and have not stopped to conserve the exceeding bounty of nature, without which our genius for enterprise would have been worthless and impotent, scorning to be careful, shamefully prodigal as well as admirably efficient. We
15 have been proud of our industrial achievements, but we have not hitherto stopped thoughtfully enough to count the human cost, the cost of lives snuffed out, of energies overtaxed and broken, the fearful physical and spiritual cost to the men and women and children
20 upon whom the dead weight and burden of it all has fallen pitilessly the years through. . . .
    With the great Government went many deep secret things which we too long delayed to look into and scrutinize with candid, fearless eyes. The great
25 Government we loved has too often been made use of for private and selfish purposes, and those who used it had forgotten the people.
    At last a vision has been vouchsafed us of our life as a whole. We see the bad with the good, the debased
30 and decadent with the sound and vital. With this vision we approach new affairs. Our duty is to cleanse, to reconsider, to restore, to correct the evil without impairing the good, to purify and humanize every process of our common life without weakening or
35 sentimentalizing it.
    There has been something crude and heartless and unfeeling in our haste to succeed and be great. Our thought has been "Let every man look out for himself, let every generation look out for itself," while
40 we reared giant machinery which made it impossible that any but those who stood at the levers of control should have a chance to look out for themselves. We had not forgotten our morals. We remembered well enough that we had set up a policy which was meant
45 to serve the humblest as well as the most powerful, with an eye single to the standards of justice and fair play, and remembered it with pride. But we were very heedless and in a hurry to be great.
    We have come now to the sober second thought.
50 The scales of heedlessness have fallen from our eyes. We have made up our minds to square every process of our national life again with the standards we so proudly set up at the beginning and have always carried at our hearts. Our work is a work of
55 restoration. . . .
    We have studied as perhaps no other nation has the most effective means of production, but we have not studied cost or economy as we should either as organizers of industry, as statesmen, or as individuals.
60 Nor have we studied and perfected the means by which government may be put at the service of humanity, in safeguarding the health of the Nation, the health of its men and its women and its children, as well as their rights in the struggle for existence.
65 This is no sentimental duty. The firm basis of government is justice, not pity. These are matters of justice.
    There can be no equality or opportunity, the first essential of justice in the body politic, if men and
70 women and children be not shielded in their lives, their very vitality, from the consequences of great industrial and social processes which they cannot alter, control, or singly cope with. Society must see to it that it does not itself crush or weaken or damage its
75 own constituent parts. The first duty of law is to keep sound the society it serves. Sanitary laws, pure food laws, and laws determining conditions of labor which individuals are powerless to determine for themselves are intimate parts of the very business of justice and
80 legal efficiency.
    These are some of the things we ought to do, and not leave the others undone, the old-fashioned, never-to-be-neglected, fundamental safeguarding of property and of individual right. This is the high
85 enterprise of the new day: To lift everything that concerns our life as a Nation to the light that shines from the hearth fire of every man's conscience and vision of the right.

32

The stance Wilson takes in the passage is best described as that of

A) an innovator sharing his groundbreaking ideas.
B) a supplicant asking his audience for rectitude.
C) a champion of economic progress and democracy.
D) an idealist seeking to redress a shortfall.

33

In context of the whole passage, paragraph 1 mostly serves to

A) introduce the position Wilson intends to argue for.
B) present a presumption which is consequently rebutted.
C) lay out a point of view which is subsequently qualified.
D) affirm the significance of a nation's achievements.

34

In lines 9-14, people who are achieving riches are mostly characterized as being

A) efficacious.
B) malicious.
C) careless.
D) regretful.

35

The main rhetorical effect of the repeated use of the word "cost" in lines 17-21 is to

A) enumerate the different ways that people have paid for advancement.
B) suggest the gradual increase of the burden people have to shoulder.
C) contrast the physical cost of an endeavor to its psychological cost.
D) convey the sense of dread that people have had to overcome.

36

As presented in paragraph 4, the "vision" (line 28) is significant in that it enables people to

A) realize that the prohibitive cost of success ultimately outweighs the benefits.
B) maintain the rate of progress while correcting its downsides.
C) approach a problem with more consideration and care than before.
D) perceive the agents behind the evils that accompany the benefits of progress.

37

Which choice provides the best evidence for the answer to the previous question?

A) Lines 22-24 ("With the great . . . eyes")
B) Lines 39-42 ("while we . . . themselves")
C) Lines 49-54 ("We have . . . hearts")
D) Lines 76-80 ("Sanitary laws . . . efficiency")

38

As used in line 46, "single to" most nearly means

A) free of.
B) fastened upon.
C) alone with.
D) distinct from.

39

In the context of the whole passage, the phrase "sober second thought" in line 49 suggests that

A) the drive towards success initially impaired people's judgment.
B) people are now willing to align their lives with moral standards.
C) a pessimistic view will have to be adopted to rebuild the nation.
D) every nation needs to reflect on its actions from time to time.

CONTINUE

40

The statement in lines 68-73 ("There can . . . with") can best be described as

A) a condition.
B) an accusation.
C) speculation.
D) incitement.

41

In lines 75-76 ("The first . . . serves"), the speaker suggests that law

A) is irreplaceable in the role it serves.
B) should be seen as a means to an end.
C) ensures justice even for those without power.
D) is seldom put to use in a meaningful way.

Questions 42-52 are based on the following passages.

Passage 1 is adapted from Arandjelovic et al., "Genetic inference of group dynamics and female kin structure in a western lowland gorilla population." ©2014. Passage 2 is adapted from Clyvia et al., "Do wild titi monkeys show empathy?" ©2014.

Passage 1

By using genetic analysis to monitor multiple groups over several years, we indirectly observed the dynamics of group formation, group dissolution and
Line individual movements in western lowland gorillas
5 (WLGs). In many species, there are clear benefits for females to reside with female kin, so much so that most mammals are female philopatric[1]. Despite low levels of feeding competition and no evidence of between-group competition for resources, related
10 female mountain gorillas exhibit more affiliative behaviors towards kin than non-kin when they live in the same group and female kin are more likely to form coalitions than non-kin in competition over food. However, no studies have yet tested to see
15 whether residing with and supporting kin improves their fitness.

Our analyses imply that female WLGs do not disperse far from their natal range as the average relatedness of females across all groups at the
20 study site was higher than expected by chance. Furthermore, we found that, assuming that all local groups are equally viable dispersal options, females co-occur in groups containing their kin more often than would be expected if they dispersed randomly.
25 At the same time, our tests can neither determine the primary driver(s) of female dispersal nor rule out that co-residency of female kin may be a secondary effect of other drivers of female dispersal decisions.

We inferred several instances of apparent natal
30 and secondary transfer where females moved between groups either separately or together, which has also been observed in other populations. Another study suggests that post-dispersal female kin associations could occur in a scenario where female half-siblings
35 (daughters of their group's silverback[2]) reach dispersal age at similar times and transfer into the same group. We have evidence here that, in at least one case, the co-occurrence of two half-siblings in a group occurred over a longer time period as
40 the elder half-sibling had already produced at least one offspring with the group's silverback when the younger half-sibling immigrated into the group. Thus, females may not need to be in the same age cohort

but may still transfer into the same group. It has also
45 been suggested that related females may co-reside in a
new group if they co-transfer after the disintegration
of their natal group.

Females, despite natal and secondary dispersal,
appear to retain associations with their same-sex
50 kin post-emigration as females co-reside in groups
containing female kin. The lack of long-term
behavioral data limits the inferences we can make
on the function of these kin relations; however,
dispersal need not be treated as an impediment to the
55 possibility of kin-biased behaviors in the species.

Passage 2
Clyvia et al. observed a potential case of
empathy in the black-fronted titi monkey (*Callicebus
nigrifrons*). Titi monkeys are highly territorial
and pairs defend their territories by duetting[3] and
60 displaying other aggressive behaviors to neighbouring
pairs at their boundaries. It was therefore surprising
to witness members of one group not only accepting
the presence of, but also socializing with an injured
male of another group. The female of the former
65 group even displayed affiliative behaviors commonly
reserved for mates.

Within the primate lineage, sympathetic concern
was first thought to be confined to the great apes,
and only recently has been considered possible for
70 monkey species. Some examples of compensatory
or compassionate care among new world primates[4]
could also be interpreted as empathetic behaviors.
However, the circumstances described in these
instances were based on interactions between group
75 members unlike the case of the injured titi monkey.
One study, for instance, reported compensatory care
for an injured juvenile spider monkey by his mother
long after weaning while another reported behavioral
responses of moustached tamarins to an injured
80 group member that allowed them to maintain contact
with this individual.

Empathy is more likely to occur when there is
social proximity and kinship between individuals as
it is thought to originate from the mother-offspring
85 bond. Though genetic kinship data for the titi
monkeys was not available, Clyvia et al. thought it
is likely that the individuals in question might be
related as home-ranges overlapped by more than one
third, which could explain the emotional engagement
90 between them. What adds to this conjecture is
a recorded case of adoption among the groups
involved in said study. Subject to familiarity, however,
they added that this does not imply that unrelated
individuals cannot perceive another individual's
95 emotional state. Even in the absence of kinship,
empathy could have appeared because of familiarity
due to overlapping home-ranges. For instance, it has
been established for bonobo monkeys that partners
sharing strong affiliative bonds were more likely to be
100 sensitive to each other's distress, even in the absence
of genetic ties.

[1] refers to the tendency to remain near a particular area
[2] adult male gorilla
[3] a loud song performed by primates
[4] the families of primates found in Central and South America

42

As used in line 20, "chance" most nearly means

A) opportunity.
B) fate.
C) possibility.
D) coincidence.

43

The sentences in lines 14-16 ("However . . . fitness")
and lines 25-28 ("At . . . decisions") are similar in that
both

A) admit to points that their research has failed to elucidate.
B) point out the lack of studies regarding kinship among gorillas.
C) present results the authors have arrived at through their tests.
D) indicate an extent of knowledge that is currently available.

44

It can be inferred that the authors of Passage 1 believe which of the following about the dispersal of female gorillas?

A) It is possible to calculate the statistical probability of accidental meetings with kin.
B) Females transferring in concert with a sibling to the same group are a rare occurrence.
C) They choose their post-dispersal groups based on the presence of kin.
D) It is mainly motivated by drivers such as quality of vegetation and alpha male.

45

Which choice provides the best evidence for the answer to the previous question?

A) Lines 7-14 ("Despite . . . food")
B) Lines 21-24 ("Furthermore . . . randomly")
C) Lines 29-32 ("We inferred . . . populations")
D) Lines 37-42 ("We have . . . group")

46

As used in line 66, "reserved" most nearly means

A) composed.
B) set aside.
C) unsociable.
D) claimed.

47

The authors of Passage 2 suggest that new world primates should be understood as

A) capable of empathy outside of groups.
B) an only recently discovered species.
C) noted for their exemplary compassion.
D) a family separate from that of the great apes.

48

Which of the following best summarizes the main point of the final paragraph of Passage 2 (lines 82-101)?

A) Geographical proximity is the main reason for the witnessed empathy.
B) The likelihood of existing blood relationship does not preclude the alternative.
C) Empathy confers advantages to its practitioners in the absence of kinship.
D) Empathy among non-great apes is predicated upon kinship and physical proximity.

49

The central claim of Passage 1 is that in spite of the dispersal of female western lowland gorillas from their kin,

A) relationships among kin continue unchanged upon reunion.
B) most will reunite with siblings since they stay near their natal range.
C) their behavior upon reunion betrays their partial sympathy.
D) competition for food and other resources remains a great issue.

50

Which choice best describes a major difference between Passage 1 and Passage 2?

A) Whereas Passage 2 is based on the assumption that groups are static, Passage 1 focuses on their dynamic aspect.
B) Whereas Passage 2 considers a variety of primate species, Passage 1 states that a behavior only occurs in a single species.
C) Whereas Passage 2 emphasizes the importance of physical proximity, Passage 1 claims that kinship is more important.
D) Whereas Passage 2 mentions kinship as a driver behind empathy, Passage 1 asserts that this might not be the only driver.

51

On which of the following points would the authors of both passages most likely agree?

A) Primates that do not display empathy are farther removed from humans than those that do.
B) Interactions between separate groups of primates are often characterized by hostilities.
C) The advantages of having kin present are reflected in the small distances that individuals travel.
D) Recognition of commonalities can change the face of an encounter between primates.

52

Which choice provides the best evidence that the authors of Passage 2 would agree to some extent with the statement in lines 7-14 ("Despite . . . food"), Passage 1?

A) Lines 70-72 ("Some . . . behaviors")
B) Lines 76-81 ("One . . . individual")
C) Lines 85-89 ("Though . . . third")
D) Lines 92-95 ("Subject . . . state")

STOP

Do not move on to the next section if you finish early.

You may review your answers in this section only.

Answer Keys & Performance Breakdown

1	(C)	Summary	19	(C)	Evidence	37	(C)	Evidence
2	(C)	Local	20	(C)	Graph	38	(B)	Vocabulary
3	(C)	Synthesize	21	(C)	Graph	39	(A)	Summary
4	(A)	Local	22	(A)	Vocabulary	40	(A)	Local
5	(B)	Evidence	23	(A)	Local	41	(B)	Local
6	(C)	Local	24	(C)	Evidence	42	(D)	Vocabulary
7	(B)	Local	25	(B)	Vocabulary	43	(D)	Synthesize
8	(C)	Evidence	26	(B)	Local	44	(A)	Local
9	(C)	Local	27	(C)	Evidence	45	(B)	Evidence
10	(D)	Local	28	(D)	Context	46	(B)	Vocabulary
11	(A)	Context	29	(B)	Graph	47	(D)	Local
12	(B)	Local	30	(A)	Graph	48	(B)	Local
13	(C)	Vocabulary	31	(D)	Graph	49	(C)	Summary
14	(D)	Local	32	(D)	Stance	50	(A)	Synthesize
15	(C)	Local	33	(C)	Context	51	(D)	Synthesize
16	(C)	Evidence	34	(C)	Local	52	(B)	Synthesize
17	(D)	Vocabulary	35	(A)	Style			
18	(A)	Local	36	(C)	Local			

■ Write down the number of correct answers for each question type.

Question Types	Number of Correct Answers
Local	/ 19
Style	/ 1
Vocabulary	/ 7
Evidence	/ 8
Context	/ 3
Organization	0 / 0
Summary	/ 3
Stance	/ 1
Synthesize	/ 5
Graph	/ 5
Total	**/ 52**

Answer Explanations

Questions 1-10

1. (C) — Summary

In the passage, Anna is mainly concerned with her feelings about Carla. The latter is, if not a role model, at least a person of influence (lines 12-13), but something about her bothers Anna (lines 15-17). Carla is the leader of their group of friends and very attractive (lines 27-33), but can also be bossy and mean (lines 47-57).

C is the best choice.

A is incorrect because in the passage, Anna does not reflect on any certain event in depth. B is incorrect. Though she was detained and jumps the fence, the passage does not suggest she does this to gain acceptance by the group. D is incorrect because Anna does not mainly hate herself in the passage.

2. (C) — Local

C is the best choice because the paragraph states that school is depressing being completely deserted, and Anna looks at dead, empty windows (forlorn). Also, she was detained. In addition, it is only Tuesday which implies the weekend is far off and elicits a sigh (frustrated).

A is incorrect because there is no instance of "exuberance." B is incorrect because "friends" are not mentioned. Rather, it says she does not have anywhere to be. D is incorrect because "amusement" and "vicissitudes" are not supported.

3. (C) — Synthesize

Lines 10-12 show that Anna jumps the fence which is against the rules. Lines 19-22 show that Anna went through detention, which implies that a teacher was angry at her.

C is the best choice.

A is incorrect because it only applies to the fence. (She handles it expertly.) B is incorrect because even with the detention, it is not suggested that she resents her teachers. D is incorrect because the detention part did not suggest anything about being influenced.

4. (A) — Local

A is the best choice because everyone else has gotten used to it (this has happened more than once) and no one says anything because it would be unthinkable (best not brought up).

B is incorrect because the passage does not show how the girls feel about their surroundings. C is incorrect because the passage does not imply that the girls find it embarrassing. D is incorrect because the passage does not suggest the behavior intimidates the girls.

5. (B) — Evidence

B is the best choice because the lines show that Anna now thought of commenting on Carla's weird behavior which had been unthinkable before.

A is incorrect because though it shows a change of heart toward Carla, it does not specify how this feeling changed. C is incorrect because though she is mad at Carla, it does not indicate a recent change. D is incorrect because it does not show a recent loss of respect.

6. (C) — Local

C is the best choice. Anna is listening to a song she "secretly enjoyed." (line 42) She does not want the others to find out.

A is incorrect because no previous occurrences are hinted at. B is incorrect because she does not want them to find out; i.e., they do not know yet. D is incorrect because a strong reaction like "ostracized" is not supported by the passage.

7. (B) — Local

B is the best choice because of lines 55-57 (see next question).

A is incorrect because even though a case could be made for mischievous in lines 19-26, "outright silly" is not supported. C is incorrect because the passage never mentions her academic performance. D is incorrect because "underhanded" (secret and deceitful) is not supported by the passage.

8. (C) — Evidence

C is the best choice because the lines state that Megan shows sympathy while all the other girls try not to laugh at Anna (loyal), but she dares not show more of a reaction. (She is cowed by Carla.)

A, B, and D are incorrect because they do not show that Megan is loyal but slightly cowed.

Answer Explanations

9. (C) — Local

The laughter is mentioned in lines 70-74. The cause was that someone's first name was printed as "Abcde Smith," which was "so absurd" (line 70) that everyone started laughing.

C is the best choice. The passage states that someone's name actually being spelled "Abcde" seems absurd, so it could be called a "surprising idiosyncrasy."

A is incorrect because Megan's laughter did not cause the others to laugh. B is incorrect because nothing suggests "a printing error." D is incorrect because the passage indicates that Carla did not create the list. (She stole it from a teacher.)

10. (D) — Local

D is the best choice because Carla, after aggravating Anna in lines 47-51 and then making everyone laugh, chooses this opportune moment (manipulative) to sweetly ask Anna (affable) if she is mad.

A is incorrect because it implies Carla is innocent and honest. B is incorrect because "confrontational" means seeking a fight or argument. C is incorrect because Carla merely asks Anna if she is mad, which is not the same as flattery.

Questions 11-21

11. (A) — Context

The second paragraph clearly spells out what happened in the example in paragraph 1. In paragraph 3, this event is connected to a psychological concept (tacit assumptions).

A is the best choice.

B is incorrect because it does not show what the paragraph does within the context of the passage. C is incorrect because it does not introduce the situation but explain it. D is incorrect because no criticism is leveled at Mr. Doe.

12. (B) — Local

B is the best choice because lines 24-26 mention that the mental construct (model) is shaped by tacit assumptions. In other words, the mental construct would be different if tacit assumptions did not exist.

A is incorrect because no mention is made of acquiring them. C is incorrect because the specified lines do not mention evolution. D is incorrect because the passage does not suggest that other terms exist.

13. (C) — Vocabulary

C is the best choice because the sentence says our minds are free to focus on problems that "warrant" dealing with (instead of questioning and analyzing every single situation). Therefore, "call for" (justify) is correct.

A and B are incorrect because they means "guarantee." D is incorrect because it means "allow."

14. (D) — Local

There are two paragraphs in the specified range. The former paragraph explains that tacit assumptions are an evolutionary advantage that frees up our mind to deal with situations that really need dealing with. The latter paragraph concedes that tacit assumptions are not always advantageous because they might lead to wrong conclusions.

D is the best choice.

A is incorrect because *replacing* tacit assumptions is not mentioned. B is incorrect because it leaves out the latter paragraph. C is incorrect because it leaves out the former paragraph.

15. (C) — Local

C is the best choice because of lines 47-51 (see next question).

A is incorrect because the passage does not indicate that Mr. Doe is a racist. B is incorrect because society's changing notions did not cause Mr. Doe to mistake the company's president. D is incorrect because the passage does not imply that President Smith acted improperly.

16. (C) — Evidence

C is the best choice. The "embarrassment and laughter" was a result of Mr. Doe mistaking the man for the president. The lines show that Mr. Doe unconsciously connected the wrong person's attributes with the role of president.

A, B, and D are incorrect because none of them show that Mr. Doe's unconscious decision caused the embarrassment and laughter.

17. (D) — Vocabulary

D is the best choice because the next sentence suggests anyone would be able to understand why he reacted the way he did. Thus, Mr. Doe's "natural" reaction was common.

A is incorrect because it means "unsophisticated." B is incorrect because it means "genuine" or "honest." C is incorrect because it means "inherent."

18. (A) — Local

A is the best choice because of lines 61-65 (see next question).

B is incorrect. Assuming that "the handicap" refers to wrong associations, then the last paragraph indicates that fewer such handicaps now exist though many are still left. This is different from "unable to overcome." C is incorrect because "dangerously" is not supported. D is incorrect because the last sentence states a host of tacit assumptions still roam our minds.

19. (C) — Evidence

C is the best choice because the lines state that Mr. Doe's reaction is not considered outlandish even though it should be considered outlandish. In other words, an objectionable behavior is broadly accepted by society.

A, B, and D are incorrect because none of them state that our mindsets are colored to an objectionable degree.

20. (C) — Graph

C is the best choice because the number of people preferring a female boss in 2007 was lower than in 2000.

A is incorrect because in the year 2007, preference for a female boss decreased even though the number of female CEOs increased. B is incorrect because of the word "steadily." D is incorrect because there is no data regarding this statement.

21. (C) — Graph

C is the best choice. The statement was made in lines 66-69. The graph supports this because according to its data, the number of female CEOs has increased over time.

A is incorrect because the graph's data makes no statement in this regard. B is incorrect because neither the passage nor the graph shows that we have overcome sexism. D is incorrect because neither the graph nor the passage shows a cause-and-effect relationship between female CEOs' success and an overturning of tacit assumptions.

Questions 22-31

22. (A) — Vocabulary

A is the best choice because the sentence mentions that material was added to plants' growth "medium." Thus, the word refers to the material (presumably some kind of soil) that surrounded the plants.

B is incorrect because it means "machine" or "method." C is incorrect because it means "condition" or "approach." D is incorrect because it means "weather" or "conditions."

23. (A) — Local

A is the best choice because of lines 35-39 (see next question).

B is incorrect because the authors do not suggest there are long term detrimental effects. C is incorrect because the lack of an atmosphere is only mentioned to occasion a lack of reactive nitrogen which is different from "most of the nutrients." D is incorrect because the authors mention that Martian soil performed better than Earth soil on average.

24. (C) — Evidence

C is the best choice because the lines state that Earth soils can be used to mimic Martian and lunar regoliths thanks to a similarity in mineral composition.

A, B, and D are incorrect because none of them show that it is possible to create interchangeable substitutes for lunar and Martian regoliths using resources from Earth.

25. (B) — Vocabulary

B is the best choice because the sentence mentions using Earth soil from the river Rhine as a "control." In context, the authors discuss using Mars and moon regolith simulants. It can be inferred that "control" in this instance means a standard to compare moon and Mars results against. This makes "standard" the best choice.

A is incorrect because it means "expert" or "power." C is incorrect because it means "management" or "administration." D is incorrect because it means

Answer Explanations

"restraint" or "disadvantage."

26. (B) *Local*

B is the best choice because of lines 50-54 (see next question).

A is incorrect because the authors do not suggest that certain plants yield more accurate results. C is incorrect because "gravity" is mentioned as a factor that diverges from the target environments (Mars and moon). D is incorrect because "water quality" was not mentioned as a factor that favors the accuracy of results.

27. (C) *Evidence*

C is the best choice because the sentence states that the small seed size ensures that plants will quickly start depending on the soil (instead of the nutrients contained within the seed). It can be inferred that from that point on, the difference in soils will influence the performance of the plants which is, after all, the aim of the study.

A, B, and D are incorrect because none of them show that the size of seeds is a factor that favors the accuracy of the study's results.

28. (D) *Context*

D is the best choice. The same sentence states that different amounts of soil were used in different pots in order to attain the same column height. Thus, "column height" was the reason for the decision to use different amounts.

A is incorrect because wanting to attain the same column height does not imply stringent requirements regarding exactitude. B is incorrect because "essential" is not supported in context. C is incorrect because "column height" does not explain a process.

29. (B) *Graph*

B is the best choice because Chart 1 shows that Martian soil, on average, yields the best results (highest rate of germination). Also, the passage states that the authors expected Earth soil to perform equally or better than extraterrestrial soils, which supports that the results are surprising.

A is incorrect because the statement that "crops suffer less from lack of hydration" is not supported. C is incorrect because the statement refers to Chart 2, not Chart 1. D is incorrect because according to the logic in D, moon simulant should show similar results to Mars simulant as it is also made of Earth soil.

30. (A) *Graph*

A is the best choice because a comparison between Chart 1 (germination) and Chart 2 (alive after 50 days) shows very minor losses for Earth and Mars regoliths, but a lot of major losses for moon regolith.

B is incorrect because the Charts do not contain sufficient data to support this conjecture. C is incorrect because "thrive for the most part" conflicts with the mediocre values for Nat2, and the poor values for Nat1. D is incorrect because the plants die the least after germination if planted in Martian soil (roughly comparable losses for Nat1 and Nat3, and a decisively bigger loss in Earth soil for Nat2).

31. (D) *Graph*

D is the best choice because both the minimum (Nat1) and the maximum (Nat3) values for Earth soil are found with naturally occurring plants.

A is incorrect because "categorically" means "unconditionally" or "without exception." However, Nit3 has a higher survival rate in Earth soil than Crop1. B is incorrect because the survival rate on moon for Crop2 is obviously higher than non-moon values for Nat1, Nit1, and Nit2. C is incorrect because the survival rate on Earth surpasses that of Mars for Nit1 and Nit2.

Questions 32-41

32. (D) *Stance*

Wilson emphasizes that while the nation has made great achievements, these have come at great human cost. He says this oversight has cost the people dearly, and that safeguarding the people, protecting them, is a matter of justice and something government should implement now.

D is the best choice.

A is incorrect because the passage does not indicate that Wilson's ideas are innovative. B is incorrect because Wilson does not beg. Rather, he asserts his proposal is the morally proper choice. C is incorrect because Wilson does not speak for progress, but rather for the victims of progress.

33. (C) — Context

Paragraph 1 states that we have achieved greatness and filled our lives with great things in abundance. The remainder of the passage emphasizes the cost at which this has been achieved.

C is the best choice.

A is incorrect because Wilson does not focus on the fact that greatness has been achieved. B is incorrect because Wilson does not deny the statements in paragraph 1. D is incorrect because the paragraph's function is to present an achievement in order to cite the price paid. The achievement in itself is not the focus of the speaker.

34. (C) — Local

C is the best choice because the lines portray people as wasteful of natural resources, prodigal, and unwilling to be careful but also efficient.

A is incorrect because "efficient" is mentioned once while negative traits are repeatedly mentioned. B is incorrect because "malicious" suggests evil intent. D is incorrect because "regretful" indicates that the people described felt regret.

35. (A) — Style

"Cost" refers to lives lost, energies overtaxed, and broken spirits of people burdened.

A is the best choice.

B is incorrect because "gradual increase" is not supported. C is incorrect because "physical cost" is not stated to be different from psychological cost. D is incorrect because "overcome" is not suggested.

36. (C) — Local

C is the best choice because "at last" (differently from before), we can approach new affairs and "correct the evil without impairing the good." The "evil" refers to the human cost of process in the previous two paragraphs, so "consideration and care" refers to taking care of the people.

A is incorrect because the paragraph states the vision enables the administration to get rid of evil, not realize something. Also, the paragraph does not mention that the cost of success will be prohibitive. B is incorrect because maintaining the speed of progress is not mentioned. D is incorrect because agents behind the evil are not mentioned. Also, perception of evil is the vision itself, but the question asks what the vision *enables* people to do.

37. (C) — Evidence

C is the best choice because the lines again state that we have "now" come to the "sober second thought." (We finally think clearly—this is like line 28.) The lines then state that we will apply the standards we are proud of and carry at our hearts (in context, it can be inferred that these are moral standards) to every process of our national lives.

A, B, and D are incorrect because they do not show a renewed spirit that involves taking care of the people.

38. (B) — Vocabulary

B is the best choice because the sentence mentions a policy meant to serve poor and rich, with an eye "single to" justice and fair play. Thus, "single to" means "focused on" or "exclusively considering."

A is incorrect because it means "devoid of." C is incorrect because it implies isolation or the absence of others. D is incorrect because it means "different from."

39. (A) — Summary

See question 32 for a short summary.

A is the best choice because "sober second thought" implies there was an intoxicated first thought (impaired judgment). The passage mentions that up to this point, progress was achieved at the cost of human suffering.

B is incorrect because the phrase implies realization which does not equal willingness to change. C is incorrect because the new view is not "pessimistic." D is incorrect because only Wilson's nation is discussed.

40. (A) — Local

A is the best choice because the sentence says the outcome in lines 68-69 is impossible to attain unless lines 69-73 ("if men . . . with") take place.

B is incorrect because no one is blamed. C is incorrect because "speculation" indicates a measure of uncertainty. D is incorrect because it means "to stir up violent behavior."

41. (B) — Local

The sentence says that laws exist to keep society healthy. This implies that laws exist for a purpose.

Answer Explanations

B is the best choice.

A is incorrect because "irreplaceable" is not suggested. C is incorrect because "those without power" is not hinted at. D is incorrect because how law is actually used is not mentioned.

Questions 42-52

42. (D) *Vocabulary*

D is the best choice because the sentence states that average relatedness was higher than expected by "chance." And the next sentence states that females co-occurred with kin more often than if they dispersed randomly. Therefore, "chance" is similar to the result of random dispersion. Thus, "coincidence" is correct.

A is incorrect because it means "lucky chance" or "convenience." B is incorrect because it means "destiny" or "predestination." C is incorrect because it means "feasibility" or "likelihood."

43. (D) *Synthesize*

The first specified sentence states that no studies have yet tested the question of improved fitness thanks to residing with kin. The second specified sentence states that the conducted tests cannot determine the primary motivation for female dispersal.

D is the best choice because "extent of knowledge" indicates limits of knowledge, i.e., that knowledge ends at a certain point and that things are unknown beyond this point.

A is incorrect because it only applies to the second sentence. B is incorrect because it does not apply to the second sentence. It also does not apply to the first sentence because stating that no studies have been conducted yet and pointing out a lack of studies are not the same. C is incorrect because neither sentence presents results.

44. (A) *Local*

A is the best choice because of lines 21-24 (see next question).

B is incorrect because while this kind of transfer is mentioned (lines 32-37), the passage does not imply that this is a rare occurrence. C is incorrect because the passage does not mention the criteria by which female gorillas choose a group to join. D is incorrect because nothing like this is suggested in the passage.

45. (B) *Evidence*

B is the best choice. According to the authors, females co-occur in groups with kin more often than would be expected if they dispersed randomly. The truth of this statement is predicated on the ability to determine how often females co-occur in groups with kin if they disperse randomly. In other words, the authors have to have a way to calculate the chance of random co-occurrence of kin in the same groups.

A, C, and D are incorrect because none of them show that it is possible to calculate the statistical probability of accidental meetings with kin.

46. (B) *Vocabulary*

B is the best choice because in context, socializing is described as an unexpected behavior. Even more unexpected (indicated by "even" in line 65) is the display of affiliative behaviors usually "reserved" for mates. This implies that usually, these behaviors are only shown to mates. Thus, "set aside" is correct.

A is incorrect because it means "calm" or "levelheaded." C is incorrect because it means "unfriendly" or "reclusive." D is incorrect because it means "demanded" or "asserted."

47. (D) *Local*

D is the best choice. The sentence that mentions "new world primates" states that compensatory or compassionate care could *also* be interpreted as empathetic behaviors. Thus, these new world primates represent *another* case of possible empathy *in addition to* the groups mentioned in the previous sentence (great apes and monkey species). Therefore, it can be inferred that new world primates are a group distinct from that of the great apes.

A is incorrect because the passage states that the instances involving new world primates were intragroup cases. B is incorrect because the passage does not suggest this. C is incorrect because "exemplary" (which means "admirable" or "excellent") is not supported.

48. (B) *Local*

The paragraph first states that the observed titi monkeys that were involved in a display of empathy were probably related due to overlapping home-ranges. This supposition was strengthened by a case of adoption among the groups in question. On the other hand, empathy could have also occurred without kinship since the individuals were familiar with each other (overlapping home-ranges again).

B is the best choice.

A is incorrect because the paragraph makes conjectures. It does not say for certain that geographical proximity was the main reason. C is incorrect because the advantages of empathy are not the main focus. D is incorrect because "predicated upon kinship" is not supported.

49. (C) — Summary

The main idea of Passage 1 is that female gorillas who transfer to new groups do not travel far, which is reflected by the amount of occurrences of related females within post-dispersal groups. This kinship is visible through positively kin-biased behaviors.

C is the best choice. Through their behavior, one can see (is betrayed) their kin-biased (partial) sympathy.

A is incorrect because "continue unchanged" is not supported. B is incorrect because "most" indicates the vast majority. The only data given in the passage is that co-occurrence of kin is higher than would be expected of random dispersal. This does not support "most." D is incorrect because the opposite was stated in the passage (lines 7-9).

50. (A) — Synthesize

For the main idea of Passage 1, check the explanation for question 49.

The main idea of Passage 2 is that the titi monkey surprisingly showed possibly empathetic behavior (stemming from either kinship or familiarity). What makes this more exceptional is that the witnessed event was an intergroup event since other known cases of primate empathy were intragroup events.

A is the best choice.

B is incorrect because Passage 1 does not state that group transfer or kin-biased behavior only occurs in gorillas. C is incorrect because Passage 1 does not compare the importance of kinship and that of physical proximity. D is incorrect because it is Passage 2 that mentions kinship might not be the only driver behind empathy.

51. (D) — Synthesize

Check the explanations for questions 49 and 50 for the main ideas of Passage 1 and Passage 2.

D is the best choice since Passage 1 states that gorillas display kin-biased behaviors and Passage 2 states that kinship makes empathy more likely to occur.

A is incorrect because it is not mentioned. B is incorrect because it is only supported by Passage 2. C is incorrect because it is only supported by Passage 1.

52. (B) — Synthesize

Lines 7-14 state that gorilla females exhibit more affiliative behaviors towards kin than non-kin when they live in the same group, and female kin are more likely to form coalitions than non-kin in competition over food. In essence, blood relations strengthen the ties among individual animals.

B is the best choice because the lines state that an injured monkey was cared for by his mother long after weaning. This implies that an animal cared for kin long after the time that she was supposed to care for him.

A, C, and D are incorrect because none of them show that blood relations strengthen the ties among individual animals.

SAT.Hackers.ac

Hackers New SAT Reading: 10 Practice Tests

TEST 10

Answer Keys & Performance Breakdown

Answer Explanations

Reading Test

65 MINUTES, 52 QUESTIONS

Mark your answers to the questions in Section 1 in the answer sheet provided.

DIRECTIONS

For each of the passages below, there are 10 or 11 questions. Choose the best answer for each of the questions after you have finished reading the passage. The answers to the questions should be based on the information that is stated or implied in the text and any associated graphics.

Questions 1-10 are based on the following passage.

This passage is from a short story. In this excerpt, a girl from an immigrant family is taking a walk on Christmas Eve.

Every exposed bit of skin stinging from the cold, she ducked into an alley promising shelter from the icy wind that drove great cloud banks westward into the
Line setting sun. It would have been a beautiful sight—the
5 sinking, quavering orb of fire painting the grey sky castles in a blast of orange against pale blue. She kept her head down, though, blowing on her fists to keep some semblance of feeling in her fingers. The sunset wasn't the only thing she was missing out on today.
10   Today was supposed to be a special day. Supposed to. Even for girls like her, though? Her fingers were going numb in the frosty air. Would that she could feel warm on the inside at least, like those Christmas songs blaring out of every speaker in every shop told
15 you to. What was it Jane had told her she was going to do again? Dinner with all of her family? *And ... presents under the tree. She mentioned candles on the table and everyone feeling warm and happy. Something along those lines. Must be nice to be from around here*
20 *and have lots of family. Must be nice to have family.* As for herself, there was only Dad. Dad wasn't from here. "Our country, no Christmas," he said every year. So he was with her "uncles" again, probably drinking. *Probably? Stop kidding yourself. Definitely drinking.*
25   "Don't you miss your mom?" Jane had once asked her. She was grateful for Jane. Really was. She at least talked to her like a normal person. The other kids in school mostly kept it polite. "Hi" and "bye" were a good start, but she wished there was something in
30 between, too. As it stood, most of her conversations were rather depressing exemplars of their kind. Being new didn't help, and looking different definitely didn't help either. She knew from experience it was going to get better, but for now, it was what it was. So she was
35 grateful for having Jane, but this question was just stupid.
   "I told you, she died when I was a baby. I don't even remember her."
   "Oh," she said. *Right*. "So how is it? Just being
40 with your dad?" She hadn't really known what to answer then. Jane had this way of asking questions that seemed innocuous enough, but were either plain moronic or really hard to answer. But this question stuck with her and actually made her think, about
45 dad and everything. And now she figured she couldn't hate her dad for being the way he was. *I guess he is having a hard time, too, without Mom.*
   With nothing better to do, she headed further into the small alley. Brownish-grey two- and three-
50 story buildings lined it, and they somehow managed to look even more ancient in the glow of the yellow streetlights. The snow getting crunched between her boots and the cobblestones was the only discernible sound over the wind.
55   Suddenly, she smelled something. Something more than the ever-present traces of smoke in the air from burning coals. She smelled cinnamon and sugar, hot cookies being baked. She could smell the smiles of the kids and mother's joy as they took them out of
60 the oven. She looked up at a window and saw a bunch of pretty little Christmas lights taped against the glass arranged just so, almost like a star, or almost like a flower, and somehow, right at that moment, she felt better inside. She felt good. Good enough, at least.
65   "Merry Christmas," she whispered to herself.

1

The passage is chiefly concerned with the girl's

A) feelings towards her life and finding a measure of peace.
B) loneliness due to her ineptitude at making school friends.
C) yearning to have a proper Christmas Eve with her friend.
D) scorn towards her father and resentment towards her classmates.

2

Over the course of the passage, the main focus of the narrative shifts from the

A) girl's recognition of being an outsider to the growing confidence in her ability to overcome her past mistakes.
B) disappointment and negativity the girl feels towards her surroundings to a quiet acceptance of her situation.
C) emphasis on the importance of family ties to the fickle and arbitrary nature of relationships with friends.
D) jealousy the girl feels towards her friend for having a working family to the realization that she still loves her friend.

3

In the context of the passage, the question "Even for girls like her, though?" is used to convey that the girl

A) deserves to enjoy a special day like Christmas more than anyone else.
B) has no right to expect anything on this day due to her own shortcomings.
C) feels that conventions like Christmas might not apply to her.
D) feels disappointed that Christmas day is too cold for her to enjoy.

4

Which choice provides the best evidence for the answer to the previous question?

A) Lines 6-8 ("She kept . . . fingers")
B) Lines 12-15 ("Would that . . . to")
C) Lines 20-22 ("As for . . . year")
D) Lines 26-28 ("She at . . . polite")

5

In lines 15-21, the girl's attitude toward her friend can best be described as one of

A) condescension.
B) loathing.
C) appreciation.
D) jealousy.

6

The main rhetorical effect of the parallel sentences in lines 19-20 ("*Must be . . . family*") is to

A) indicate the happiness the girl feels for her friend Jane.
B) specify more clearly which aspect the girl feels she is lacking.
C) emphasize that her immigrant background bothers her.
D) imply that the girl's mother passed away leaving her lonely.

7

In the passage, the phrase "kept it polite" (line 28) primarily refers to

A) asserting one's clear dislike towards someone.
B) maintaining only a minimum of civility.
C) displaying good manners towards others.
D) treating someone like a real friend.

CONTINUE →

8

As described in lines 31-34 ("Being new . . . was"), the girl's attitude towards her situation can best be described as

A) dejected.
B) forbearing.
C) helpless.
D) withdrawn.

9

The passage indicates that Jane's question in lines 39-40 ultimately has which effect on the girl?

A) It makes her ponder and elicits a measure of compassion.
B) It strikes her as impossible to answer because it is innocuous.
C) It reaffirms her opinion of Jane not being very intelligent.
D) It strengthens the respect and gratitude she feels for Jane.

10

The smells in lines 55-60 can best be characterized as being

A) nostalgic.
B) intoxicating.
C) wistful.
D) evocative.

Questions 11-21 are based on the following passages.

These passages discuss a system of labor referred to as sweatshops.

Passage 1

In the early to mid-1800s, a system of subcontracting tailoring work was described as the *sweat system* in England. The *sweater* would direct the arduous production in dirty, dangerous, and low-
5 paying conditions. These *sweatshops* rightly incurred criticism regarding the exploitation of the workers it attracted—packed into small, unsanitary spaces without proper ventilation or safety standards and taking home paltry wages. Eventually, such criticism
10 in the UK and the U.S. contributed greatly to the inception of labor laws and safety regulations. Sadly, the very societies which nowadays benefit from worker protection (to a great degree, at least), fuel the same archaic malpractices abroad with their mindless
15 hunger for cheap consumption.

The material lifestyle of the Occident could not flourish without underpaid Asian sweatshop workers. A great share of the articles we purchase and consume—branded clothes, electronics, and even
20 food items—are cheaply produced somewhere on the other side of the globe. We know that. What we aren't sufficiently aware of, however, is that our strong dollars and euros empower us to buy so much of them thanks to the fact that nearly none of our currency
25 ends up in the workers' hands. This drastic fall in production costs is an amazingly lucrative proposition for major Western companies which have accordingly based their manufacturing arms in Asia.

While the fact that sweatshop workers are
30 underpaid is nothing new, *how* underpaid they are is, for lack of a better word, stunning. Increasing a worker's wages by 100% would raise the retail price of the garment produced by not even 2%. Or, put differently, a woman producing a jersey that retails
35 for US $150 stands to make a few cents for her work. Ironically, consumer studies have shown that customers, properly educated, are willing to pay more than a 10% premium on items guaranteed to come from a safe and legal manufacturing environment.

40 A popular misconception often brought up is that sweatshops are necessary symptoms of a country's transition into prosperity and as such should be seen as an intermediate step to eliminating poverty. What is often brushed aside is the hard fact that people
45 must spend the majority or all of their earnings on

basic necessities such as food and housing. This hand-to-mouth situation does not offer any exits for the worker. On a real, individual basis, sweatshops do not eliminate poverty even in cases where workers
50 voluntarily choose to work there.

We have largely cleaned up our act within our borders, but now we have to make ourselves truly aware of the fact that the clothes on our skin and the cheap electronics we enjoy drive the very problem we
55 have freed ourselves from.

Passage 2

It is easy to understand why sweatshops are vilified, and it is also easy to jump on the train and call for changes: laborers work in unsafe conditions, safety standards are often unheard of, coercion and
60 violence abound, and, of course, the only benefit laborers receive is mere subsistence pay.

The reality, however, is more complicated: Sweatshops are driven by incentives to invest in developing countries precisely because of certain
65 preexisting conditions such as available low-wage labor. If minimum wage levels were to increase substantially, an exodus of investment would ensue. In other words, companies would relocate to other, more lucrative locations. (If Asia is not substantially
70 cheaper, why not relocate to a country in the Americas and save on shipping time and costs?) In such a scenario, the region's workers would be laid off and would have to look for alternatives.

Though sweatshops naturally seem atrocious
75 to us, laborers still choose to work there, which means it is better than the alternatives—in many cases, prostitution or no work at all. We cannot compare sweatshops to American jobs unless we have American jobs to offer to sweatshop workers. We have
80 to compare sweatshops to other local opportunities.

To gain a little perspective, countries like Taiwan and South Korea provide proof that sweatshops, albeit ugly, represent a possible route to prosperity. Unlike countries that have—understandably—resisted
85 this economic exploitation by Western interests, the aforementioned nations that have paid this price have, as a result of their bitter exertions, now joined the ranks of the developed world.

Intuitively, heeding calls to boycott certain
90 brands and companies for their reliance on sweatshop labor seems justified. But withholding the dollars that would otherwise flow in that direction would ultimately hinder development, not help.

11

The primary purpose of both passages is to

A) criticize sweatshops for their inhumane working conditions.
B) argue that sweatshops are not completely objectionable.
C) put forward an evaluation of sweatshops and their effects.
D) chronicle the history of sweatshops including their current incarnation.

12

According to paragraph 1 in Passage 1, a long-term effect of the *sweat system* in the early to mid-1800s was

A) the introduction of measures to protect workers.
B) the complete abolition of worker exploitation.
C) an inability to find laborers willing to work.
D) a marginalization of more expensive Western products.

13

In lines 29-31, the author of Passage 1 mainly distinguishes between

A) a fact and the degree it exhibits.
B) tolerable and unacceptable facts.
C) Western and Eastern standards.
D) recent and new developments.

14

It can be inferred from lines 36-39 that consumers

A) are partially unaware of the payment conditions in sweatshops.
B) are happy to overpay on an item if the item's quality is guaranteed.
C) do not care about the origin of a product as long as the price is right.
D) could drastically change a sweatshop worker's life by paying a premium.

15

Within the context of Passage 1, the "clothes" and the "cheap electronics" in lines 53-54 refer to the

A) results of an unfair arrangement.
B) fruits of human advancement.
C) vestiges of a distant past.
D) basic necessities for survival.

16

The author of Passage 2 indicates that a rise in minimum wage levels (lines 66-67) would ultimately

A) benefit laborers as they would be able to leave privation behind.
B) make a country more competitive in attracting investment capital.
C) burden the workers since their workplaces would disappear.
D) attract more skilled labor which would enhance production quality.

17

As presented in Passage 2, the author of Passage 2 would most likely view criticism of sweatshops as

A) entirely justified.
B) a necessary evil.
C) readily understandable.
D) ludicrous and harmful.

18

Which choice provides the best evidence for the answer to the previous question?

A) Lines 62-66 ("The reality . . . labor")
B) Lines 77-80 ("We . . . opportunities")
C) Lines 89-91 ("Intuitively . . . justified")
D) Lines 91-93 ("But . . . help")

19

Would the author of Passage 1 agree that nations have "as a result of their bitter exertions, now joined the ranks of the developed world" (lines 87-88, Passage 2)?

A) Yes, because examples like South Korea and Taiwan corroborate this.
B) Yes, because low wages allow for faster development of a nation.
C) No, because coercion and violence do not belong in the developed world.
D) No, because low wages make it impossible for workers to better their lot.

20

The author of Passage 2 would most likely respond to the assertion in Passage 1, lines 36-39 ("Ironically . . . environment") by arguing that

A) paying a premium does not guarantee that the money will actually go to the worker.
B) encouraging educated consumption will protect sweatshop laborers abroad.
C) paying a premium could hurt the sweatshop workers instead of protecting them.
D) boycotting brands that support sweatshop labor would ultimately hurt the consumers.

21

Compared to Passage 1, Passage 2 focuses more on

A) the common worker's indigence.
B) blaming Western consumption habits.
C) the overall advancement of a nation.
D) the need to expand sweatshops.

Questions 22-32 are based on the following passage and supplementary material.

This passage discusses biodiversity loss on our planet.

To an individual, our planet naturally appears rich and abundant. We instinctively assume that somewhere, behind that curved horizon, there will
Line always be more. In my mind, I used to conjure up
5 vast stretches of untouched rainforest, savannah, and other iconic shrines that, in their vastness and majesty, safeguarded that which we call "nature." But nowadays, these mental panoramata can no longer remain pristine. Given the way Earth's habitable zones
10 have been saturated by us, and considering the sheer density of populations, our existence alone degrades the bounty of our environment. It could be said that humankind has finally achieved a level of magnitude that enables us to leave permanent and irreversible
15 footprints all over our planet.

Prionailurus iriomotensis, commonly known as (or rather, more commonly known as) the Iriomote Cat, is one of the many species being crushed under our pervasive feet. Classified as a subspecies of the
20 Leopard Cat, it is about the size of a domestic cat and wears a dusky brown coat. Stripes on the head and spots on the side of the coat are reminiscent of its parental lineage. These cats are exclusive to Iriomote, a small Japanese island measuring a mere 284 km^2.

25 These felines are listed as one of the world's most critically endangered species. Unlike whales, they have not been actively hunted. Rather, it seems that, as true in many other cases, our presence and following our way of life alone has largely led to this
30 outcome. It is true that, there only existing a single population of this species, inbreeding has affected the genetic stock and contributed to the doom this species faces, but this problem has been exacerbated by interbreeding with domestic cats which has diluted
35 the genetic material and by diseases transferred from the same. And this is compounded by habitat loss driven by human development projects on this small island. These latter factors have ensured that there is less genetic material to go around in the first
40 place which does anything but lead the cat out of its naturally occurring dire straits.

Let this little friend stand in for countless other species that we, unwittingly, displace or destroy simply by existing and expanding to new areas and
45 imposing upon them our ways of life, carrying with us flora and fauna dear to us which then invades and often dominates this conquered habitat. Today, the final 100 or less cats vanishing into the dusk of their existence are not alone on this anthropogenic
50 journey over the brink. Hundreds, possibly thousands of species vanish every year, a rate that has been estimated to be at least 1,000 times higher than the background extinction rate[1].

It is true. If you sail on, something new
55 unfailingly crests the horizon. When sailing was still the preferred mode of transportation, that something might have included nature untouched or people living in such numbers and living in such ways as to not seriously distort the balance of life. Today,
60 however, all that you will encounter is more people who have, in turn, driven out, displaced, or in some other way driven to extinction their own Iriomote Cats. Such diversity loss has silently accompanied our complete conquest of the globe.

[1] the rate at which species would go extinct if humans were not around

Chart
Causes of Animal Extinctions in Region A

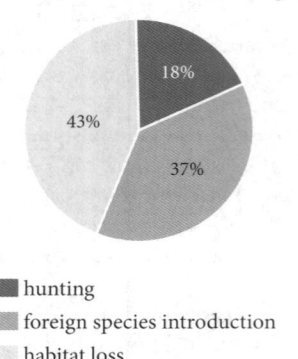

- hunting
- foreign species introduction
- habitat loss

Graph
Habitat Loss vs. Species Loss in Region A

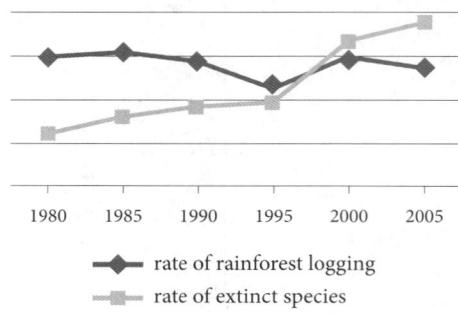

- rate of rainforest logging
- rate of extinct species

22

The stance the author takes is best described as that of

A) an alarmed observer calling for increased awareness of a problem.
B) an interested scholar pointing out an issue that has sparked intense controversy.
C) an anxious bystander lamenting the way history has proceeded.
D) a sober idealist advocating certain policies to rectify an affair.

23

The passage indicates that the "mental panoramata can no longer remain pristine" (lines 8-9) due to the fact that

A) these images were unrealistic and only existed in the author's mind.
B) climate change has affected all of the habitats that were conjured up.
C) humans have intentionally spoiled the riches of nature.
D) there are effectively no regions left that are free of humans.

24

Which choice best supports the author's claim that our existence alone degrades the bounty of our environment?

A) Lines 7-9 ("But . . . pristine")
B) Lines 38-41 ("These . . . straits")
C) Lines 42-44 ("Let this . . . areas")
D) Lines 59-63 ("Today . . . Cats")

25

The tone employed in the last sentence of paragraph 1 ("It could . . . planet") could best be described as

A) sarcastic.
B) reverent.
C) cavalier.
D) flippant.

26

Which choice provides the best evidence for the answer to the previous question?

A) Lines 1-4 ("To an . . . more")
B) Lines 16-19 ("*Prionailurus* . . . feet")
C) Lines 34-38 ("interbreeding . . . island")
D) Lines 55-59 ("When . . . life")

27

The passage suggests that the "felines" (line 25) are critically endangered mainly because

A) interbreeding with other cat species has been encouraged.
B) their habitat is too small to support genetic diversity.
C) they bear a strong resemblance to a dangerous cat species.
D) they happen to share their habitat with human beings.

28

The primary purpose of the statement in lines 30-33 ("It is true . . . faces") is to

A) exemplify how humans have contributed to a species' demise.
B) suggest that genetic diversity is an essential necessity for survival.
C) concede that humans might not be at fault for the fate of these cats.
D) acknowledge the fact that non-human factors also play a role.

29

As used in line 48, "dusk" most nearly means

A) minority.
B) terminus.
C) bleakness.
D) sunset.

30

The passage suggests which of the following about the time "When sailing was still the preferred mode of transportation" (lines 55-56)?

A) Preserving nature was of the highest priority.
B) There might have been places devoid of humans.
C) People avoided living too closely together.
D) Humans lacked the means to extinguish other species.

31

Which of the following points made in the passage is supported directly by the chart?

A) The mere presence of humans increases the rate of animal extinctions.
B) Most animal extinctions are side effects of other human activities.
C) Habitat loss is the prime killer of animals in any region.
D) All native species will eventually succumb due to human activities.

32

Which statement is best supported by the data in the graph?

A) The rate of animal extinctions was the highest when the rate of logging picked up after 1995.
B) The correlation between logging rate and extinction rate supports the opinion that habitat loss kills the most animals.
C) The decline in rainforest logging prior to 1995 was followed by a decade of increased logging rates.
D) In order to lower the rate of animal extinctions, more measures might be necessary than lowering the rate of logging.

CONTINUE →

Questions 33-42 are based on the following passage.

This passage is adapted from President Woodrow Wilson's address to Congress in 1914. Prior to this, U.S. sailors were arrested and humiliated by Mexican General Huerta's forces in Mexico. Mayo's demand for a formal apology which included a gun salute in honor of the U.S. flag was denied.

It is my duty to call to your attention to a situation which has arisen in our dealings with the General Victoriano Huerta at Mexico City which calls for action, and to ask your advice and cooperation in acting upon it.

On the 9th of April a paymaster of the U.S.S. *Dolphin* landed at the Iturbide Bridge landing at Tampico with a whaleboat and boats' crew to take on certain supplies needed by his ship, and while engaged in loading the boat was arrested by an officer and squad of men of the army of General Huerta. . . . Admiral Mayo regarded the arrest as so serious an affront that he was not satisfied unless the flag of the United States be saluted with special ceremony by the military commander of the port.

The incident cannot be regarded as a trivial one, especially as two of the men arrested were taken from the boat itself—that is to say, from the territory of the United States—but had it stood by itself it might have been attributed to the ignorance or arrogance of a single officer. Unfortunately, it was not an isolated case.

A series of incidents have recently occurred which cannot but create the impression that the representatives of General Huerta were willing to go out of their way to show disregard for the dignity and rights of this Government . . . The manifest danger of such a situation was that such offences might grow from bad to worse until something happened of so gross and intolerable a sort as to lead directly and inevitably to armed conflict. It was necessary that the apologies of General Huerta and his representatives should go much further, that they should be such as to attract the attention of the whole population to their significance, and such as to impress upon General Huerta himself the necessity of seeing to it that no further occasion for explanations and professed regrets should arise.

I, therefore, felt it my duty to sustain Admiral Mayo in the whole of his demand and to insist that the flag of the United States should be saluted in such a way as to indicate a new spirit and attitude on the part of the Huertistas.

Such a salute General Huerta has refused, and I have come to ask your approval and support in the course I now propose to pursue. This Government can, I earnestly hope, in no circumstances be forced into war with the people of Mexico. . . . If armed conflict should unhappily come as a result of his attitude of personal resentment toward this Government, we should be fighting only General Huerta and those who adhere to him and give him their support . . . But I earnestly hope that war is not now in question.

I believe that I speak for the American people when I say that we do not desire to control in any degree the affairs of our sister Republic. Our feeling for the people of Mexico is one of deep and genuine friendship, and everything that we have so far done or refrained from doing has proceeded from our desire to help them, not to hinder or embarrass them.

We would not wish even to exercise the good offices of friendship without their welcome and consent. The people of Mexico are entitled to settle their own domestic affairs in their own way, and we sincerely desire to respect their right. The present situation need have none of the grave implications of interference if we deal with it promptly, firmly, and wisely.

No doubt I could do what is necessary under the circumstances to enforce respect for our Government without recourse to the Congress, and yet not exceed my constitutional powers as President; but I do not wish to act in a manner possibly of so grave consequence except in close conference and cooperation with both the Senate and House.

I, therefore, come to ask your approval that I should use the armed forces of the United States in such ways and to such an extent as may be necessary to obtain from General Huerta and his adherents the fullest recognition of the rights and dignity of the United States, even amidst the distressing conditions now unhappily occurring in Mexico.

There can in what we do be no thought of aggression or of selfish aggrandizement. We seek to maintain the dignity and authority of the United States only because we wish always to keep our great influence unimpaired for the uses of liberty, both in United States and wherever else it may be employed for the benefit of mankind.

Simplified Timeline of Events
Surrounding the Tampico Affair

1914	• President General Huerta struggles to defend his authority in the Mexican Revolution. • U.S. warships are deployed in the area to ensure the safety of U.S. assets and citizens on Mexican soil.
1914 Apr. 9	• mistaken arrest of U.S. sailors in Tampico by Mexican forces • U.S. admiral demands an proper apology. • Mexican President General Huerta refuses. • Diplomatic relationships deteriorate.
1914 Apr. 20	President Wilson addresses Congress (passage).
1914 Apr. 22	• Congress approves the use of military force. • U.S. forces seize and occupy the Mexican port town of Veracruz which is one of Huerta's supply lines.
1914 July	General Huerta resigns partly due to outcome of Tampico.
1917	• Mexico refuses to participate in World War I alongside the U.S. due to anti-American resentments.

33

The passage suggests that if General Huerta had properly apologized as the situation demanded,

A) the apologies would have attracted undue attention from the greater population.
B) the U.S. would not consider the use of force to extract due recognition.
C) General Huerta would have lost crucial footing among his followers.
D) armed conflicts with the U.S. could have been avoided in the past.

34

Which choice provides the best evidence for the answer to the previous question?

A) Lines 16-19 ("The incident . . . States")
B) Lines 30-34 ("It was . . . significance")
C) Lines 45-47 ("This Government . . . Mexico")
D) Lines 77-81 ("use the . . . States")

35

Within the context of the passage, the fourth paragraph (lines 22-37) mainly serves to

A) suggest that General Huerta's motives might have been misunderstood.
B) justify a course of action that is about to be proposed.
C) emphasize the need for restraint in dealing with General Huerta.
D) indicate that deliberate provocations have led to armed conflict.

36

As used in line 53, "question" most nearly means

A) doubt.
B) discussion.
C) remonstration.
D) query.

37

As used in line 59, "proceeded" most nearly means

A) travelled.
B) originated.
C) emitted.
D) carried out.

38

Wilson suggests that Mexico should be viewed as

A) a benevolent and sagacious neighbor.
B) a discrete, autonomous entity.
C) an ally in the quest for independence.
D) inconsequential to U.S. affairs.

39

According to the passage, the "constitutional powers as President" (line 72) could best be described as

A) considerable.
B) subordinate.
C) boundless.
D) magnanimous.

40

The last paragraph indicates that President Wilson seeks to take action because

A) maintaining the dignity of his nation is imperative on the global stage.
B) many stand to benefit if the U.S. is a well-respected nation.
C) the U.S. is unable to exert influence without its dignity.
D) the exalted goals the U.S. pursues justify aggression and egotism.

41

Which choice is supported by the information in the table?

A) Misunderstandings have often been the cause of armed conflict.
B) The U.S. wanted to avoid alienating the majority of Mexicans.
C) The Tampico Affair proved crucial to the outcome of World War I.
D) The U.S. was able to mobilize its fighting forces very quickly.

42

Based on the information in the table, Wilson's stated directive of "fighting only General Huerta and those who adhere to him" (lines 50-51) could best be described as

A) ill-advised.
B) fruitless.
C) impractical.
D) astute.

Questions 43-52 are based on the following passage and supplementary material.

This passage was written in 1993.

   In today's world, we are often far removed from the basic raw materials that are then processed into technological gadgets which facilitate our comfortable
Line lives. These technologies enter our lives as plastic-
5 clad appliances, fully formed and ready to be plugged in. It is safe to say that most of us do not really think about copper mines or rare earth metal deposits on a daily basis. And yet, our modern lifestyles are fundamentally dependent on minerals extracted
10 from beneath the earth's surface. As more and more people are now demanding a higher lifestyle, the task of efficiently prospecting such materials grows ever more important.
   One might assume that with today's advances in
15 science and technology, pinpointing and exploiting underground resources would be easy. Just think of how far our eyes now penetrate into space, discerning planets in solar systems light-years away! The truth, however, is that Mother Earth has shown formidable
20 resistance to our exertions. Her secrets are clutched in an iron grip whose fingers have to be laboriously pried open one by one. So while we are discussing Mars missions and our telescopes are pointed at galaxies that are stupendously far removed from our
25 vantage point, we have not even scratched the surface in the other direction: the center of our planet lies more than 6,370 kilometers beneath our feet, yet the deepest mine that has been constructed barely reaches four kilometers coreward.
30   Still, looking to space exploration in search of parallels is not unfitting. There is a colossal disparity in scientific knowledge between recognizing that the night sky is filled with other suns, and augmenting that insight with specific, instrument-based data
35 on each of them. Consider the sheer multitude of celestial objects in our solar system alone, and how many of them remain to be explored and analyzed even though we presume to know our own galactic backyard pretty well. Similarly, while we are able to
40 say that we are aware of the fundamental anatomy of our planet, getting the specifics for any given cubic foot of mass beneath the surface is a different story entirely.
   Aside from the fact that digging underground
45 is slow, arduous, and dangerous, searching for ore is further complicated by its limited availability. There is only a finite amount of each mineral to be found (since compared to ore formation processes, human life spans are insignificant). And of these limited
50 amounts, the most obvious and easily accessible deposits have already been exploited over the course of human history. So it stands to reason that over time, open mining pits will become increasingly rare, and true mines will have to reach farther and deeper.
55   Nevertheless, the field of ore geology is still very young, and we can rightfully expect significant strides in the future. It was only in the sixteenth century that the first serious treatise concerning ore deposits was published by Georgius Agricola, presenting an
60 alternative to pure speculation. The late eighteenth century saw the rise of two opposing theories. James Hutton, a "plutonist," posited that molten magma and its movement was central to ore genesis, whereas Abraham Werner, a "neptunist," hypothesized that
65 sediments in ancient oceans were responsible for depositing the ores where we find them today. Though both were too general and neither disproved the other, their discussion proved seminal to the advancement of ore geology. By the twentieth
70 century, chemistry had matured enough as a science to contribute greatly to the theory of ore genesis, and many relevant, more specialized theories have now been proposed. Theories that we can now test with the help of computer simulations which allow
75 us to negate the immense spans of time geological processes normally involve. Such advances will ultimately enable us to efficiently explore our planet's crust in search of the materials we require.

43

The main purpose of the passage is to

A) examine the differences between two different kinds of exploration.
B) explain the various methods scientists use when searching for ore.
C) describe some challenges and the outlook of an endeavor.
D) explain why the field of mineral exploration remains unpopular.

44

The author implies which of the following about searching for minerals?

A) It is a formidable task because of our comparative ineptitude for exploring solid material.
B) It does not pose a real challenge any longer thanks to scientific advances and modern tools.
C) It has become ever more important because we depend its success for our basic needs.
D) It has been neglected in favor of space exploration which was deemed more feasible.

45

In context, the words "sheer" (line 35) and "alone" (line 36) have mainly which effect?

A) They convey dismay at our presumptive nature.
B) They contrast a level of ignorance to its boundaries.
C) They express confidence in future research.
D) They compare our achievements to our failures.

46

The passage suggests that prospecting minerals and space exploration have which of the following in common?

A) Both have resulted in big pictures lacking information on the details.
B) They are hampered by our presumptive beliefs that we know more than we actually do.
C) Physical distance represents one of the main obstacles to gleaning more information.
D) Both are needed to guarantee better lifestyles across the globe.

47

Which choice provides the best evidence for the answer to the previous question?

A) Lines 8-10 ("And yet . . . surface")
B) Lines 16-20 ("Just think . . . exertions")
C) Lines 35-39 ("Consider . . . well")
D) Lines 39-43 ("Similarly . . . entirely")

48

The parenthetical remark in lines 48-49 is most likely mentioned to

A) underscore the fact that humans do not contribute to ore formation.
B) reconcile a seeming contradiction regarding a limited amount.
C) suggest that the activities of humans leave no lasting trace on nature.
D) explain why ore exploration is a time-consuming and dangerous activity.

49

As used in line 58, "serious" most nearly means

A) severe.
B) meaningful.
C) crucial.
D) somber.

50

The author's main purpose in including information on ore availability and open pit mining is to

A) support the idea that space exploration and mineral exploration are disparate.
B) concede that some of the challenges scientists face could have been avoided.
C) introduce the idea that ore exploration is a difficult undertaking.
D) add to the notion that mineral exploration presents a formidable challenge.

51

According to the passage, which of the following is true of ore geology?

A) It has yet to develop into a more mature science.
B) It was conceived by two opposing ideas.
C) It is an as yet unproven field of science.
D) It is uniquely important to a large number of people.

52

Which choice provides the best evidence for the answer to the previous question?

A) Lines 10-13 ("As more . . . important")
B) Lines 55-57 ("Nevertheless . . . future")
C) Lines 61-66 ("James . . . today")
D) Lines 69-71 ("By the . . . genesis")

STOP

Do not move on to the next section if you finish early.

You may review your answers in this section only.

Answer Keys & Performance Breakdown

1	(A)	Summary	19	(D)	Synthesize	37	(B)	Vocabulary
2	(B)	Organization	20	(C)	Synthesize	38	(B)	Local
3	(C)	Context	21	(C)	Synthesize	39	(A)	Local
4	(C)	Evidence	22	(C)	Stance	40	(B)	Local
5	(D)	Local	23	(D)	Local	41	(D)	Graph
6	(B)	Style	24	(C)	Evidence	42	(B)	Graph
7	(B)	Local	25	(A)	Local	43	(C)	Summary
8	(B)	Local	26	(B)	Evidence	44	(A)	Local
9	(A)	Local	27	(D)	Local	45	(B)	Context
10	(D)	Local	28	(D)	Context	46	(A)	Local
11	(C)	Synthesize	29	(B)	Vocabulary	47	(D)	Evidence
12	(A)	Local	30	(B)	Local	48	(B)	Context
13	(A)	Local	31	(B)	Graph	49	(B)	Vocabulary
14	(A)	Local	32	(D)	Graph	50	(D)	Context
15	(A)	Summary	33	(B)	Local	51	(A)	Local
16	(C)	Local	34	(D)	Evidence	52	(B)	Evidence
17	(C)	Local	35	(B)	Context			
18	(C)	Evidence	36	(B)	Vocabulary			

■ Write down the number of correct answers for each question type.

Question Types	Number of Correct Answers
Local	/ 21
Style	/ 1
Vocabulary	/ 4
Evidence	/ 7
Context	/ 6
Organization	/ 1
Summary	/ 3
Stance	/ 1
Synthesize	/ 4
Graph	/ 4
Total	**/ 52**

Answer Explanations

Questions 1-10

1. (A) *Summary*

A is the best choice because the girl feels cold and lonely thinking about her father not being there for her on Christmas Eve and that she is envious of her friend who is apparently spending a nice day with her family. She also remembers her dead mother at this point. Later, she feels better at seeing pretty Christmas decorations in windows and imagining the happiness inside.

B is incorrect because "ineptitude at making school friends" is neither the main reason for her loneliness nor the main focus. C is incorrect because she envies her friend for spending Christmas with her family. D is incorrect because "scorn" is too strong and "resentment" is not supported.

2. (B) *Organization*

B is the best choice (see explanation for question 1).

A is incorrect because no "past mistakes" is mentioned. C is incorrect because "the importance of family ties" is not directly emphasized. Also, the only friendship that is mentioned (with Jane) is not described as "fickle and arbitrary." D is incorrect because the main focus, rather than on her friend, is on her feelings towards her own family that are brought out thanks to her friend.

3. (C) *Context*

C is the best choice because the indicated question implies that she is different in some way. That difference comes up in lines 20-22 where it is stated that her only family is her father and, being from another country, he does not want to celebrate Christmas. So Christmas is not a special day for "girls like her."

A is incorrect because the passage does not state that she feels she *deserves* a special day. B is incorrect because the passage does not mention "shortcomings" that caused her situation. D is incorrect because "girls like her" does not refer to the weather.

4. (C) *Evidence*

C is the best choice (see explanation for previous question).

A, B, and D are incorrect because none of them explain how the indicated question means that Christmas does not apply to the girl.

5. (D) *Local*

D is the best choice because in the specified lines, the girl recalls what a nice Christmas her friend said she was going to have, and she thinks how it "must be nice" for her friend not once but twice.

A is incorrect because it means *arrogance*. B is incorrect because it is too extreme. C is incorrect because she does not feel grateful in these lines.

6. (B) *Style*

B is the best choice because the first sentence mentions being from here and having family, while the second sentence only repeats family. This implies that what she envies her friend for the most is family.

A is incorrect because the sentences indicate envy. C is incorrect because to the girl, being "from here" is less important than having family. D is incorrect because this specific information is not given here.

7. (B) *Local*

B is the best choice because "kept it polite" is contrasted to talking to her like a normal person. Therefore, keeping it polite is the opposite, and the next sentence specifies that this means only greeting someone without additional conversation.

A is incorrect because not saying much is not asserting one's dislike. C is incorrect because only greeting someone and displaying good manners are not the same. D is obviously incorrect.

8. (B) *Local*

B is the best choice because the specified lines state that she knows her situation will get better, but not right now. Thus, she is patient because she knows things will get better in the future. "Forbearing" means "patient."

A is incorrect because "dejected" is too negative in context. C is incorrect because being helpless implies needing help. However, she knows her situation will get better, so she does not need help. D is incorrect because it means that the girl was unsociable which is not implied in these lines.

Answer Explanations

9. (A) — Local

A is the best choice. Even though at first, the girl does not have an answer for the question, in the end it makes her think (lines 44-45) about her dad and how he is also having a hard time without her mother (a measure of compassion).

B is incorrect. The question's seemingly innocuous nature does not result in her inability to answer. Also, this is not the ultimate effect. C is incorrect because it is not the ultimate effect of the question. D is incorrect because nothing such is stated.

10. (D) — Local

D is the best choice because the smells make her imagine what is being baked. She also imagines smiles of kids and happiness due to the smells.

A is incorrect because she is not thinking about her past. B is incorrect because a heady kind of excitement is not supported by the girl's reaction. Rather, her reaction is quiet. C is incorrect because it means "longing" and "melancholy."

Questions 11-21

11. (C) — Synthesize

C is the best choice. Passage 1 in essence states that sweatshops are a form of worker exploitation that benefits Western countries and will not help workers escape poverty. Passage 2 asserts that sweatshops might seem atrocious, but they have actually raised developing countries out of poverty, so boycotting sweatshops would hinder developing countries. Therefore, both passages evaluate sweatshops and their effects.

A and B are incorrect because they only apply to Passage 1 and Passage 2 respectively. D is incorrect because merely recounting the history is not the primary purpose of either passage.

12. (A) — Local

A is the best choice because of lines 9-11 (after "Eventually").

B is incorrect because "complete abolition" is not the same as saying that a great degree of workers benefits from worker protection. C is incorrect because the paragraph does not suggest that it was a problem to find workers willing to work. D is incorrect because this is not suggested in paragraph 1.

13. (A) — Local

A is the best choice because *that* they are underpaid (fact) is known while *how* underpaid (degree) they are is shocking.

B is incorrect because it implies there are two different sets of facts. C is incorrect because Western and Eastern standards are not contrasted. D is incorrect because "recent and new" is not supported, either.

14. (A) — Local

A is the best choice because the specified lines state that properly educated (condition) consumers are willing to pay more money for items from legal manufacturing environments. This implies that there are consumers who are not properly educated. Therefore, "partially unaware" is correct.

B is incorrect because "quality" is not the issue discussed. C is incorrect because it is the opposite of what the passage states. D is incorrect because the passage does not suggest paying a premium would drastically change workers' lives.

15. (A) — Summary

This question is posed within the context of the whole passage. The "problem" referred to in the same sentence is the reliance on sweatshops. Thus, the "clothes" and "cheap electronics" are products (results) of an unfair agreement (sweatshops).

Therefore, A is the best choice.

B is incorrect because Passage 1 would not describe sweatshops as human advancement. C is incorrect because "vestiges of a distant past" implies these items are very old. D is incorrect because the author does not connect sweatshops to the manufacture of basic necessities.

16. (C) — Local

C is the best choice because of lines 71-73. (The region's workers would be laid off.)

A is incorrect because leaving privation behind is not stated in the passage. B is incorrect because the passage indicates the opposite: there would be an exodus of capital. D is incorrect because nothing such is mentioned.

17. (C) — Local

C is the best choice because of lines 89-91 (see next question) and because of lines 56-61.

A is incorrect because the author of Passage 2 ultimately believes that sweatshops help developing nations. B is incorrect because even though the author of Passage 2 would call sweatshops a necessary evil, he would not call *criticism* thereof a necessary evil. D is incorrect because no such extreme opinion is voiced in Passage 2.

18. (C) — Evidence

C is the best choice because it states that intuitively, calls to boycott sweatshops seem justified.

A, B, and D are incorrect because they do not show that the author of Passage 2 would think criticism of sweatshops is readily understandable.

19. (D) — Synthesize

D is the best choice because the quoted lines basically mean that sweatshops (bitter exertions) enabled nations to develop. Passage 1 asserts that this is not true in paragraph 4. D is best supported by lines 43-50.

A and B are obviously incorrect. C is incorrect because Passage 1 does not use coercion and violence as obstacles to development.

20. (C) — Synthesize

C is the best choice because lines 36-39 state that people are willing to pay more money if they know the product does not come from a sweatshop. In essence, this refers to boycotting sweatshops. The author of Passage 2 would contend that sweatshops can actually help developing nations prosper, and that boycotting sweatshops can hinder such development.

A is incorrect because Passage 2 does not focus on money distribution. B is incorrect because the author of Passage 2 does not think buying less from sweatshops will benefit the workers. D is incorrect because Passage 2 states the workers will be hurt, not the consumers.

21. (C) — Synthesize

C is the best choice (see explanation for question 11).

A and B are incorrect because they represent Passage 1's position. D is incorrect because Passage 2 does not recommend expanding sweatshops.

Questions 22-32

22. (C) — Stance

C is the best choice because the passage highlights the fact that humans now populate all of our planet's habitable zones and inevitably damage our environment. This expansion of the human species could be called "the way history has proceeded."

A is incorrect because the author does not encourage increased awareness in the passage. He merely recounts the current state of affairs. B is incorrect because of "intense controversy." D is incorrect because no "policies to rectify" is brought up.

23. (D) — Local

D is the best choice (see next sentence).

A is incorrect because it is not stated that these panoramata were unrealistic. B is incorrect because "climate change" is not mentioned. C is incorrect because of "intentionally."

24. (C) — Evidence

C is the best choice because the lines state that we have unwittingly destroyed countless species simply by existing and expanding to new areas.

A and B are obviously incorrect. D is incorrect because "our existence alone" is not supported by these lines.

25. (A) — Local

A is the best choice because of lines 16-19 (see next question).

B is incorrect because "reverent" means "very respectful." C is incorrect because it means "condescending." D is incorrect because it means "silly."

26. (B) — Evidence

B is the best choice because the last sentence of paragraph 1 describes humankind's expansion like a great feat: humankind has "finally achieved a level of magnitude." At the same time, the result of this is that many species are being crushed under our pervasive feet (lines 18-19).

A, C, and D are incorrect because they do not show that the sentence in question is sarcastic.

Answer Explanations

27. (D) — Local

D is the best choice because the passage states that our presence and following our way of life alone has largely led to the critical endangerment (lines 28-29).

A is incorrect because of "encouraged." Also, it is not the main reason. B is incorrect because the passage does not specify that there only exists one species due to the size of the island. C is incorrect because it is not mentioned as a reason for endangerment.

28. (D) — Context

D is the best choice because before and after the specified lines, the author lists how humans have contributed to the endangerment of the cats whereas within the specified lines, the author lists a natural cause.

A is obviously incorrect. B is incorrect because the word "essential" is not supported. C is incorrect because for this to be true, genetic diversity or inbreeding would have to be described as the crucial factor in the cats' fate.

29. (B) — Vocabulary

B is the best choice because the sentence mentions cats vanishing into the "dusk of their existence," i.e., cats going extinct. Therefore, "dusk" means "end," like terminus.

A and D are obviously incorrect. C is incorrect because it means "gloom," "despair," or "darkness."

30. (B) — Local

B is the best choice because the passage mentions "nature untouched."

A is incorrect because "highest priority" is not supported. C is incorrect because it implies the intent to leave space between habitations, which is not supported. D is incorrect because it is not mentioned.

31. (B) — Graph

B is the best choice because hunting (killing animals directly) only makes up 18%. The other activities do not involve killing animals directly.

A is incorrect because it has no data on the rate of extinctions. C is incorrect because of the word "any." D is incorrect because the chart has no data on "all" species.

32. (D) — Graph

D is the best choice because even when the rate of logging fell over time, the rate of extinctions steadily grew. Therefore, according to the data, reducing logging activities will not lower animal extinction rates.

A is incorrect because the rate of animal extinctions was the highest when the rate of logging decreased in 2005. B is incorrect because the graph does not have comparative data on other causes of extinction. C is incorrect because the period between 2000 and 2005 also saw a decline in logging rates.

Questions 33-42

33. (B) — Local

B is the best choice because of lines 77-81 (see next question).

A is incorrect because no undue attention is mentioned. C is incorrect because losing the support of his followers due to apologizing is not mentioned. D is incorrect because armed conflicts in the past are not mentioned.

34. (D) — Evidence

D is the best choice because the lines state that Wilson "should use the armed forces . . . to obtain from General Huerta . . . the fullest recognition of the rights and dignity of the United States." Logically, had General Huerta properly apologized, such use of force would not be considered.

A, B, and C are incorrect because they do not show that the U.S. considers the use of force because Huerta did not apologize as the situation demanded.

35. (B) — Context

B is the best choice because the specified lines in essence state that General Huerta has been repeatedly disrespectful of the U.S. to such a degree it might lead to armed conflict, and that adequate apologies by the General are necessary to prevent further provocations. In the next paragraph, Wilson therefore upholds Admiral Mayo's demand that the General apologizes (which the General refused). Therefore, Wilson now proposes to Congress the use of armed forces to extract this apology.

A is incorrect because the fourth paragraph agrees with the rest of the passage. Saying something was a misunderstanding implies a change of perspective. C is incorrect because the specified paragraph shows no reason for restraint; it rather serves as a justification for the use of arms. D is incorrect because no armed conflict has taken place.

36. (B) — Vocabulary

B is the best choice because the sentence says "I . . . hope that war is not now in question." Therefore, "question" is an option under consideration.

A is obviously incorrect. C is incorrect because it means "objection." D is incorrect because it means "inquiry."

37. (B) — Vocabulary

B is the best choice because the sentence says "everything that we have so far done . . . has proceeded from our desire to help them." So "proceeded" here means "come from" or "originate."

A and C are incorrect because the sentence discusses a motivation for actions. D is incorrect because it means to "complete an activity" or to "execute."

38. (B) — Local

B is the best choice because of lines 63-65.

A is incorrect because Wilson calls only the U.S. "benevolent," and he does not describe Mexico as "sagacious" which means "wise." C is incorrect because it implies that the U.S. is fighting for independence. This is not suggested. D is incorrect because the U.S. is seeking apologies from Mexico.

39. (A) — Local

A is the best choice because the passage states that Wilson could have pursued his plan (involving the use of armed forces) using his presidential powers alone without the help of Congress.

B is therefore incorrect. C is incorrect because it means "infinite" which is extreme. D is incorrect because it means "giving" and "kind."

40. (B) — Local

B is the best choice because according to the last paragraph, the U.S. wishes to have influence "for the uses of liberty . . . wherever . . . it may be employed for the benefit of mankind."

A is incorrect because "imperative" is too strong. Wishing to have enough influence to do good is not the same as making dignity an absolute requirement. C is incorrect. Wilson implies U.S. influence would diminish without dignity and authority. This does not necessarily mean, however, that the U.S. would be unable to exert influence. D is incorrect because it is opposite to what the passage states in lines 83-84.

41. (D) — Graph

D is the best choice because the U.S. military seized Veracruz on the same day (April 22) that Congress approved the use of military force.

A is incorrect because the word *often* is not supported by the information in the table. B is incorrect because this information cannot be found in the table. C is incorrect because even though Mexico did not participate as a result of the Tampico Affair, there is no indication that this crucially affected the outcome of the war.

42. (B) — Graph

B is the best choice because the table indicates that even three years after Tampico, Mexico refused to fight alongside the U.S. due to anti-American resentments. Therefore, Wilson's effort to avoid indiscriminate fighting was not appreciated.

A is incorrect because the information in the table does not suggest that Wilson's intent was unwise or imprudent. C is incorrect because the table does not suggest that discriminating between Huerta's faction and other Mexicans was not feasible. D is incorrect because the information in the table does not suggest that Wilson's intent was shrewd or perceptive.

Questions 43-52

43. (C) — Summary

C is the best choice. The passage first states that ore exploration is important. Then it describes some of the difficulties that it presents and finally claims that it will get easier in the future as science develops.

A is incorrect because space exploration is used to emphasize certain aspects of ore exploration. The differences between the two, however, are not the main focus of the passage. B is incorrect because concrete methods to find ore are not the focus. D is incorrect because the passage does not focus on the field's popularity.

Answer Explanations

44. (A) Local

A is the best choice. The second paragraph states that we have been quite successful at exploring space, but that we "did not even scratch the surface in the other direction" (which is down through the crust of our planet).

B is incorrect because the passage does not mention that searching for minerals does not pose a real challenge any longer. C is incorrect because the passage does not state that we need to prospect minerals to cover our basic needs (such as food, water, and shelter). D is incorrect because the passage does not state that ore exploration has been neglected in favor of space exploration.

45. (B) Context

Within the sentence, "sheer" describes a large number of objects, many of which are unexplored, while "alone" describes a limited area which is our solar system.

Therefore, B is the best choice.

A and C are incorrect because the words in question do not convey "dismay" or "confidence." D is incorrect because the words in question do not serve to evaluate our past attempts at exploration.

46. (A) Local

A is the best choice because of lines 39-43 (see next question).

B is incorrect because presumption is not brought up as an obstacle to exploration, and it is only mentioned in connection with space exploration. C is incorrect because "physical distance" is only mentioned as a problem when exploring for ore. D is incorrect because only ores are mentioned as a requirement for better lifestyles.

47. (D) Evidence

D is the best choice because the lines state that we roughly know the makeup of our planet, but we do not know every small detail. The word "similarly" shows that this principle also holds true for ore exploration.

A, B, and C are incorrect because none of them show that the two types of exploration result in big pictures lacking in information on the details.

48. (B) Context

B is the best choice because the specified remark explains the sentence which contains it. That sentence states that there is only a finite amount of minerals. This characteristic of being finite contradicts the fact that ore is formed. However, the specified remark continues to suggest that our lives are too short for this to be of import. So *practically*, minerals are a finite resource.

A is incorrect because the specified remark does not mention human contribution to ore formation. C is incorrect because the context does not mention that humans leave no lasting trace on nature. D is incorrect because the specified remark does not serve to explain the time-consuming and dangerous nature of ore exploration.

49. (B) Vocabulary

B is the best choice because the sentence contrasts a "serious" treatise against pure speculation.

A is incorrect because it means "harsh," "stern," or "difficult." C is incorrect because it means "critical" or "essential." D is incorrect because it means "solemn" or "depressing."

50. (D) Context

"Ore availability" is a problem, and "open pit mining" (or the increasing scarcity thereof) is a symptom of this problem. The previous paragraphs list challenges that ore exploration brings with it whereas the next paragraph states that it will get easier in the future.

Therefore, D is the best choice.

A is incorrect because the information about ore availability and pit mining does not suggest that space exploration and mineral exploration are completely different. B is incorrect because the specified part does not discuss avoidable problems. C is incorrect because the previous paragraphs already introduced this idea.

51. (A) Local

A is the best choice because of lines 55-57 (see next question).

B is incorrect because even though the two opposing theories were seminal, they did not bring the field into being (lines 68-69). C is incorrect because the passage does not support that it is an "unproven" field of science. D is incorrect because though important, "uniquely" important is not supported.

52. (B)   Evidence

B is the best choice because the lines say the field is still very young (not yet mature) and there will be significant advances in the future.

A, C, and D are incorrect because none of them support this idea.

SAT.Hackers.ac

How to Score Your Test

Convert your score by using the Scaled Score Conversion Table (use the "New SAT" column), and mark your converted scores in the graph.

Scaled Score Conversion Table

New SAT Reading Test					
Raw Score (out of 52, new SAT)	New SAT Score	Old SAT Score	Raw Score (out of 52, new SAT)	New SAT Score	Old SAT Score
52	400	790	25	460	460
51	400	790	24	440	440
50	390	760	23	440	440
49	380	720	22	420	420
48	380	720	21	420	420
47	370	700	20	400	400
46	370	700	19	400	400
45	360	680	18	380	380
44	350	660	17	380	380
43	350	660	16	370	370
42	340	640	15	370	370
41	330	610	14	340	340
40	330	610	13	340	340
39	320	590	12	310	310
38	320	590	11	280	280
37	310	570	10	280	280
36	310	570	9	270	270
35	300	550	8	260	260
34	300	550	7	260	260
33	290	530	6	250	250
32	290	530	5	240	240
31	280	520	4	220	220
30	280	520	3	210	210
29	270	500	2	200	200
28	260	480	1	200	200
27	260	480	0	200	200
26	250	460			

Individual Score Overview

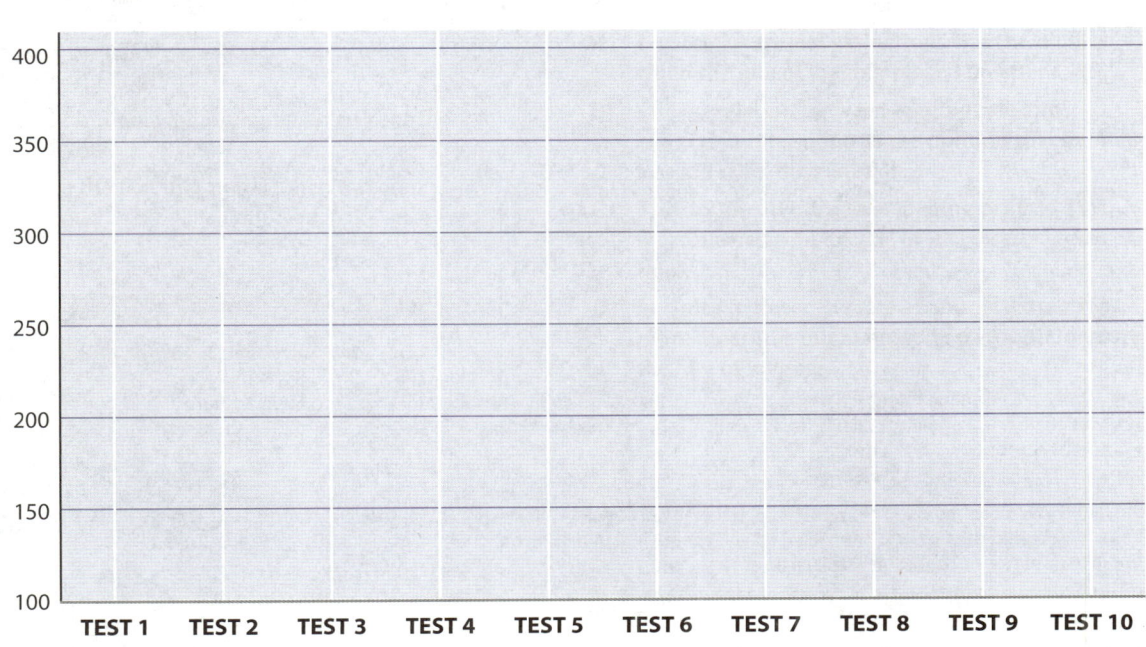

Additional Attribution and Copyright Information

TEST 5 / Pages 126-127:
Passage 1 has been adapted and modified from the following source: Low, C. and Hanley, D.: A perspective on the importance of within-tree variation in mortality risk for a leaf-mining insect, Web Ecol., 12, 27-32, doi:10.5194/we-12-27-2012, 2012. ©2012 Creative Commons Attribution 3.0 License.

http://www.web-ecol.net/12/27/2012/we-12-27-2012.html

Passage 2 has been adapted and modified from the following source: Marañón, T., Pugnaire, F. I., and Callaway, R. M.: Mediterranean-climate oak savannas: the interplay between abiotic environment and species interactions, Web Ecol., 9, 30-43, doi:10.5194/we-9-30-2009, 2009. ©2009 Creative Commons Attribution 3.0 License.

http://www.web-ecol.net/9/30/2009/we-9-30-2009.html

TEST 6 / Page 155:
The passage has been modified from the following source: Vignoli, L. and Luiselli, L.: Better in the dark: two Mediterranean amphibians synchronize reproduction with moonlit nights, Web Ecol., 13, 1-11, doi:10.5194/we-13-1-2013, 2013. ©2013 Creative Commons Attribution 3.0 License.

http://www.web-ecol.net/13/1/2013/we-13-1-2013.html

TEST 7 / Page 179:
The passage has been modified from the following source: Marti, R., Gascoin, S., Houet, T., Ribière, O., Laffly, D., Condom, T., Monnier, S., Schmutz, M., Camerlynck, C., Tihay, J. P., Soubeyroux, J. M., and René, P.: Evolution of Ossoue Glacier (French Pyrenees) since the end of the Little Ice Age, The Cryosphere, 9, 1773-1795, doi:10.5194/tc-9-1773-2015, 2015. ©2015 Creative Commons Attribution 3.0 License.

http://www.the-cryosphere.net/9/1773/2015/tc-9-1773-2015.html

TEST 8 / Page 197:
The passage has been adapted and modified from the following source: Pugnaire, F. I., Chapin III, F. S., and Hardig, T. M.: Evolutionary changes in correlations among functional traits in Ceanothus in response to Mediterranean conditions, Web Ecol., 6, 17-26, doi:10.5194/we-6-17-2006, 2006 ©2006 Creative Commons Attribution 3.0 License.

http://www.web-ecol.net/6/17/2006/we-6-17-2006.html

TEST 9 / Page 221:
The passage has been modified from the following source: Wamelink GWW, Frissel JY, Krijnen WHJ, Verwoert MR, Goedhart PW (2014) Can Plants Grow on Mars and the Moon: A Growth Experiment on Mars and Moon Soil Simulants. PLoS ONE 9(8): e103138. doi:10.1371/journal.pone. 0103138 ©2014 Creative Commons Attribution License.

http://journals.plos.org/plosone/article?id=10.1371/journal.pone.0103138

TEST 9 / Pages 226-227:
Passage 1 has been modified from the following source: Arandjelovic, M., Head, J., Boesch, C., Robbins, M. M., and Vigilant, L.: Genetic inference of group dynamics and female kin structure in a western lowland gorilla population (Gorilla gorilla gorilla), Primate Biol., 1, 29-38, doi:10.5194/pb-1-29-2014, 2014. ©2014 Creative Commons Attribution 3.0 License.

http://www.primate-biol.net/1/29/2014/pb-1-29-2014.html

Passage 2 has been modified from the following source: Clyvia, A., Kaizer, M. C., Santos, R. V., Young, R. J., and Cäsar, C.: Do wild titi monkeys show empathy?, Primate Biol., 1, 23-28, doi:10.5194/pb-1-23-2014, 2014. ©2014 Creative Commons Attribution 3.0 License.

http://www.primate-biol.net/1/23/2014/pb-1-23-2014.html

Answer Sheet
- TEST 1 -

COMPLETE MARK ●

EXAMPLE OF INCOMPLETE MARKS

You are advised to use a No. 2 pencil. Make heavy, dark marks that completely fill in the circle. When changing an answer, fully erase the original mark. Your score may be affected by incomplete marks or partial erasures.

■ Section 1

	A B C D		A B C D		A B C D		A B C D
1	○ ○ ○ ○	14	○ ○ ○ ○	27	○ ○ ○ ○	40	○ ○ ○ ○
2	○ ○ ○ ○	15	○ ○ ○ ○	28	○ ○ ○ ○	41	○ ○ ○ ○
3	○ ○ ○ ○	16	○ ○ ○ ○	29	○ ○ ○ ○	42	○ ○ ○ ○
4	○ ○ ○ ○	17	○ ○ ○ ○	30	○ ○ ○ ○	43	○ ○ ○ ○
5	○ ○ ○ ○	18	○ ○ ○ ○	31	○ ○ ○ ○	44	○ ○ ○ ○
6	○ ○ ○ ○	19	○ ○ ○ ○	32	○ ○ ○ ○	45	○ ○ ○ ○
7	○ ○ ○ ○	20	○ ○ ○ ○	33	○ ○ ○ ○	46	○ ○ ○ ○
8	○ ○ ○ ○	21	○ ○ ○ ○	34	○ ○ ○ ○	47	○ ○ ○ ○
9	○ ○ ○ ○	22	○ ○ ○ ○	35	○ ○ ○ ○	48	○ ○ ○ ○
10	○ ○ ○ ○	23	○ ○ ○ ○	36	○ ○ ○ ○	49	○ ○ ○ ○
11	○ ○ ○ ○	24	○ ○ ○ ○	37	○ ○ ○ ○	50	○ ○ ○ ○
12	○ ○ ○ ○	25	○ ○ ○ ○	38	○ ○ ○ ○	51	○ ○ ○ ○
13	○ ○ ○ ○	26	○ ○ ○ ○	39	○ ○ ○ ○	52	○ ○ ○ ○

Answer Sheet
- TEST 2 -

COMPLETE MARK ●

EXAMPLE OF INCOMPLETE MARKS

You are advised to use a No. 2 pencil. Make heavy, dark marks that completely fill in the circle. When changing an answer, fully erase the original mark. Your score may be affected by incomplete marks or partial erasures.

■ Section 1

#	A B C D	#	A B C D	#	A B C D	#	A B C D
1	○ ○ ○ ○	14	○ ○ ○ ○	27	○ ○ ○ ○	40	○ ○ ○ ○
2	○ ○ ○ ○	15	○ ○ ○ ○	28	○ ○ ○ ○	41	○ ○ ○ ○
3	○ ○ ○ ○	16	○ ○ ○ ○	29	○ ○ ○ ○	42	○ ○ ○ ○
4	○ ○ ○ ○	17	○ ○ ○ ○	30	○ ○ ○ ○	43	○ ○ ○ ○
5	○ ○ ○ ○	18	○ ○ ○ ○	31	○ ○ ○ ○	44	○ ○ ○ ○
6	○ ○ ○ ○	19	○ ○ ○ ○	32	○ ○ ○ ○	45	○ ○ ○ ○
7	○ ○ ○ ○	20	○ ○ ○ ○	33	○ ○ ○ ○	46	○ ○ ○ ○
8	○ ○ ○ ○	21	○ ○ ○ ○	34	○ ○ ○ ○	47	○ ○ ○ ○
9	○ ○ ○ ○	22	○ ○ ○ ○	35	○ ○ ○ ○	48	○ ○ ○ ○
10	○ ○ ○ ○	23	○ ○ ○ ○	36	○ ○ ○ ○	49	○ ○ ○ ○
11	○ ○ ○ ○	24	○ ○ ○ ○	37	○ ○ ○ ○	50	○ ○ ○ ○
12	○ ○ ○ ○	25	○ ○ ○ ○	38	○ ○ ○ ○	51	○ ○ ○ ○
13	○ ○ ○ ○	26	○ ○ ○ ○	39	○ ○ ○ ○	52	○ ○ ○ ○

Answer Sheet
- TEST 3 -

COMPLETE MARK ●

EXAMPLE OF INCOMPLETE MARKS

You are advised to use a No. 2 pencil. Make heavy, dark marks that completely fill in the circle. When changing an answer, fully erase the original mark. Your score may be affected by incomplete marks or partial erasures.

■ Section 1

#	A B C D	#	A B C D	#	A B C D	#	A B C D
1	○ ○ ○ ○	14	○ ○ ○ ○	27	○ ○ ○ ○	40	○ ○ ○ ○
2	○ ○ ○ ○	15	○ ○ ○ ○	28	○ ○ ○ ○	41	○ ○ ○ ○
3	○ ○ ○ ○	16	○ ○ ○ ○	29	○ ○ ○ ○	42	○ ○ ○ ○
4	○ ○ ○ ○	17	○ ○ ○ ○	30	○ ○ ○ ○	43	○ ○ ○ ○
5	○ ○ ○ ○	18	○ ○ ○ ○	31	○ ○ ○ ○	44	○ ○ ○ ○
6	○ ○ ○ ○	19	○ ○ ○ ○	32	○ ○ ○ ○	45	○ ○ ○ ○
7	○ ○ ○ ○	20	○ ○ ○ ○	33	○ ○ ○ ○	46	○ ○ ○ ○
8	○ ○ ○ ○	21	○ ○ ○ ○	34	○ ○ ○ ○	47	○ ○ ○ ○
9	○ ○ ○ ○	22	○ ○ ○ ○	35	○ ○ ○ ○	48	○ ○ ○ ○
10	○ ○ ○ ○	23	○ ○ ○ ○	36	○ ○ ○ ○	49	○ ○ ○ ○
11	○ ○ ○ ○	24	○ ○ ○ ○	37	○ ○ ○ ○	50	○ ○ ○ ○
12	○ ○ ○ ○	25	○ ○ ○ ○	38	○ ○ ○ ○	51	○ ○ ○ ○
13	○ ○ ○ ○	26	○ ○ ○ ○	39	○ ○ ○ ○	52	○ ○ ○ ○

Answer Sheet
- TEST 4 -

COMPLETE MARK ●

EXAMPLE OF INCOMPLETE MARKS

You are advised to use a No. 2 pencil. Make heavy, dark marks that completely fill in the circle. When changing an answer, fully erase the original mark. Your score may be affected by incomplete marks or partial erasures.

■ Section 1

	A B C D		A B C D		A B C D		A B C D
1	○ ○ ○ ○	14	○ ○ ○ ○	27	○ ○ ○ ○	40	○ ○ ○ ○
2	○ ○ ○ ○	15	○ ○ ○ ○	28	○ ○ ○ ○	41	○ ○ ○ ○
3	○ ○ ○ ○	16	○ ○ ○ ○	29	○ ○ ○ ○	42	○ ○ ○ ○
4	○ ○ ○ ○	17	○ ○ ○ ○	30	○ ○ ○ ○	43	○ ○ ○ ○
5	○ ○ ○ ○	18	○ ○ ○ ○	31	○ ○ ○ ○	44	○ ○ ○ ○
6	○ ○ ○ ○	19	○ ○ ○ ○	32	○ ○ ○ ○	45	○ ○ ○ ○
7	○ ○ ○ ○	20	○ ○ ○ ○	33	○ ○ ○ ○	46	○ ○ ○ ○
8	○ ○ ○ ○	21	○ ○ ○ ○	34	○ ○ ○ ○	47	○ ○ ○ ○
9	○ ○ ○ ○	22	○ ○ ○ ○	35	○ ○ ○ ○	48	○ ○ ○ ○
10	○ ○ ○ ○	23	○ ○ ○ ○	36	○ ○ ○ ○	49	○ ○ ○ ○
11	○ ○ ○ ○	24	○ ○ ○ ○	37	○ ○ ○ ○	50	○ ○ ○ ○
12	○ ○ ○ ○	25	○ ○ ○ ○	38	○ ○ ○ ○	51	○ ○ ○ ○
13	○ ○ ○ ○	26	○ ○ ○ ○	39	○ ○ ○ ○	52	○ ○ ○ ○

Answer Sheet

- TEST 5 -

COMPLETE MARK	EXAMPLE OF INCOMPLETE MARKS	
		You are advised to use a No. 2 pencil. Make heavy, dark marks that completely fill n the circle. When changing an answer, fully erase the original mark. Your score may be affected by incomplete marks or partial erasures.

Section 1

	A	B	C	D		A	B	C	D		A	B	C	D		A	B	C	D
1	○	○	○	○	**14**	○	○	○	○	**27**	○	○	○	○	**40**	○	○	○	○
2	○	○	○	○	**15**	○	○	○	○	**28**	○	○	○	○	**41**	○	○	○	○
3	○	○	○	○	**16**	○	○	○	○	**29**	○	○	○	○	**42**	○	○	○	○
4	○	○	○	○	**17**	○	○	○	○	**30**	○	○	○	○	**43**	○	○	○	○
5	○	○	○	○	**18**	○	○	○	○	**31**	○	○	○	○	**44**	○	○	○	○
6	○	○	○	○	**19**	○	○	○	○	**32**	○	○	○	○	**45**	○	○	○	○
7	○	○	○	○	**20**	○	○	○	○	**33**	○	○	○	○	**46**	○	○	○	○
8	○	○	○	○	**21**	○	○	○	○	**34**	○	○	○	○	**47**	○	○	○	○
9	○	○	○	○	**22**	○	○	○	○	**35**	○	○	○	○	**48**	○	○	○	○
10	○	○	○	○	**23**	○	○	○	○	**36**	○	○	○	○	**49**	○	○	○	○
11	○	○	○	○	**24**	○	○	○	○	**37**	○	○	○	○	**50**	○	○	○	○
12	○	○	○	○	**25**	○	○	○	○	**38**	○	○	○	○	**51**	○	○	○	○
13	○	○	○	○	**26**	○	○	○	○	**39**	○	○	○	○	**52**	○	○	○	○

Answer Sheet
- TEST 6 -

COMPLETE MARK ● | **EXAMPLE OF INCOMPLETE MARKS** | You are advised to use a No. 2 pencil. Make heavy, dark marks that completely fill in the circle. When changing an answer, fully erase the original mark. Your score may be affected by incomplete marks or partial erasures.

■ Section 1

#	A	B	C	D		#	A	B	C	D		#	A	B	C	D		#	A	B	C	D
1	○	○	○	○		14	○	○	○	○		27	○	○	○	○		40	○	○	○	○
2	○	○	○	○		15	○	○	○	○		28	○	○	○	○		41	○	○	○	○
3	○	○	○	○		16	○	○	○	○		29	○	○	○	○		42	○	○	○	○
4	○	○	○	○		17	○	○	○	○		30	○	○	○	○		43	○	○	○	○
5	○	○	○	○		18	○	○	○	○		31	○	○	○	○		44	○	○	○	○
6	○	○	○	○		19	○	○	○	○		32	○	○	○	○		45	○	○	○	○
7	○	○	○	○		20	○	○	○	○		33	○	○	○	○		46	○	○	○	○
8	○	○	○	○		21	○	○	○	○		34	○	○	○	○		47	○	○	○	○
9	○	○	○	○		22	○	○	○	○		35	○	○	○	○		48	○	○	○	○
10	○	○	○	○		23	○	○	○	○		36	○	○	○	○		49	○	○	○	○
11	○	○	○	○		24	○	○	○	○		37	○	○	○	○		50	○	○	○	○
12	○	○	○	○		25	○	○	○	○		38	○	○	○	○		51	○	○	○	○
13	○	○	○	○		26	○	○	○	○		39	○	○	○	○		52	○	○	○	○

Answer Sheet
- TEST 7 -

COMPLETE MARK ●

EXAMPLE OF INCOMPLETE MARKS

You are advised to use a No. 2 pencil. Make heavy, dark marks that completely fill in the circle. When changing an answer, fully erase the original mark. Your score may be affected by incomplete marks or partial erasures.

■ Section 1

	A B C D		A B C D		A B C D		A B C D
1	○ ○ ○ ○	14	○ ○ ○ ○	27	○ ○ ○ ○	40	○ ○ ○ ○
2	○ ○ ○ ○	15	○ ○ ○ ○	28	○ ○ ○ ○	41	○ ○ ○ ○
3	○ ○ ○ ○	16	○ ○ ○ ○	29	○ ○ ○ ○	42	○ ○ ○ ○
4	○ ○ ○ ○	17	○ ○ ○ ○	30	○ ○ ○ ○	43	○ ○ ○ ○
5	○ ○ ○ ○	18	○ ○ ○ ○	31	○ ○ ○ ○	44	○ ○ ○ ○
6	○ ○ ○ ○	19	○ ○ ○ ○	32	○ ○ ○ ○	45	○ ○ ○ ○
7	○ ○ ○ ○	20	○ ○ ○ ○	33	○ ○ ○ ○	46	○ ○ ○ ○
8	○ ○ ○ ○	21	○ ○ ○ ○	34	○ ○ ○ ○	47	○ ○ ○ ○
9	○ ○ ○ ○	22	○ ○ ○ ○	35	○ ○ ○ ○	48	○ ○ ○ ○
10	○ ○ ○ ○	23	○ ○ ○ ○	36	○ ○ ○ ○	49	○ ○ ○ ○
11	○ ○ ○ ○	24	○ ○ ○ ○	37	○ ○ ○ ○	50	○ ○ ○ ○
12	○ ○ ○ ○	25	○ ○ ○ ○	38	○ ○ ○ ○	51	○ ○ ○ ○
13	○ ○ ○ ○	26	○ ○ ○ ○	39	○ ○ ○ ○	52	○ ○ ○ ○

Answer Sheet
- TEST 8 -

COMPLETE MARK ●

EXAMPLE OF INCOMPLETE MARKS ◐ ◯✓ ◉ ⊗ ◯

You are advised to use a No. 2 pencil. Make heavy, dark marks that completely fill in the circle. When changing an answer, fully erase the original mark. Your score may be affected by incomplete marks or partial erasures.

■ Section 1

	A B C D		A B C D		A B C D		A B C D
1	○ ○ ○ ○	14	○ ○ ○ ○	27	○ ○ ○ ○	40	○ ○ ○ ○
2	○ ○ ○ ○	15	○ ○ ○ ○	28	○ ○ ○ ○	41	○ ○ ○ ○
3	○ ○ ○ ○	16	○ ○ ○ ○	29	○ ○ ○ ○	42	○ ○ ○ ○
4	○ ○ ○ ○	17	○ ○ ○ ○	30	○ ○ ○ ○	43	○ ○ ○ ○
5	○ ○ ○ ○	18	○ ○ ○ ○	31	○ ○ ○ ○	44	○ ○ ○ ○
6	○ ○ ○ ○	19	○ ○ ○ ○	32	○ ○ ○ ○	45	○ ○ ○ ○
7	○ ○ ○ ○	20	○ ○ ○ ○	33	○ ○ ○ ○	46	○ ○ ○ ○
8	○ ○ ○ ○	21	○ ○ ○ ○	34	○ ○ ○ ○	47	○ ○ ○ ○
9	○ ○ ○ ○	22	○ ○ ○ ○	35	○ ○ ○ ○	48	○ ○ ○ ○
10	○ ○ ○ ○	23	○ ○ ○ ○	36	○ ○ ○ ○	49	○ ○ ○ ○
11	○ ○ ○ ○	24	○ ○ ○ ○	37	○ ○ ○ ○	50	○ ○ ○ ○
12	○ ○ ○ ○	25	○ ○ ○ ○	38	○ ○ ○ ○	51	○ ○ ○ ○
13	○ ○ ○ ○	26	○ ○ ○ ○	39	○ ○ ○ ○	52	○ ○ ○ ○

Answer Sheet
- TEST 9 -

COMPLETE MARK ●

EXAMPLE OF INCOMPLETE MARKS

You are advised to use a No. 2 pencil. Make heavy, dark marks that completely fill in the circle. When changing an answer, fully erase the original mark. Your score may be affected by incomplete marks or partial erasures.

■ Section 1

1. A B C D
2. A B C D
3. A B C D
4. A B C D
5. A B C D
6. A B C D
7. A B C D
8. A B C D
9. A B C D
10. A B C D
11. A B C D
12. A B C D
13. A B C D
14. A B C D
15. A B C D
16. A B C D
17. A B C D
18. A B C D
19. A B C D
20. A B C D
21. A B C D
22. A B C D
23. A B C D
24. A B C D
25. A B C D
26. A B C D
27. A B C D
28. A B C D
29. A B C D
30. A B C D
31. A B C D
32. A B C D
33. A B C D
34. A B C D
35. A B C D
36. A B C D
37. A B C D
38. A B C D
39. A B C D
40. A B C D
41. A B C D
42. A B C D
43. A B C D
44. A B C D
45. A B C D
46. A B C D
47. A B C D
48. A B C D
49. A B C D
50. A B C D
51. A B C D
52. A B C D

Answer Sheet
- TEST 10 -

COMPLETE MARK ●

EXAMPLE OF INCOMPLETE MARKS

You are advised to use a No. 2 pencil. Make heavy, dark marks that completely fill in the circle. When changing an answer, fully erase the original mark. Your score may be affected by incomplete marks or partial erasures.

■ Section 1

#	A B C D	#	A B C D	#	A B C D	#	A B C D
1	○ ○ ○ ○	14	○ ○ ○ ○	27	○ ○ ○ ○	40	○ ○ ○ ○
2	○ ○ ○ ○	15	○ ○ ○ ○	28	○ ○ ○ ○	41	○ ○ ○ ○
3	○ ○ ○ ○	16	○ ○ ○ ○	29	○ ○ ○ ○	42	○ ○ ○ ○
4	○ ○ ○ ○	17	○ ○ ○ ○	30	○ ○ ○ ○	43	○ ○ ○ ○
5	○ ○ ○ ○	18	○ ○ ○ ○	31	○ ○ ○ ○	44	○ ○ ○ ○
6	○ ○ ○ ○	19	○ ○ ○ ○	32	○ ○ ○ ○	45	○ ○ ○ ○
7	○ ○ ○ ○	20	○ ○ ○ ○	33	○ ○ ○ ○	46	○ ○ ○ ○
8	○ ○ ○ ○	21	○ ○ ○ ○	34	○ ○ ○ ○	47	○ ○ ○ ○
9	○ ○ ○ ○	22	○ ○ ○ ○	35	○ ○ ○ ○	48	○ ○ ○ ○
10	○ ○ ○ ○	23	○ ○ ○ ○	36	○ ○ ○ ○	49	○ ○ ○ ○
11	○ ○ ○ ○	24	○ ○ ○ ○	37	○ ○ ○ ○	50	○ ○ ○ ○
12	○ ○ ○ ○	25	○ ○ ○ ○	38	○ ○ ○ ○	51	○ ○ ○ ○
13	○ ○ ○ ○	26	○ ○ ○ ○	39	○ ○ ○ ○	52	○ ○ ○ ○